# CHASING THE DRAGON

## One Woman's Struggle Against the Darkness of Hong Kong's Drug Dens

# JACKIE PULLINGER

### WITH ANDREW QUICKE

**Chosen**

*a division of Baker Publishing Group*
Minneapolis, Minnesota

First British edition published by Hodder and Stoughton in Great Britain in 1980.
First American edition published by Servant Publications in 1982.
Second British edition published by Hodder and Stoughton in 2006.
Second American edition published by Regal Books in 2006.

Published by Chosen Books
11400 Hampshire Avenue South
Bloomington, Minnesota 55438
www.chosenbooks.com

Chosen Books is a division of
Baker Publishing Group, Grand Rapids, Michigan

Chosen Books edition published 2014
ISBN 978-0-8007-9703-4

Previously published by Regal Books

Printed in the United States of America

The Library of Congress has cataloged the original edition as follows:
    Pullinger, Jackie.
    Chasing the dragon / Jackie Pullinger with Andrew Quicke.
        p. c.m.
    Originally published: London: Hodder and Stoughton, 1980, in series:
    Hodder Christian paperbacks.
    ISBN 0830743820
        1. Pullinger, Jackie. 2. Missionaries—China—Hong Kong—Biography. 3. Mis-
    sionaries—England—Biography. I. Quicke, Andrew. II. Title.
    BV3427.P8A3 2004
    266'.0092—dc22                                                    2003028164

This story is factual, but for obvious reasons, some names have been changed.

19   20   21   22   23        9   8   7   6   5

*For my family, especially my father.*

*The great dragon was hurled down—that ancient serpent
called the devil, or Satan, who leads the whole world astray.
He was hurled to the earth, and his angels with him. . . .
"Now have come the salvation and the power and the
kingdom of our God, and the authority of his Christ.
For the accuser of our brothers . . . has been hurled down."*

Revelation 12:9-10

# CONTENTS

# INTRODUCTION

Of course, *Chasing the Dragon* backfired on me. I had written it in the hope of recording history and inspiring hope. Having disposed of one decade, I had hoped to get on with more life. Instead I was invited to retell the story again and again, whereas I had meant that you, the reader, might see that the same God could impart His heart and His power in your city and write your own books.

In 1989, the announcement of the Walled City's impending demise prompted the telling of the life and death of the Kowloon Walled City in *Crack in the Wall*. The book was intended as a collection of cameos suitable for the coffee table. Like *Chasing the Dragon*, it was again a history and gave, among other things, the continuing saga of the Walled City's Triad boss and his eventual quiet turning to Christ.

We have little evidence as to what happened to those whom Jesus healed in the Gospels. The accounts, for the most part, stop suddenly. This new edition will not finish their stories but is an attempt to update our situation. The first edition covered about 10 years, and the new material in this edition overviews more than 20 years in two chapters. I hope you will forgive the time swings. It all seems like yesterday.

The Walled City has gone. Even Hang Fook Camp, our urban squat, has gone. So where can you find us today if you visit Hong Kong? Hopefully, in all the streets and blocks. We will probably be unnamed, for we care not to extend our work but rather His kingdom. There are many more adventures to be had.

There are many more battles to be fought. It would be such fun to be a part of them rather than just read of them. So go! Write your own books. Go!

Jackie Pullinger
2001

# PREFACE

I first met Jackie Pullinger in 1968 when I went to Hong Kong to make a film for BBC television. Thanks to a friend's introduction, she came to my hotel to tell me about her work in the Walled City, which was then just beginning. As I had run a youth club myself in the East End of London, I was fascinated by what she told me. When I went to see the Walled City with her, I found that it was exactly as she described it.

Over the years, Jackie and I kept in touch by letter, and year by year her work developed. Yet those outside Hong Kong who had ever heard of Jackie Pullinger were very few until the *Sunday Times* wrote about her work in 1974. Thereafter followed a question in Parliament about the status of the Walled City; articles by Reuters, UPI and other international agencies; and a 50-minute film by the British TV company, ATV, in 1978.

When Jackie went to England to talk about the work, I asked her if together we could write a fuller account of all that had happened. With some reluctance she agreed, and I revisited Hong Kong in 1979. However, Jackie did not approve of my first draft, and so she rewrote the whole book herself when she came to stay with our family in California.

Some of the names and places in the book have been changed to protect the characters concerned, nearly all of whom are still living in Hong Kong. Apart from that, everything happened as Jackie describes it. It is her story, but many of the events described can be verified from other sources.

My thanks are due to the many people who helped us complete this book against a tough time schedule. Among many, I would mention Marjorie Witcombe and Mary Stack in Hong Kong, who lent us their homes; Susan Soloman in California; my brother Edward and his friends at the World Bank in Washington, where the manuscript was completed; and, most important of all, my wife, Juliet, who did a magnificent job of editing and advising throughout.

Andrew Quicke
London
April 1980

# GLOSSARY

| | |
|---|---|
| *amah* | a Chinese servant |
| *congee* | a rice porridge, often eaten for breakfast |
| *daih lo* | Big Brother |
| *daih lo* | Big Mother, the senior Chinese wife |
| *for-gei* | waiter or worker |
| *fui-goih* | repent |
| *gong-sou* | a talk between rival Triads to attempt a settlement over gang affairs |
| *"Hai bin do ah?"* | "Where do you come from?" |
| *Hak Nam* | darkness—often used as a name for Hong Kong's Walled City |
| *kai ma* | godmother (this term and the next are used to define a close relationship between an older woman and a child she takes to be her own) |
| *kai neui* | goddaughter |
| *lap-sap* | rubbish |
| *mama-san* | a name for a woman who is in charge of various girl prostitutes or bar girls |
| *"M'gong?"* | "Not talking?" |
| *mintoi* | eiderdown |
| *"Moe yeh"* | "Nothing" |
| *pahng-jue* | lord of the hut or master of a drug den |
| *pin-mun* | illegal business |
| Poon Siu Jeh | "Pullinger" in Chinese |
| *sai lo* | Little Brother |
| Seui Fong, 14K and Ging Yu | Names of different Triads that are illegal in Hong Kong |
| *siu yeh* | a snack |
| *tin-man-toi* | weatherman, meaning watchman |
| *wunton* | dumplings stuffed with shrimp and pork |

*"Yau moe gau chor"*    "You must be off your head"
*"Yauh"*                "I'm here"
*"Yeh sou ngoi nei"*    "Jesus loves you"

**Note:** One U.S. dollar was worth HK $6.89 in 1966.

# 1

# THE TRAIL OF BLOOD

The guard spat into the alley but nodded quite kindly and allowed me to pass. I left him there squatting in his soiled T-shirt. Having no further interest in me, he removed one of his flip-flops and returned to picking his black toenails. The entrance he was so ceremoniously guarding was almost hidden, and I had to squeeze between two dark buildings as I crept into this strange Chinese "city" so feared by the people of Hong Kong.

The darkness blindfolded me for a moment, and although I knew the way well by this time, I stepped very cautiously along the narrow lane that was barely wide enough for one to walk. I kept my eyes lowered on the ground for two reasons: to avoid stepping on nameless horrors, and so fall into the open sewer, and to avoid presenting an upturned face to the windows above, which intermittently spewed their refuse onto the street below. I clapped my hands to make the rats run, but some of them were so tame that they sat arrogantly in what they obviously regarded as their territory; it took several loud claps to shift them.

Then I saw it—a small spot of red gleaming in the filthy mud, and a little way ahead several more drops. It was certainly fresh blood. My stomach gripped into a tight knot, for I feared that I knew whose blood it was. Ah Sor had been given to me by a magistrate to look after as a son for one year. Then a Triad group, nicknamed *Seui Fong,* came after him to slash him over some unfinished gang business. It seemed that they had found him. As I hurried on, I saw glistening patches ahead and stepped past two more *tin-man-toi*—the watchmen for the Triad gangsters who controlled the Walled City. They knew me and yielded as I passed; their faces showed nothing.

I turned a corner into another street, indistinguishable in its foul broken-walled buildings from the last except that it contained the main gambling den operated by the brothers of the 14K gang. I continued past the evil archways of the opium dens where more watchers leaned, nodding and dozing and seeing nothing. The gap between the hovels here was barely an arm's stretch wide, so I stepped into a doorway to avoid bumping into a crazed looking dope addict who was walking somewhere very quickly.

Up the next street, the patches of blood lay in clusters. I couldn't run in this stinking maze—it was too slippery and dark—but I was impatient to find the source of the blood. Yet I dreaded it, too.

I reached the main street, one of the few that were lit inside the Walled City. I had to walk more carefully now as I passed another gambling den, slimy outside with urine-soaked earth. The prostitutes recognized me and called from their orange boxes outside the blue film theatre. "Miss Poon, Poon Siu Jeh, will you help us?" They put out their hands, the backs of which were scarred with needle marks—their aged faces almost without hope. Then I turned into my little alley to the room I rented and opened at night to welcome the Chinese gangsters.

Outside, I found a large dark puddle. The shadowy people around looked unconcerned. "Please, what's happened?" I asked fearfully.

An old Cantonese man shook his head and muttered, "Nothing, nothing." But the others looked away. In a place controlled by Triads, you keep your hands over your eyes to survive. It is safer to see nothing—to not be involved. Then a woman appeared with a broom and a bucket and swept the blood down the street until it was absorbed and obliterated. Several barefoot children, babies strapped to their backs, played as if nothing were happening.

Full of fear for Ah Sor, I unlocked the iron gate—a protective feature of all Hong Kong dwellings, however poor—and went into our small clubroom. It was dark, damp smelling and hard to keep clean, as there was no water supply for the inhabitants of the Walled City. What water they needed had to be carried in buckets from taps and stand pumps outside. Terrible things crawled out of the sewers and across the clubroom walls. I was always more afraid of the large cesspool spiders than the gangsters, but that night as I sat alone in our room, my thoughts were on Ah Sor.

His mother had sold him as a baby to a childless opium addict who was frightened of going to hell without a son to worship his dead spirit. Thus, Ah Sor grew up with a desperate sense of betrayal—longing to be loved, but unable to recognize it when offered. In fact, "Granny"—the addict's mother—loved Ah Sor fondly, but as she was also a seller of heroin, her influence on his life could hardly be called refining.

To counterbalance his sense of total unbelonging, Ah Sor joined a Triad gang. It gave him prestige and a place to belong. He grew up fighting and earned his first spell in juvenile prison at the age of 13. Over the years I had come to know of his life and problems and had tried to help him, but he continued to go in and out of prison and was as hopelessly hooked on drugs as was his addict stepfather. I felt that I really loved him, but this love had not changed his life a bit, and so I sat on one of our crude handmade benches in the club and did the only thing I could—I prayed.

Five minutes later, a girl burst into my room, panting, "Miss Poon, go to the hospital immediately, Elizabeth Hospital—they called for you!"

"Who is it there—is it Ah Sor?" I was so relieved that there was some news at last.

"I just have to tell you to go quickly—something about dying." The girl disappeared into the dingy labyrinth. She was only a message carrier and knew nothing more.

I locked up and collected a couple of boys I knew on the way out. We raced back through the alleys as fast as we could, and once outside the Walled City, they hailed a taxi.

"Quickly, quickly, Elizabeth Hospital! Maybe our friend die!!
More quickly!"

Hong Kong taxis need no encouragement to speed, and our
driver mentally slew the other drivers. He zigzagged in and out
of the traffic lanes, driving deliberately with only one hand on
the steering wheel, never slowing but crashing on his brakes at
the last moment. My hands were clenched—I was praying and
thinking and racing all at the same time. *Maybe my friend die*,
I thought in Cantonese. What a miserable kind of half-life
Ah Sor had lived, and how I longed to show him something
better. If only he could know that somebody cared.

"God, please save his life—let him be saved," I prayed. The
driver was, by now, bouncing up and down in his seat with
excitement, and for several terrifyingly long moments he took
his eyes completely off the road and swung around in his seat
to observe the macho impression he was making on us. By this
time, we were all praying out loud. As if finding the Casualty
Department were a surprise, our taxi screeched to a sudden
halt, and we leaped out to find Ah Sor before he died.

But it was not Ah Sor who was dying. It was Ah Tong. It was
his blood that had left that sinister trail along the streets. I had
only known Ah Tong by reputation as one of the most depraved
gang leaders. He lived off prostitution and used his gang followers, such as Ah Sor, to make collection from the brothels.
Even among his own kind he was despised because he used to go
to parties, seduce young girls and then sell these ruined lives
into the rackets.

As we waited in the passage outside his ward, I learned more
of the story. Apparently, the *Seui Fong* gang had hidden down a
dark alley near my room, armed with knives and water pipes.
This was reciprocal warfare over a brother who had been wronged
years previously. The target was Ah Sor.

As Ah Sor moved toward the street with Ah Tong and another brother, he was unaware of the ambush. A knife glinted; the
gang jumped and made for their victim. But Ah Tong saw them
coming and threw himself in the way to protect Ah Sor. Ah

Tong's arm was slashed until it was nearly severed before the attackers left him lying in a pool of his own blood. Ah Sor, with the other brother, ran home, fetched a *mintoi* (Chinese eiderdown) and wrapped up their protector, their gang boss. They staggered with him along the streets until they reached an exit and could take a taxi. After delivering their burden to the hospital, they fled. (There are police at hospitals who ask questions about gang fights, and they did not want any report of this incident.)

Another brother relayed this story before he, in turn, disappeared, but the only information I could extract from the nurse was that the patient would almost certainly lose his arm, if not his life.

Sitting there on the hard hospital seat, I thought over what I had heard. I grew more and more impressed with the behavior of the man I had yet to see. All right, he was evil and lived a revolting life, but I felt he had also shown a rare degree of love. Jesus said, "Greater love has no one than this, that he lay down his life for his friends."[1] Ah Tong had been ready to die.

I rang up some friends and told them to come to the hospital, and we stayed there all night praying for Ah Tong's life. When his family turned up, they stood aghast at our totally incomprehensible behavior. What were we, good people—Christians even—doing praying for their son? To them he was bad. He had left their home young, ran the streets, organized the gangs, and merited only a turning by on the other side.[2]

At last, the sister gave us permission to enter the ward. I heard the Chinese nurses telling each other, "They're pastors, come to pray." Dressed as I was in old jeans and a sweater, I could understand their curious stares. We were hardly a conventional group come to administer the last rites in the middle of the night.

I stood by the bedside and looked at Ah Tong. He lay desperately pale from loss of blood, with drips in his uninjured arm and a huge wad of dressing over the sutured injury. He was deeply unconscious still. Afraid to disturb his bandages, we cautiously laid our hands on him and prayed for him in Jesus' name. He did not immediately sit up, although I believed he might, and as long as we were there he did not recover consciousness.

The bulletins from the hospital each day thereafter, however, were extraordinary. It seemed that Ah Tong was making amazing progress—almost miraculous? And then, to our joy and with the incredulous consent of the medical staff, he was discharged. His release was within five days of the attack. He had made a remarkable recovery, keeping not only his life, but also the full use of his arm.

Anyone would think that after this miracle Ah Tong might be pleased to see one of his intercessors, but far from it. In the following months, if he ever spotted me in the dark and dreary alleys, he would run as if I were the Chief Inspector after him. He was afraid to see me. But I did get several messages from him saying "thank you."

"Thank me for what?" I asked the message bearer—a yellow-toothed youth with a grown-out perm.

"He believes your prayers saved his life." The boy was sniffing and sweating and clearly in need of a fix, but he looked at me with respect. Anything his boss believed, he was prepared to believe, too. But if Ah Tong believed that my prayers saved him, why did he run from me? The illogicality of it all puzzled me for some time. Months afterward, I found the pathetic reason behind it all. He was an addict, and he needed a shot of heroin several times a day. All the time he had been in the hospital, his girlfriend, whom he had originally raped and sold into a live sex show when she was 14, had been bringing him drugs.

Ah Tong knew I was a Christian. He knew that Christians were "good people," and he knew that drug addicts were "bad people." So, in his mind, it was wrong for him to express his gratitude in person. He felt dirty—not clean enough for those good Christians.

It wasn't until several years later that Ah Tong fell across the doorstop of my little Walled City room. It was nearly the middle of the night. I do not think he had come through any conscious decision. He looked at me with devil-tormented eyes and blurted out, "Poon Siu Jeh, I'm desperate. I've tried to kick it so many times, but I can't get off drugs. Can you help me?"

"No, I can't," I said, "but I have good news for you. Jesus can. I think you should understand something about Jesus' life. Some years back you were willing to die for your brother, Ah Sor, and I've never forgotten that. You did something very wonderful."

Ah Tong's brows were drawn in concentration as he listened, and his face mirrored his disappointment, hope and puzzlement.

"What would you think about dying for someone in the other gang?" I asked.

"Tcha!" A lump of spit shot from his mouth and he looked bitterly at me. "You must be joking! Your brother is one thing, but no one dies for his enemy!"

"That is just what Jesus did. He not only died for his own gang but also for everyone in the other gangs. He was the Son of God. He never did wrong but healed people and made them whole—and He died for His enemies—for us. If we believe in Him, He will give us His life because He loves us."[3]

I do not think the drug-riddled mind of Ah Tong understood all of the doctrine of redemption. He was crazy for drugs and this had been a long speech, but I could see that something had happened. He was absolutely amazed at the idea that Jesus loved someone like him. For the first time in years, something—or someone—had penetrated his mean heart, and he was moved.

I hurried him out of the Walled City, down to the Kowloon waterfront, across the harbor on the ferry and up to the small flat on Hong Kong Island. He knew we were going to the "church," but quite what he had in mind I do not know, for he looked stunned as we entered the apartment.

It was minute by Western standards and not like a church at all. He was standing in what was obviously the living/dining room, which was bright and cheerfully decorated—even curtained. Everything was so clean and beautiful, and it felt like a home, not a church. But most extraordinary of all were the people, who were all smiling. There seemed to be a lot of Westerners as well as a lot of young Chinese men, all of whom Ah Tong recognized.

There were men he had known in jail; there were men he had fought with or against. There were men with whom he had taken drugs. But now they were all shining and happy and fat with good health. They began to tell him that they believed in Jesus and that Jesus' power had changed their lives.

"Yeow—even you here too?" he said as he greeted another friend.

"Yup, it's true, Ah Tong." (They spoke in the equivalent of Cantonese Cockney.)

"You know us—we'd never use this 'holy' talk if we didn't really believe. I mean—well, you'd expect Miss Poon and those priests to spout the Bible and all that, but they've never kicked drugs—they don't know what it's like. It got so the pain, the screaming agony, was so bad that I prayed to Jesus like they told us, and it worked! My pain went away and I felt really changed, and—well—sort of new. I got this strength, like—it's called the Holy Spirit, and I spoke in a new language and I didn't have any pain at all."

It was a bit incoherent, but Ah Tong clearly thought, *If they can, so can I. If Jesus did it for him, He can do it for me.*

Ah Tong told us he would believe that Jesus was God and ask Him to change his life. Then he prayed, and as he did so, his desperately thin and pain-lined face softened and relaxed. He smiled.

The other former crooks looked at one another joyfully. Once more, they were taking part in a miracle. Ah Tong had received the gift of speaking in a language he had never learned and found that praying came easily. Joy filled his eyes, and as he lay on his bunk bed, he grew more and more at peace. We all joined him and sat with him until he slept soundly.

Ah Tong stayed on in the house. There was no need for him to go "cold turkey," an experience that so tortures the human body that it can result in an addict's death. (The term is derived from the fact that when an addict is withdrawing from drugs without medication, as well as severe and painful symptoms, there are also fits of cold shivers that cause "turkey" skin.) We gave him no medication, not even aspirin. We did not even give him cigarettes to help him in his withdrawal from heroin. Every time he began to feel a slight pang, he went back to praying and using his new language. His withdrawal period was pain-free. No vomiting, no cramps, no diarrhea, no shivers. With this miracle, Ah Tong began a new life.

# SLOW BOAT TO CHINA

I mmigration control boarded the ship. I stood first in the queue, longing to disembark and get on with my adventure. Earlier that morning I had dressed, once again locked my bags ready for disembarkation, and gone up on deck. The sight took my breath away. All the places we had passed by earlier on the voyage seemed so flat by comparison. Here was perspective. Here were mountains shimmering and fading into the mist in an Oriental painting. I found myself filled with peace, and as I recognized that this was the place God had chosen, I said, "Thank You."

So now I stood, waiting and looking across the South China Sea at the Pearl of the Orient, Hong Kong. Around us was the harbor, separating Victoria Island and the Kowloon Peninsula. It was thronged with small crafts: little fishing *sampans* bobbing up and down as they were sculled with peculiar skill by slant-eyed girls; lighters gaily painted in red, blue, yellow and green, hurrying to unload the freight ships anchored in the channel; and the *wallah wallahs* offloading their crew.

Ferry boats moved between outlying islands carrying shift workers, and crowding the waterfronts were the ancient junks bringing food to the Colony from mainland China. They looked oddly old-fashioned, for behind them, along the shoreline, rose row upon row of magnificent modern skyscrapers clinging to the sides of the mountain on Hong Kong Island, right up to the peak where they disappeared into ethereal clouds.

Close at hand, behind the dockyards with their warehouses (strangely named "godowns"), I saw glimpses of Chinese streets, their signs displayed in large characters hanging horizontally from the buildings. They looked quaint, exciting, hinting of the exotic East acclaimed by tourist guides. As I lifted my eyes, I saw more mountains behind them in the distance on the Kowloon side. These were the hills of the Nine Dragons in the New Territories that stretched away to the border with Mao's China, a mere 20 miles away. Hong Kong, from the water on a sunny morning, looked beautiful; but it was a façade.

The immigration officer did not echo my eagerness. He took from me my completed forms, which stated that I was entering the Colony to work, and settled down to question my replies. They did not make him happy.

"Where you live?"

"I don't actually have anywhere to live yet."

"Where your friends?"

"I haven't got any of those here yet."

"Where you work?"

"Well, no—I don't have a job either."

The young Cantonese looked at me darkly. His Hong Kong English had managed the interrogation fine so far, but my answers were not according to the book. He must have thought I looked a bit pathetic, so he tried some supplementary questions.

"Where your mother?" He was quite kind now.

"She's in England."

"Where your return ticket?"

"Oh, I haven't got one of those." I said this quite blithely. Having a one-way ticket had not worried me, and I could not see why he was so concerned.

Finally, he brightened—we were in a place where one commodity usually solves most problems. "How much money you got?"

I felt quite pleased, as I considered myself rather well off. By dint of limiting my soft drinks on the month's journey out, I had arrived with almost what I had when I boarded the ship. "About HK $100," I said proudly.

"Not enough," the man snapped. "Hong Kong velly expensive place! That money not enough three days!" And he bustled off importantly in his fine peaked cap and starched shorts to find his superior. They consulted a moment, and then came back at me in officialdom. "Even though you Blitish," said the Chief, "we refuse you permission to leave the ship. Wait here."

I gathered that they thought I was a prostitute looking for easy earnings from U.S. troops on "rest and recreation" trips from Vietnam. With no means of support, no home, no friends, no nothing, I was left to watch all the other passengers land, wondering what they were going to do with me. Into my mind flashed horrible visions of their locking me up in the ship's hold and sending me back to England in disgrace. I would have to meet all my friends who would say, "Told you so! Fancy setting off round the world and leaving all the plans to God—very irresponsible!" What was I going to do? How had I landed here in the first place?

My mother had only been expecting one of us and when, as an end-of-war bonus, she gave birth to twins, my father was granted 48 hours compassionate leave. It must have been a disappointment for him, hoping for a rugby team and ending up with four girls instead. So I tried to make it up to him by behaving like a tomboy. I loved climbing and running, boys' toys and bicycles, and later I developed a passionate interest in rugger and scrum halves.

One of my first memories is from when I was four. I was leaning against the radiator in our home in Sutton, outside London, thinking, *Is it really worth being good?* I knew there was a choice, but I wondered if it paid to be good. So I went on sitting on the radiator—it made a lovely hollow noise when you banged it—and thinking. I ended up deciding that whatever I did was bound to be found out by someone some day. There would be a reckoning.

About a year later, my twin, Gilly, and I were sitting in Sunday School when a proper missionary came to talk to us. She was dressed up like the pictures of missionaries in Victorian children's books, complete with long dark skirt and hair pulled back in a bun. Pointing at each one of us sitting on our baby chairs, she fluted, "And could God want you on the mission field?" I remember thinking the answer to that question could not be no because, of course, God wanted everyone on the mission field. What exactly a mission field was I had no idea; I had a dim picture of myself sitting at the door of a mud hut, a sort of White Queen in Africa, feeling worthy. There were people like that in a missionary booklet I had seen.

I later told a friend at our little junior school that I wanted to be a missionary. It was a disastrous mistake. I soon found that everyone expected me to be better than everyone else. "But I thought you were going to be a missionary?" they would say accusingly when I was naughty. I always felt this was cheating somehow—it did not seem quite fair. So I learned very early that in England it is better to keep quiet about these things.

So I invented a series of careers to throw people off the scent— a conductor, the first woman to climb Everest, a circus performer. But occasionally I was found out. Once when a school friend's mother gushed, "So, you're the one who's going to be a mission- ary, aren't you?" I went very pink and hoped no one would men- tion it again.

However, privately, some things still bothered me. One day Gilly and I were walking over the railway bridge on our way back from meeting Nellie, our friend and the family daily help. As usual we had scrounged lime green penny lollies off her, but I had hardly got past the bit where it stuck to your tongue when an awful thought appeared: *What are we doing on the earth? What is life all about?* It seemed to me that I was trapped. I could not live just how I pleased, because it was possible that God was there after all and that one day I would have to explain every- thing I had done to Him. This was not a happy thought.

Then there was the problem of sin. I had seen the school register and the mark the students got against their name every day. Lying on the tennis lawn, I looked up at the sky and imag- ined God was up there with a big book. It had all our names in it, and every time you did something wrong, you got a mark.

I had a look at my column, and it was terribly long. I think it went on for pages. Well, there was nothing to be done, because there was a song in Sunday School about being stuck with your sins:

> God has blotted them out
> I'm happy and glad and free!
> God has blotted them out
> let's turn to Isaiah and see.[1]

I did not understand "blotting out," so it wasn't until years later that I knew what we were singing. I thought of that big book with all my sins stretching for lines and lines and God with a piece of blotting paper carefully blotting them in. At last a solution occurred to me. Because youth was in my favor, I decided, *If I never do anything wrong again, ever, ever, perhaps one day I will catch up to Winston Churchill! He is the goodest person on the earth, but he is very old, so if I stop sinning now maybe we will end up about equal!*

I made another mistake during my first term at boarding school. My twin and I were sitting at the end of the table, eating the compulsory piece of brown bread for tea. The head of our table was a tall girl named Mirissa; she told me off for not cutting my bread in half before eating it. I thought I would try to atone for the brown bread by making polite conversation, but, unfortunately, I chose the wrong topic. Having heard the first Billy Graham broadcast a short time previously, I mentioned how impressed I had been with the evangelist. "Mass emotion!" she drawled disdainfully and dismissed the subject. (I was in such awe of the seniors that ever after when such matters cropped up in school, I would sneer, "Mass emotion!")

Confirmation came around, and it was our grade's turn to be "done." I was rather serious about all this, feeling that I was one of the few who really believed in God. The others were only doing it for the dresses and the Confirmation Tea, to which we could invite relatives and godparents. My real fear was that the vicar would ask us individually what we believed before we

could get through, but I need not have worried—he never did.
So that was all right. But I had to ask him a question first:
"What should I think about when the bishop puts his hands
upon my head?"

The vicar thought for a moment. "Ah—I should er . . .
er—pray!" he concluded triumphantly. Gilly and I walked forward in our school-issue white dresses and knelt down. The
bishop laid hands on us—I can only remember walking back to
my seat filled with joy. Actually, I felt like laughing—like split-
ting my sides. *How improper—this was a confirmation service, and
this was the solemn bit. Laughing was for the tea afterward.* I found my
service sheet and covered up my face so that no one should see
me smiling in the pew, and then quickly put my head down in
an attitude of prayer. I had hoped to carry off the ceremony
looking both reverent and graceful—there did not seem to be
any connection between the service and this unseemly gladness. I was giving my life to God; I had expected nothing back.

My next move was to find the classified phone directory,
look up missionary societies, take the address of the first one and
write them a letter. "I'm thinking of becoming a missionary,"
I wrote, "and I think I should start preparing now. What subjects
should I take?" They responded by joining me to their postal
youth fellowship. It was lovely getting extra mail at boarding
school breakfast, but I had to make sure I leaned across the label
on the brown envelopes so that no one would find out where my
letters came from.

I worked during the holidays in Father's factory, gave coaching lessons, or delivered letters for the Post Office at Christmas.
For several years, I held the unofficial title of "our Number 1
Post-girl of the year," and I was even elected Miss Croydon
(South) 1960. My princely wage was US $.24 per hour, plus
luncheon vouchers; these I exchanged at the Post Office Canteen
for Woodbine cigarettes. I was a woman of the world!

I later moved on to the Royal College of Music, where I discovered very quickly that musicians regard love as the food of
music and had a hard time eluding a persistent horn player.

I did have a great predilection for the brass section, however, and I spent an unfortunate amount of my time trailing them around from pub to rehearsal to concert to pub. I sat on their instrument cases in the train and did very little practice on my piano or oboe.

From time to time, I passed the Christian Union notice board and got a twinge of conscience. But those Christians looked wet, pimply and feeble and were mostly organists, anyway. Not my scene at all. They sat in a holy huddle by themselves in the canteen and looked unattractive, like those awful people who came up to me and asked if I was "saved" or "washed in the blood." I did not know what they were talking about and did not want to, either. They looked grim—no makeup—and wore felt hats. Although they assured me I would change once I "knew Jesus," I certainly did not want to change into one of them.

Instead, I went to a series of parties where the chosen forms of recreation were sordid or boring. "Well, what did you come for then?" The men flung this at me when I declined the alternatives. I always went, hoping to meet the man of my dreams, and it was a long time before I realized that he was not likely to be at such parties.

I was sitting drably on my commuter train dragging back home from college one day when I met two old school friends. They took one look at me and invited me to a London flat for coffee with a fabulous man who talked about the Bible. So I went. He was fabulous. But so was everyone there. I could not get over it—they looked quite normal like me! The girls were made-up, and one of them was talking about bikinis. The men were discussing car racing—and yet all of them were there because they wanted to study the Bible. It was the first time in my life that my toes did not curl up when someone talked to me about Jesus. I could discuss God easily in that flat.

I was upset to hear, though, about *heaven* and *hell*, which I had thrown out with the mass emotionalism years before. But more disturbing was hearing that no one could go to God except through Jesus.[2] The words themselves were not as much of a shock as my discovery that it was Jesus who said them. I was constrained either to accept what Jesus said about Himself or to forget about the Christian faith. Among my social set, the worst sin was to be narrow, but Jesus' words offered no compromise.[3]

Reluctantly, I told Him I would believe what He had said—although I did not like it much. I was converted.

My life became fuller than I had believed possible. I had not entered a narrow life after all. Shortly after, a man on my suburban line leaned across the carriage and asked if I believed in God. "No," I replied, "I know Him; it's different. I know peace; I know where I'm going."

My new life also brought difficulty. After one particular Bible study, the girls sat praying—thanking God for their certainty of going to heaven. I opened my eyes and peeped at them. They were all smiling and genuinely happy. I was appalled. For if we believed that we were going to heaven because of Jesus, surely the converse was true also—that some people would not be going. The girls sat down to eat risotto, but I dashed out, thinking, *How can you just sit there believing what you do? What about the people who haven't heard? Risotto?*

This resulted in my taking part in the kind of scene that I would have despised before my conversion. I found myself playing the piano for a youth squash evangelical tea party in Waddon. It was a Saturday afternoon, and I should have been at the Rugger International at Twickenham, yelling "shove" with the best of them. Instead, I was singing salvation songs and eating sausage-sizzles in Waddon. It was then that I was sure my life had really taken a new direction!

Having gained my degree, I was enjoying a career teaching music. I wanted to give my whole life somewhere; I was free. Since I was not especially in love at the time, there was nothing to stop me from giving all my time in one place. The missionary idea came back.

So I wrote to Africa (that's where missionaries go)—to schools, societies and broadcasting companies. And they all wrote back no—they did not want me. One group explained, "If you could teach English and math, then we could find a place for you, but we can't afford musicians out here yet. Maybe in a few years."

Undeterred, I sought the best advice going. My idea was to get hold of the visiting speaker (or the good-looking curate) after a meeting and ask for a private audience.

"What do you think I should do with my life?" I asked earnestly of each one.

"Have you prayed about it?" they always replied. It was maddening, because I had prayed about it, but God did not give me a clear answer. My Bible told me to trust and He would lead me.[4] I used to dash down to fetch the post in the mornings, thinking guidance would come that way. But the replies were always negative.

One night, I had a dream in which the family were all crowded around the dining room table looking at a map of Africa. In the middle of the different colored countries was a pink one. I leaned over to see what it was called. It said "Hong Kong." I did not really believe this, but I did not want to show my ignorance.

"Ah," I tried to sound nonchalant, "I never knew Hong Kong was there."

"Yes, of course, it is, didn't you know?" said my Aunty Dotty in a superior tone, and I did not dare argue.

When I woke up, I wrote to the Hong Kong government explaining that I was a qualified musician and that I would like a teaching post. They wrote back saying that applications accompanied by three named references had to be handled through the Ministry of Overseas Development—and that they had no jobs for musicians. Then, I tried my old Missionary Society, stating that I wanted to go to Hong Kong. Impossible, they said—they did not accept would-be missionaries until the age of 25, so I would have to wait.

"But I think Jesus might come back before I'm 25," I said. "Couldn't I go sooner? I don't mind not being called a missionary—can't I teach in one of your schools?" They said there was no way. I seemed to have misinterpreted my dream. I went to pray in a tiny, peaceful village church. There, I saw a vision of a woman—holding out her arms beseechingly as on a refugee poster. I wondered what she wanted—she looked desperate for something. Was it Christian aid?

Then words moved past like a television credit. "What can you give us?" What did I honestly think I could give her? If I was going to be a missionary, what was I going to give anyone? Was it my ability to play the piano and oboe? Was I to pass on the benefit of my nice English background or my education? Was I to be a channel for food, or money or clothing? If I only gave her those things, then when I went away she would be hungry again. But the woman in the picture had been hungry for a food she did not know about.

Then it came to me that what she needed was the love of Jesus; if she received that, then when I left her she would still be full and, even better, she would be able to share it with other people. I now knew what I had to do, but I still did not know where I was supposed to do it.

Not long afterward, I met a factory worker from West Croydon who had been with us on the sausage-sizzle mission.

"You got any answers yet?" He knew I was praying about the future.

"No," I said apologetically.

"You wanna come to our meeting?" he said, nodding his head knowingly. "We always get answers in ours."

What kind of monopoly on God did he think he had in West Croydon? I was furious, but I was also intrigued to know what was going on at his meeting. So one Tuesday night, I took the bus over.

When I arrived, someone told me confidentially not to be surprised if anything odd happened. Nervously, I sat myself near the door—apparently they were going to use "spiritual gifts" at their meeting, and I wanted to be in a good position to get away if necessary.

I was not sure what to expect, and I thought maybe someone would prophesy in a loud voice, "You'll meet a man who'll give you a ticket for such and such a country on such and such a date," and that would be God's way of answering me.

The meeting, however, was orderly and calm, with normal prayers and songs. One or two people who were present did speak in a strange language that I did not understand and others explained what they meant. But there was no booming voice from God talking to me.

Then it came.

It was not a great booming voice at all. Someone was speaking quite quietly, and I was completely sure that it was meant for me.

"Go. Trust me, and I will lead you. I will instruct you and teach you in the way which you shall go; I will guide you with my eye."[5] There it was, what He had been saying all along, but now it was underlined. I was sure that God had my life in hand and that He was about to lead me somewhere.

There was no doubt that West Croydon got answers, but they did not tell me how I could receive spiritual gifts myself. I went home to wait. God had quite clearly promised to guide me, but I still did not know where to go. I gave in my notice for all my jobs so that I would be free to leave after the summer term—and I tried to pray by my bedside a bit more.

Still no answers.

During the Easter holidays I went to help in Richard Thompson's Shoreditch parish for a week. As a minister, he had known me for some time, and I felt as though he was in a position to give counsel. I well remember the carpet in his study, for I spent a good time staring at it before plucking up courage to speak. Then I told him that God and I had reached a stalemate; He had told me clearly to go. I knew why I was to go, but He would not tell me where. So how could I go?

Richard's reply was extraordinary. "If God is telling you to go—you had better go."

"How can I—I don't know where to go. All my applications have been rejected."

"Well, if you've tried all the conventional ways and missionary societies and God still is telling you to go, you had better get on the move."

I felt frustrated.

"If you had a job, a ticket, accommodation, a sick fund and a pension, you wouldn't need to trust Him," Richard continued. "Anyone can go that way whether they are Christians or not. If I were you, I would go out and buy a ticket for a boat going on the longest journey you can find and pray to know where to get off."

I did not exactly hear bells, but this was the first time in all those months of searching that anything made sense.

"It sounds terrific—but it must be cheating, because I'd love to do that." I still had the idea that anything to do with God had to be serious. I was sure that Christians always had to take the hard way and that enjoyment was no part of suffering for their faith.

But Richard Thompson told me that it was quite scriptural. Abraham was willing to leave his country and follow Jehovah to a promised land without knowing where he was going, because he trusted.[6] In the same way, thousands of years later, Gladys Aylward journeyed in faith to China.

"You can't lose if you put yourself completely in God's hands, you know." Richard was quite serious. "If He doesn't want you to get on the ship, He is quite able to stop you—or to make the ship go anywhere in the world." I had visions of being storm-driven like St. Paul. I might land on a little desert island where one person wanted to hear about Jesus. It was an exciting proposition.

"Maybe you will go all the way round the world just to talk to one sailor about Christ, or maybe you will go as far as Singapore to play the piano for a week of youth meetings and then come back."

Richard's advice was extraordinary, but completely wise. Never at any time did he lead me to the impression that I was to get on a ship, grow a bun and get off as a missionary ready to do a "work." He never suggested that I had to achieve anything at all; I had simply to follow wherever God led. I, too, felt that I could not lose on this adventure.

So I went out and, after counting up my money, found the cheapest ship on the longest route passing through the most countries on its way. It went from France to Japan. I bought a ticket and was all set.

Of course, there were my parents and friends and others to deal with. Understandably, some were skeptical. My father, very rightly, insisted that I think long and carefully on my "slow boat to China." What right had I to give my religion to people in other countries when they had perfectly good religions of their own? Each parent was content about my trip but worried about the other. So I prayed, and one evening I heard them convincing each other that it was all right.

The telephone book missionary society was less keen. "Very irresponsible advice for a vicar to give a young girl," they cautioned. And I suppose it would have been had it not been the Holy Spirit who gave Richard Thompson the words.

The day I left was one of those days when everything goes wrong. The taxi ordered to drive us the 20 miles to London appeared an hour late and then got stuck in a traffic jam on Vauxhall Bridge. I remember my mother frantically chewing white stomach pills. Gasping, I settled into the boat-train carriage with my nightmare of luggage and one minute to spare. Richard Thompson came running up the platform shouting, "Praise the Lord!" in a very un-English fashion, and the train pulled out.


The immigration officer turned back to me in annoyance. For a moment, I was afraid that I had come all this way to Asia merely to be repatriated. Then I remembered that morning's reading, "Behold your name is written on the palms of God's hands." If my name was written there, then God knew all about me. So perhaps the whole purpose of the journey was that I should get arrested in Hong Kong and locked up in the ship's hold, and then I could convert the jailer. I could not lose.

"Wait a minute," I said, suddenly remembering my mother's godson. "I do know someone here. He's a policeman." The effect was dramatic; the police were highly regarded back in 1966, and anyone who knew a policeman who ranked higher than mere immigration officials was clearly okay. On their faces I read, "All this bother from a stupid girl who is well connected all along."

They thrust my passport at me, muttering angrily that I could land on condition that I search for work immediately. As far as they were concerned, my money would not last three days in Hong Kong.

# THEY CALL IT DARKNESS

The Walled City is guarded day and night by a ceaseless
army of watchers. As soon as a stranger approaches, the
watchers pass the word. Their flip-flops flapping, the boys
run between the noodle stalls, through doorways, across narrow
alleys and up staircases. Grass Sandal whispers to Red Bamboo
Pole, who respectfully communicates the news to Golden Paw.
The leaders of the crime syndicate have colorful names, but
their activities are sordid. To strangers, the real business of the
Walled City is invisible; doors close, shutters clang shut, joss
sticks camouflage the strange, pungent smell of opium.

One name for the Walled City in Chinese is *Hak Nam*, in
English, "darkness." As I began to know it better, I learned how
true this name was; the Walled City was a place of terrible darkness, both physical and spiritual. Journalists get good copy out
of it, but when you meet the men and women who have to live
and suffer in such a place, you can be broken by compassion.

I had thought I was going to one of those Chinese walled
villages in the guidebooks—sort of quaint, but poor.

Mrs. Donnithorne had invited me to visit her nursery school
and church, but she had not prepared me for what I was to see.
We got a lift as far as Tung Tau Chuen Road on the edge of the
city. The street was lined with countless dentists' parlors, which
were equipped with ancient and modern drilling equipment,
their windows filled with gold and silver teeth. There were teeth
in bottles, teeth on velvet cushions, teeth even on the tips of big
whirring fans. This was the street of the illegal dentists; illegal

because none of the amateur mouth doctors is allowed to practice in Hong Kong proper.

Behind these tawdry shops rose the ramshackle skyscrapers of the Walled City; it seemed impossible to find a way in. But the frail old lady who was my guide knew exactly where to go; we squeezed through a narrow gap between the shops and started walking down a slime-covered passageway. I will never forget the darkness and the smell—a fetid smell of rotten foodstuffs, excrement, offal and general rubbish. The darkness was startling after the glaring sunlight outside. As we walked on between the houses, their projecting upper stories almost touched each other above us so that only occasionally would the daylight penetrate in strong shafts of brightness among the shadows. I felt like I was in an underground tunnel.

As we went, my guide gave me a running commentary. On my right was a plastic flower factory; on my left an old prostitute who was too old and ugly to get work. So instead, the prostitute employed several child prostitutes to work for her; one seemed mentally retarded, another was a child she had bought as a baby and brought up to take over the bread-earner's role when she grew too old. They had plenty of customers; in that depraved street the ownership of child prostitutes was regarded as a good source of income. "Auntie Donnie" told me to keep my head down in case someone chose to empty his chamber pot as we were passing below. Next, we reached the door to the illegal dog restaurant, where the captured beasts were flayed to death to provide tender dog steaks; then we came upon the pornographic film-show house, a crowded lean-to shed.

There was legitimate business, too. Workmen carrying loads of freshly mixed cement on their heads hurried down the alleys. Women clutching huge sacks of plastic flowers staggered out from tiny workrooms where the clank of plastic-pressing machines never ceased. There was no Sabbath day of rest here; five days' holiday a year was considered quite sufficient. Whole families were involved in keeping the plastic presses running day and night. For Chinese children, when they were not studying, the duty to work all hours for their parents was paramount.

*How can such a place exist inside the British Crown Colony of Hong Kong?* Over 80 years ago when Britain apportioned to herself not only the Chinese island of Hong Kong but also the mainland Peninsula of Kowloon and the Chinese territories behind it, one exception was made. The old walled village of Kowloon was to remain under Chinese Imperial Administration, complete with its own Mandarin magistrate administering Chinese law.

Later, however, the British traders complained and the concession was unilaterally withdrawn; the Chinese magistrate died—he was never succeeded by either Chinese or British—and lawlessness inside the Walled City came to stay. The city became a haven for gold smuggling, drug smuggling, illegal gambling dens and every kind of vice. The confusion over its ownership meant that the police could not enforce the law and, indeed, would not even enter the infamous city. Even today, they go in large groups if they are hunting particular criminals, and usually the man they want effectively disappears into its sordid alleyways.

The area was large in population, small in size. A mere six acres sheltered 30,000 people (or double that; no census has ever found the true number). The housing was appalling; no building regulations could be enforced, so crazy-angled apartment blocks without sanitation, water or lighting straddled the streets. A maze of tangled wires was graphic evidence of the fact that their electricity was tapped from the public supplies outside the Walled City. But you cannot steal sanitation, so excrement had to be emptied into the stinking alleys below. At street level there were two toilets for all 30,000 people; the "toilets" consist of two holes over overflowing crawling cesspools—one for women, one for men.

It seemed unlikely that a place like the Walled City would have schools and churches. But in this appalling place where children were born and brought up, Mrs. Donnithorne had found premises and begun a general primary school. The teachers were not properly qualified, but they had attended secondary school to fourth or fifth form level. The school was small, but it had morning and afternoon shifts and taught several hundred pupils. On the very first day that I visited the school, Auntie Donnie asked me to teach there. Without thinking, I said, "Yes," and she immediately said, "How often?" Before I had fully realized what I was getting myself into, I had agreed to teach percussion band, singing and English conversation three afternoons a week.

I soon found the Chinese education system to be so miscast that very often the brightest got fed up and dropped out. The system demanded that you learn all your lessons by heart. Every month, every term and every year there were exams. Should a child fail annual exams, he or she had to repeat the whole of the year's lessons. It was not unusual to come across children who had taken the Primary One exam at the end of their first year no less than three times. I formed a theory that it was the bright ones who got bored with the system and jumped off the ladder while the duller ones climbed up.

Percussion band and singing are not too difficult to teach even if there is little or no conversation. However, when it came to teaching English conversation I was a complete failure.

All the teaching in the school was highly regimented. I would read out, "John and Mary went into the wood," and the students would repeat after me in unison, "John and Mary [it came out "Mairly"] went into the wood" without comprehension. Traditionally, understanding in Chinese education is not held to be important, but learning is considered vital, and they all learn to repeat what the teacher says like machines.

My attempts to enliven their stories by acting out what was happening were completely misunderstood; we had a classroom riot every time. No one had ever tried to teach them to participate in stories and dramatic ideas; the freedom that I tried to show them resulted in classroom anarchy within a matter of minutes. So I sadly went back to reading out sentences from the book—the sure way to maintain calm.

Once a week, one of the classrooms was converted into a church for a Sunday night service. So Miss Poon—I now proudly

:

had a Chinese name—played the harmonium. This meant pedaling at 50 mph or so to produce an accompaniment that could be heard against the singing—otherwise, having started on a particular note, they would continue to sing in that key quite regardless of the one I was playing in. I usually gave in and joined them.

Mostly, the worshipers were older Chinese women—some with babies wrapped tightly to their backs—and I discovered that many of them, being illiterate, came to church for a reading lesson. The singing leader had a sort of rehearsal before each hymn, pointing out the characters (the written form of Chinese—one sign for each word) one by one. They all sang loudly and enthusiastically. Then the Bible woman gave the teaching in Cantonese; I could not understand a word of it at that stage, but I felt that I shared in the worship.

Among the crowd of Chinese faces on my debut night, one woman stuck out remarkably. She was an elderly vegetable seller; she had a deeply lined face, with her hair combed straight back and a large circular comb stuck on her head. She had only two teeth, which showed prominently since she was always smiling. She came up and tugged me by the sleeve enthusiastically. Beside her was her half-blind husband—so she pulled him along, too. She chattered on, beaming at me and tugging still. I asked someone to translate what she was saying. It was, "See you next week—see you next week."

I wanted to tell her that I could not come every week; it was a long journey across the harbor and through Kowloon to the Walled City for a Sunday evening. It meant that I got back late. This was not good, as I had to be up very early the next morning to teach.

But then I found that I could not possibly say all that to her. She would only understand that I was there or I was not; so I decided that for her sake I would be there every week.

By now, I had regular jobs teaching in a primary school in the mornings (which I held for six months), helping Auntie Donnie three afternoons a week in her primary school, playing for the Sunday service, and arranging music programs for various welfare organizations. This filled up my time. I had been offered a superb job teaching music by a prestigious boarding school at the other end of the island; they additionally offered to refund my fare out. But it was clear I could not combine teaching there with my work in the Walled City.

I do not find that I am very good at guidance, but on this occasion I had been reading a verse in the Bible that said, "For he was looking for the city which has foundations, whose architect and builder is God."[1] As I read that verse, I felt quite sure that I should carry on teaching inside the Walled City.

The second time I went into the Walled City, I had this wonderful feeling inside; like the thrill you get on your birthday. I found myself wondering why I was so happy. And the next time I went into the Walled City, I had exactly the same sensation. This was not reasonable—of all the revolting places in the world. And yet nearly every time I was in that underground city over the next dozen years, I was to feel the same joy. I had caught a glimpse of it at confirmation, and again when I had really accepted Jesus into my life—and now to find it in this profane place?

"There's a drug addict," said Auntie Donnie as we walked down the street to her school one morning. I had no idea at that stage what being a drug addict meant. Did he jump at you, or steal your watch, or throw fits? He was a pathetic looking man slowly sorting through a pile of waste item by item to see if there was anything of value. He seemed very ill; his face was waxy and he looked more like a 70-year-old than a 35-year-old.

He wore a soiled T-shirt, a pair of cotton shorts and battered plastic sandals. Most Chinese people keep themselves meticulously clean, but Mr. Fung was filthy, his teeth were brown and broken, and his fingernails were disgusting. His rough crew cut, a grey shadow over his skull, was a sure sign that he had recently come out of prison. For Mr. Fung, though, prison was somewhere to sleep—a place with regular meals, which was more comfortable than his present existence, sleeping in the streets and eating scraps collected at restaurant doors.

But food and sleep were not important to Mr. Fung. He lived to "chase the dragon." This Chinese way of drug taking has a magic ritual all its own—a sort of devilish liturgy that is sacred. Once inside a drug den, addicts would take a piece of silver tinfoil; on it, they would place the small sand-colored grains of heroin. After heating the foil with a slow-burning spill of screwed up toilet paper, the heroin would gradually melt into a dark brown treacle. The addicts would then put the outer casing of a matchbox into their mouth to act as a funnel through which to inhale the fumes. They would keep the pool of treacle moving from one end of the silver foil to the other, following it with their mouth. This is "chasing the dragon."

Mr. Fung never chased the dragon in public but in drug dens or lavatories. It was a full nine months before I actually saw it for myself. And I soon discovered that not all drug takers looked like Mr. Fung. Some were very well dressed; they regarded their neat appearance as evidence that they were not enslaved to the dragon. As I was going into the city, quite frequently I saw Mr. Fung. *Should I learn to say "Good morning, how are you?" or "Do you have a problem?"* In any case, I could not understand his reply, even had he confided in me. I wondered whether I should do something about him and others like him. I hoped someone was doing something.

Prostitution, unlike drug abuse, was seldom concealed. The first prostitute I met used dark mauve lipstick and mauve nail varnish—a macabre combination with her thin grey face and emaciated body. She spent her whole life squatting in a street so narrow that the sewer tunnel ran by her heels. I never saw her in any other position. When she ate, she remained squatting there with her rice bowl and her chopsticks, waiting for customers.

Farther down, other women sat on orange boxes, and one even had a chair. It was hard to tell their ages, because most of them were drug addicts too. The score marks on the backs of their hands showed that they were mainlining—directly injecting heroin into the veins. Day after day, I walked past them and could not tell whether they were asleep or awake; they nodded all day, showing the yellow of their eyes in a heroin haze.

One day I tried touching the little one. I had learned to say, "Jesus loves you" (*Yeh sou ngoi nei*), and my heart went out to her. But she cringed away from me. Looking at the expression on her face, I suddenly realized that she was feeling sorry for me because she thought I had made a mistake. She seemed to be saying, "You're a good girl and shouldn't be talking to the likes of us! You're a nice Christian, dear; maybe you don't know who we are." She put up the barrier, and I did not know how to cross it. She was embarrassed that a clean girl had made an error and touched a dirty one.

Some of the older prostitutes were clearly involved in procuring. As men came out of the blue film theatre, these *mama-sans* would literally pull them in. You could hear them saying, "She's very young and very cheap," as they pushed them up the wooden flight of steps. Compared with the prices charged in other places by the more glamorous Susie Wongs, these prostitutes were cheap indeed at HK $5 each. Not, of course, that the girls were allowed to keep all this money—most prostitutes were controlled by Triad gangs, and these brothels were only allowed to operate by the gang controlling that area. The Triads also supplied the young girls.

There were two girls I saw occasionally, as I taught percussion band next to their sordid room. One was a cripple and the other was mentally retarded. They were both prisoners. They never went anywhere without a *mama-san* accompanying them. They were visited up to three times an hour, and I reckoned they might be dead of disease by the time they were 20 or so.

Later, an English-speaking Triad member explained how these two girls, and others like them, would have been introduced to the trade. A group of young men would hold a party and invite girls along. Some of them had been warned about what might happen; others were innocent victims. At the party, the new girls would be seduced; if they resisted they were

sometimes forcibly raped. Usually, each member of the gang
would take his girl off with him and stay with her for a few
days. When the girl was attached to him and thoroughly accus-
tomed to sex, he signed her over to a brothel. One girl could
bring in enough money to support several men.

Other girls became prostitutes because their parents could
not afford to feed and clothe them. One mother told me, "It
wasn't really selling my daughter, you know. My husband left
me, and as there were no social security payments in Hong Kong
I had nothing to live on. I couldn't afford to raise my baby
myself, so I gave her to this woman who wanted a child, and she
gave me HK $100 lucky money. It was just lucky money."

Of course, this woman knew what she was doing—she was
selling her daughter into prostitution for at least her teenage
years. After that, most former child prostitutes escaped from
their owners and made careers of their own, practicing the only
trade they knew. Child prostitutes could start their careers as
early as nine years old.

Respectable people thought of the girls as the scum of the
earth, but I knew that it was only by the grace of God that I had
been born in a different place. I tried to work out how I could
reach girls like these—guarded as they were. Eventually, I shelved
the problem by hoping one day to find a concerned man who
would pay the hourly rate but share the good news of Christ in
that time. Maybe he and I could work out a plan of escape if any
of the girls wanted to get out.

# THE YOUTH CLUB

Sometimes I think that Chan Wo Sai was the real reason why I started the Youth Club. He was a most unattractive 15-year-old with about as many problems in life as anyone could have—personal problems, educational problems, home problems, background problems and no prospects at all.

I first got to know him when I was teaching English and singing on one of my three afternoons a week at Oiwah Primary School. I was teaching the children "Ten Green Bottles"—a less sexy song I can hardly think of—yet there was Chan Wo Sai getting really "sent" by a traditional English nursery rhyme in a language he could not speak. Chan Wo Sai was rolling his eyes and clicking his fingers; then he got up and began to slide across the classroom toward me in a sexy, hip-thrusting motion like a bad Chinese movie actor. I hurriedly ordered him back to his place and changed to another song. As soon as class ended, I went to find out where he came from. The story was both simple and sad.

Chan Wo Sai was born in the Walled City. His mother was a prostitute and his father a drunkard. They lived in a sort of cockloft; to find him I had to go down the narrow passage where the prostitutes were living, along the main street where the older woman pimps spent all day waiting, and then left at the blue film theatre and down a very muddy path to a collapsed building. Here, beyond a heap of stones, he lived with his whole family in half of a room that had been added on to another building. The walls were crumbling off.

There were more prostitutes next door. He'd known about them for as long as he could remember. He was in no way shocked by them; they were just part of his life. Indeed, he thought their activities were very funny. His horizons were limited to the brothel next door, the gambling dens down the road and the opium dens beyond. There was nowhere in the Walled City where you could go and do anything neutral, let alone take part in constructive activity. So I tried to get to know him, to help him with his problems.

This was difficult, because I could hardly speak a word of Cantonese. All I had managed to learn as of yet were a few sentences. I could say "good morning" and "have you eaten yet?" but that was about all. And to make life still more difficult, Chan Wo Sai had a speech impediment, which made conversation hard even for fluent Cantonese speakers. Our great point of contact was the drum pad I gave him; it is a sheet of rubber stuck on a wooden board on which you can practice, with drumsticks, making a noiseless drum. The drum pad provided the perfect excuse for going to see him regularly. He was supposed to practice with it, but he seldom did, and in any case he had the most hopeless sense of rhythm. But he was pleased to find that someone was interested in him. This was the first time in his life that anyone had shown care for him.

As time went on, I found myself constantly thinking about him, which alarmed me. My English mind had been trained to think that love for a boy must be romantic, and because I was a Christian, that sort of love would eventually lead to marriage. Yet that, of course, was impossible and ridiculous; my mind told me that he was a very ugly boy with a hopeless background. But I really did love him, and I prayed for him continually. I got to the point where I could quite seriously and willingly have given my life for him.

After some time, I was able to understand—and was surprised by—what I saw in myself. It was as if God had given me a special love for him and that I was meant to show it, although it was not necessarily an emotion that should or could be returned. This love was for his good; it was quite different from any love for other people that I had before, in which I had always wanted something in return. I had never before loved somebody entirely for his benefit without caring what he felt for me. So it was really for Chan Wo Sai that I opened a club just for young people.

Of the various groups of people in need in the Walled City, none were worse catered to than the young teenagers. At least the younger children had the chance to go to primary school, and most Chinese parents, no matter how poor, encouraged this. But the young teenagers had nothing; getting into secondary school was almost impossible for a Walled City boy, even if his parents could afford it, which was unlikely.

Teenagers often found work in the sweated-labor plastic factories where the hours were unlimited and the pay pitiful. Then, disheartened by the life of ceaseless work, they dropped out. Many boys, and sometimes girls, left home to find shelter in some one-room hovel where lots of others, all following the same path, slept. Soon, with nothing to do, they drifted into crime; the Triad gangs often provided the only other employment available.

My involvement with Chan Wo Sai grew during the summer of 1967, when all of China was thrown into confusion by the activities of the Red Guards. The fever crossed the border into Hong Kong; trouble was skillfully stirred by local agitators. Knowing nothing about politics, I remained blissfully unaware of what was going on, although there were riots all over the colony.

I did discover, however, that some of the Walled City boys were being paid to pick up stones and throw them. I felt that they could just as easily be persuaded to come on a picnic. So one hot, humid day in June, I said to Auntie Donnie rather pompously, "I think the Lord would have me start a youth club." I had visions of a handpicked team of handsome helpers from Hong Kong Island who would sweep in with a beautifully organized program while I sat back and applauded. I envisaged a room open evenings and weekends; it would be a place where young people could play table tennis and take part in all the other normal activities available to boys and girls in a big city. It equally could be a place where they would hear about Jesus. I envisaged committee discussions, prayer meetings, program planning and further discussion. Auntie Donnie was more practical. "Good, I've been praying for that for years," she said. "When do you start? Next week?"

We started one week later. I had not yet put together my handpicked team, and we did not have anywhere to meet. But I soon borrowed a room from the school on Saturday afternoons. Gordon Siu, a young Chinese man I had met at the Youth Orchestra, became a tower of strength and an invaluable translator. He was also realistic: Unlike some of the Chinese leaders who expected a youth club to be a sort of extended Bible lecture, Gordon helped us hire coaches, came on picnics and went roller skating with us. Soon school ended, and none of the pupils had much to do. The prospect of the boys being caught up in the riots stimulated me to develop the activities further.

Saturday afternoons grew into a complete summer program, with organized picnics, hikes and visits to the forestry plantations. What started that summer became a regular program that happened every July and August for some years after.

The first to come to the Youth Club were the 13- and 14-year-olds; they began to bring friends from outside. Everyone knew from the beginning that I was there because I was a Christian and that events would start or end with a short talk. They did not like the Jesus bit at all; for them, anything to do with Christianity was either full of prohibition or middle class. They had no idea who Jesus really was. Worse, they believed that if you could not read, you could not be a Christian, because to them being a Christian was something to do with the Big Book.

Some young people told me that they could not come to the Youth Club. "We smoke and we drink," they said. "We go to films and we gamble—and we know Christians don't do any of those things." It soon became clear that the blocks to belief were often the result of a culture gap, which local Chinese Christians did nothing to overcome.

All too soon, Chan Wo Sai dropped out of school. At 15, he was one of the oldest boys in Primary fourth form, and he was at least four years behind. He decided not to finish that year of schooling; a new blue film theatre had just opened in the Walled City, and he got a job selling the tickets.

To the inexperienced teacher from England, dropping out of primary school seemed a terrible thing to do. I spent all summer trying to persuade the hostile boy to go back. Eventually, he humbled himself and went to see his teachers, but they refused to take him back. Their explanations horrified me: One said, "Well, Jackie, we were only too pleased when he left, because we could not control him. He upset not only the teachers but also the whole of the class. Good riddance to him."

Theirs was a mission school, not a profit-oriented private academy. These were Christian teachers, and I had imagined that when they met once a week for prayer meetings, they prayed for the difficult and troublesome boys like Chan Wo Sai. But the truth was that most of the teachers had barely completed secondary school themselves; they had said they were Christians just to get the job and were incapable of handling anything other than entirely docile classes. For Chan Wo Sai, his departure was effectively the end of his education—he could not go to another school without retaking the Primary Four exam.

The only alternative was to find him a vocational training school that would teach him some skill. However, he proved ineligible for such courses, either because he was too old or because he had not completed primary school and could not speak English. Together we trudged around schools and factories seeking further training or an apprenticeship, and in every case we were turned away. Against Chan Wo Sai the gates were shut, even though he was only 15.

What was to happen to him? He had dropped out of school, and selling tickets at the blue film theatre was as far as he was ever going to go. There was nothing I could do for him except keep this club going. Several of his dropout friends joined the gangs. They discovered that there they had a role. If they proved themselves, they were given respect and responsibility. They were given a rank and treated as people of importance. In the gangs they found a degree of care, consideration and closeness that they certainly found nowhere else. In school and church, success in exams was equated with righteousness: "Be a good boy—don't go around with bad people, but study hard and pass your exams." The school had said it. The Church had said it. Their parents had said it. For the boys like Chan Wo Sai, it was terribly boring to be told the same thing again and again, and they hated hearing it. The gangs and my club were the only places where they did not hear the sentence of failure and rejection.

The Youth Club was indeed unlike any other activity organized in the Walled City. Nobody made any money out of it; no gangsters controlled it, and years later they even sent guards to protect it from those who wanted to smash the place up. The club went through various addresses, but inside it was always the same—a bare room with some game equipment (like table tennis and darts), crude benches and a bookshelf with Christian books bought by me, which no one could read.

Nicholas was another boy I got to know very well during this time. Both his father and mother had been on charges for selling drugs, and the whole family lived in one of the nastiest houses I have ever been in. Half of it was literally a pigsty—for their neighbors kept a pig below. The two eldest girls were prostitutes, and there always seemed to be a lot of babies around. I never found out which baby belonged to which mother. Some were Nicholas's brothers and sisters—others his nephews and nieces. They all lived in a room the size of a broom cupboard that stank.

The church members resented Nicholas because, like Chan Wo Sai, he was such a bad influence in the school. Of course, they knew about the bargirl sisters and that the father was a hopeless opium addict. In their eyes, the fact that I was welcoming Nicholas to our club gave the Christian Church a bad name—I should not even be seen with him.

I knew what Nicholas was like. He was vile and always a pain; he had Triad connections right from the beginning and later graduated to becoming a heroin addict and, necessarily, a pusher. But I loved him, even if unreasonably, for Jesus had come into the world for him, which too was unreasonable.

So I made a point of befriending him. I visited him at home all hours of the day for weeks and months and years. I was terribly concerned about him and grieved for him—perhaps more deeply than for any other person over the years. I found him in drug dens; I went to him when he was arrested; I prayed with him in the police station and in the prison before his trial; I helped him with his trial. But none of my efforts changed him.

I learned that any sense of "righteousness" was lacking in that place of darkness. Crime, dishonesty and corruption were considered "right" as long as they paid. But this attitude did not stop its supporters from adopting a cliché-loaded morality in my presence. They felt it was correct, as I represented the Church, the Establishment.

"Isn't he a bad boy," Nicholas's mother would say to me in front of him. "Miss Pullinger—you must teach him a good way and take him to your church and the Youth Club." It was nauseous prating, and I hated it. Then she would moan, "Can't understand why my children are bad. I had them baptized and sent them to church." This from a woman who measured grains of white powder into little packets for sale to junkies.

Later on, one of the younger sisters, Annie, also became a bargirl. Then, incredibly, she scored the ultimate by making a wonderful marriage. Her husband was a *for-gei* and a collector of rake-off money for the police. Annie was ever so pleased about marrying him, because he had his own private car. Annie's mother was delighted, too; although the nightclubs, ballrooms and brothels owned and run by the son-in-law's family were only low class, at least they were successful.

One day as I was walking down the street, an old man ran up to me. He was an opium den owner—an important man in the Walled City. He had the skeleton face of an opium addict, with gray-tinged hollow cheeks from a lifetime of taking the sweet stuff. He was beside himself with rage. "Poon Siu Jeh—Miss Poon," he cried. "You must complain to the police!"

"Why should I complain?" I asked him.

"They've closed all the opium dens." He was outraged and indignant.

"I'm delighted the police have closed the opium dens," I replied. "Why do you want me to complain?"

"Because they've let the heroin dens stay open, and we've all paid them the same money. It's not fair!"

No right and wrong. Just fair and unfair.

A young man named Joseph was one of the earliest Youth Club presidents. Unlike Nicholas and Chan Wo Sai, he had no overt connections with vice. His father had remarried when he was six, and his new wife did not like her stepchildren, so she did not feed them. Joseph and his sister, Jenny, were sent out to beg with plastic bowls or to grub through a rubbish heap for food. They were rescued by a pastor in the New Territories and sent to Mrs. Donnithorne's Mission School. Having finished primary school, Joseph got himself a room and worked as a coolie whenever he could. His sister soon joined him there.

Characters such as Nicholas would drop in on him and stay the night, and his room became a breeding ground for gangsters. His sister, Jenny, however, was in moral danger. At 15, she was very pretty and reveled in release from her highly supervised Christian hostel. Now she could talk all night with her brother's friends—or go out with them. She was not at school, and it was great fun. I thought that if she remained in Joseph's room, there was only one way she could go.

I could not offer them both a home, as I was already sharing my Hong Kong room with another Walled City girl, Rachel. But I thought I could squeeze Jenny in, so I bullied her out of the Walled City to live with me. I found her a secondary school and bought the uniform, the books and the lunches. She was not grateful; she wanted to be back in the Walled City, and she caused many headaches during the next year that she lived with us.

One of our regular attendees, Christopher, lived in the Walled City in a house that could only be described as a loft. To find it, you had to walk down a narrow street where no light penetrated; the houses were built so close to each other that it was like going down a tunnel. When you reached a couple of hencoops made from soft drink crates, you had found their home. It was very, very smelly. Beside the coops and up some wooden ladders you reached the living level; you had to open Christopher's door from underneath, exactly like a trap door. There was just one room over the chickens; should it catch fire everyone would be burned to death. Escape was impossible except by lifting the door and going down the wooden ladder. The family sleeping quarters were behind a curtain; there you found a pair of wooden bunk beds, one on top of the other. Everyone slept in these two beds—everyone being six brothers and sisters, plus the parents.

The rest of the single room was taken up with huge piles of plastic objects, which Christopher's mother assembled. She earned about HK $1 a day for this work. All the children had to help her assemble these plastic parts; they began working as soon as they were three or four years old. Christopher's younger sister did not finish primary school; she was sent to work in a factory as soon as she was 13. She was badly paid for the sweated labor and every dollar and cent she earned had to be given to her mother—she was not allowed to keep anything for herself. Although already exhausted by a 10- or 12-hour day and a crowded bus journey, when she eventually returned home, she had as many as 4 more hours of work ahead of her sewing on sequins. One sweater would take her up to a week to complete; when finished it would bring another HK $3 in wages, all of which would be kept by her mother.

When Christopher went to work, all his money went to his mother, too. It was an unwritten law in Chinese families that the parents were paid back by their offspring for supporting them; their ambition was to retire and live off their children. Christopher's mother used to say, "I bore you, I brought you up, and I sent you to school. I paid out everything for you . . . now you children should be paying me back for having had you." The Chinese children, I knew, found the process of starting work very depressing, as it meant that they entered into a lifetime's debt. They got no pride from their paycheck, because they never saw any of it. Their parents got the lot. Christopher's mother saved all this money and later on bought herself a flat outside the Walled City.

The reason why so many Chinese families are large is an economic one. Parents have far bigger families than they can afford to maintain so that they will be rich in their old age. It seemed to me that family love and solidarity were based not so much on mutual love and respect as on economic advantage.

Christopher's younger sister, Ah Lin, finally rebelled at such exploitation. She met a boy at her factory who liked her, but her mother forbade her to go out with him. She was not allowed to come to the Youth Club either because our program was mostly recreational. Had we provided sewing lessons or English classes, it would have been permitted; but enjoyment, pure and simple, was to be no part of her life. Instead, the girl's task was to stay at home and look after the babies, or assemble plastic parts, or carry water.

Eventually the drudgery became too much. Ah Lin left home at age 14 and went to live with the boy. Her mother recaptured her and locked her up at home, saying that she was a bad girl. She was beaten for what she had done; her action had not only brought shame on the family but also was considered an attack on the family earnings. And her mother continued to refuse to let her go anywhere outside the home. Treated like chattels, it was not surprising that many girls made the jump into prostitution rather than remain imprisoned at home.

My mission was to help the Walled City people to understand who Christ was. If they could not understand the words about Jesus, then we Christians were to show them what He was like by the way we lived. I remembered He had said, "Whoever forces you to go one mile, go with him two."[1] So this was the beginning of what I called walking the extra mile. There seemed to be a lot of Christians who did not mind walking one, not many who could be bothered to walk two, and no one who wanted to walk three. Those in need that I met seemed to need a marathon.

I became even more involved with the boys, their families and their problems. It meant walking with them in a practical way so that they could see and know who Jesus was. One example of this was when one of the boys asked me to help his sister get into a secondary school. The usual process was to queue up for a day merely to obtain an admission form to take the entrance examination. If the school was Protestant and discovered that the applicant had studied in a Catholic primary school, he or she would not get a form, and the queuing would begin at another school.

The boy's family thought that the way I would help would be by going to the headmistress and saying, "Look, I'm so and so and I know so and so; can you get this girl in?" I did it the opposite way around and queued up for whole days with the ordinary people—which surprised them, as this was not at all their idea of how I was supposed to help.

Oftentimes there were problems regarding identity cards, as many who lived in the Walled City had not been registered at birth. They thought that I could have a word with the authorities and a card would be issued. Instead, if asked to help, I would go with them and sit all day at the government office to help them make the correct application. I had to do all this during the holidays, as by now I was teaching music full-time at an Anglo-Chinese girls' college, St. Stephen's.

For several years, I had many followers who reckoned that if they hung around for long enough they might get a baptism certificate or a document that would enable them to get to America. They were real "rice Christians." Perhaps they could get an introduction to a priest who needed someone to clean in a convent, or they could grab any of the side perks they thought they could get from a church. They began to treat me as they treated other missionaries; they thought I was a pushover. They were careless with my property and equipment and were continually asking to borrow money. They simply did not believe me when I told them that I did not have any. The conversations were always the same, and they went like this . . .

"Poon Siu Jeh, I haven't got a job and I've run out of money."

"But I'm afraid I haven't got any money."

"Oh, but you must have—you're terribly rich."

"No, no, really, I haven't got any money."

"Oh yes you have, because you've got a church in America like the rest of them."

"No, really, I haven't got a church in America. Actually, I come from England, but no church sent me."

At this point another jumbo jet would lurch low across the rooftops as it came in to land at Kaitak airport, which was close to the Walled City. Indeed, the Walled City must have been directly under the flight path, because in the summer months the tourist-filled jets came over every couple of minutes, making conversation impossible as they thundered overhead.

The plane noise would die away and our conversation would continue.

"Huh, one day I expect you'll get into one of those and fly back to where you came from."

"No, there's no danger of that," I would reply honestly, "because I haven't got enough money to get on one."

"Well, your parents can send you the money anyway—there is plenty of money where you came from—we've seen how all those English people live it up."

"No," I said, "you're wrong about that—my parents haven't got any money either." There would be a pause, and then Ah Ping would join the conversation. Ah Ping thought more than the others; his remarks were always more to the point, more understanding and more desperate.

"Maybe you haven't got any money now, but you could always get away from here if you had to get away. We can't. There is nowhere else for us to go; we're stuck on the edge of the sea, and the only escape is into it. But you Westerners—you can fly away when you want to, and then you can forget all about us."

"No, Ah Ping. I'm not planning to fly away and forget all about you."

Ah Ping could really talk when he got warmed up. I respected his honesty, for few Chinese ever tell Westerners what they really feel about them. "You Westerners—you come here and tell us about Jesus. You can stay for a year or two, and your conscience will feel good, and then you can go away. Your Jesus will call you to other work back home. It's true that some of you can raise a lot of money on behalf of us underprivileged people. But you'll still be living in your nice houses with your refrigerators and servants, and we'll still be living here. What you are doing really has nothing to do with us. You'll go home anyhow, sooner or later."

This kind of conversation took place many times; it was an indictment of those evangelists who flew into Hong Kong, sang sweet songs about the love of Jesus on stage and on Hong Kong television, and then jumped back into their planes and flew away again.

"Fine," said Ah Ping to me savagely one day. "Fine for them, fine for us too, we wouldn't mind believing in Jesus too if we could get into a plane and fly away round the world like them. They can sing about love very nicely, but what do they know about us? They don't touch us—they know nothing."

Sometimes I tried talking to the men who guarded the gambling dens, but when I told them that Jesus loved them, they just nodded. "Yeah, yeah, how nice. That means nothing to us." And of course, it did not mean anything to them, as most of them had no idea who Jesus was or what love was. I went on—preach, preach, preach about how Jesus could give them a new life, but no one seemed to understand.

# LIGHT IN THE DARKNESS

Jesus did not promise running shoes in the hereafter to the lame man. He made him walk. He not only preached but also demonstrated that He was God. He made blind men see, deaf men hear and dead men return to life. Some Christians claimed that these things still happened, and I certainly needed to find them.

My missionary friends could not help me much. Most of them were well over 40; many had spent their lives in China and now felt lost. They did not expect people to be converted, and they explained this by saying that there was a spiritual cloud hanging over China that covered Hong Kong, too. Some missionaries had all sorts of cultural hang-ups that infected me, until I found myself worrying over such questions as to whether I should wear sleeveless summer dresses and whether it was wrong to go bathing on Sundays. I got in the ridiculous situation where I was more concerned to please these missionary friends than to find out what God wanted me to do. I did not belong to any missionary society, was not sponsored by any group at home and, in reality, had all the freedom anyone could want; yet I was feeling bound and ineffective.

One day, I went to play the harmonium in the chapel. There, I found out that a Chinese couple was to lead the service. As soon as I saw them, I knew they had it. What "it" was I did not know—but even watching them praying, I sensed a vitality, a power. Immediately, I wanted to know what made them so different. After the service, I made a beeline for the couple. They spoke hardly any English, and I knew hardly any Chinese. Yet soon, it was clear what they were trying to convey.

"You haven't got the Holy Spirit."

A little indignantly, I replied that I had. They replied that I had not, and so the futile argument continued as we walked out of the Walled City and back to my bus stop.

*Of course I have the Spirit*, I thought to myself. *I couldn't believe in Jesus if I didn't*. So what were we arguing about? These people obviously had something I needed, which I had recognized even without understanding their sermon. They called it having the Holy Spirit, and I wanted to call it something else. I quit the quarrel over terminology—receiving the Spirit, being filled with the Spirit, baptism of the Spirit, the power of the Spirit, second blessing, or what have you.[1] If God had anything more for me, I wanted to receive it. I would sort out the theological terms later. So I made an appointment to go to the young couple's flat the next day.

Their flat proved to be a one-room affair, exactly like thousands of flats all over the colony. There was one table, and on it were placed a plate of oranges and a plate of wet flannels. The oranges are a traditional Chinese food for a celebration; they were for when I had "received" the Holy Spirit, while the flannels were for me to cry into.

Whatever was going to happen next was obviously meant to be a very emotional experience. My heart began to bump a bit, because I was not at all sure what to expect. Then I sat down, and the couple laid their hands on my head, saying over and over again in pidgin English, "Now you begin speaking, now you begin speaking, now you begin speaking."

But nothing happened; they thought I was going to burst into "the gift of tongues," but it had not worked.

Some of the West Croydon group had spoken in tongues, and I had heard of other friends who had received this gift, but no one had ever been willing to discuss it. The idea of a new language in which you could speak fluently and express all the thoughts of your heart to God was wonderful.[2] But I thought that it was something that you had to be rather advanced and spiritual to get. I shut my mouth firmly. If God was going to give me this gift, He was going to do it, not me.

"Now you begin speaking, now you begin speaking."

I was acutely embarrassed and began to get cross with them. I felt hotter and hotter and more and more uncomfortable. Here I was not speaking in tongues, and they were going to be so disappointed that nothing had happened. They need not have prepared the wet flannels and the oranges—they were not going to need either plate. Eventually, I could not stand it any longer, so I opened my mouth to say, "Help me, God." And then it happened.

As soon as I made the conscious effort to open my mouth, I found that I could speak freely in a language I had never learned. It was a beautiful articulate tongue, soft and coherent in that there was a clear speech pattern with modulated rise and fall. I was never in any doubt that I had received the sign that I had asked for. But there was no accompanying exultation. I had imagined being lifted up into praise and glory, but it was a most unemotional experience.

The Chinese pair were delighted that I had spoken, although a little surprised that I was not in a flood of tears. However, they cried to make up for it, and their old mother had a good weep too. I still felt extremely embarrassed and left their house as soon as I could. I was very glad that this experience had not happened to me in front of British people.

As I got to the door, they said, "Oh, you can expect the other gifts of the Spirit to appear now." At the time, I did not understand what they meant.

Every day for the next week or so, I waited for the gift of healing or the gift of prophecy to pop up. These were the only other gifts of the Spirit I had heard about, although I now know there are nine.[3] I knew that in England two of the ministers I most respected used these gifts, and they certainly were most effective in their ministry. I also knew that there was an MP's wife who had the gift of healing. They followed Bible teaching carefully, so there was no doubt in my mind as to the rightness of the gifts or their usefulness, but I did not know how you knew when you had received them. How do you know if you have healing?

I remained puzzled, too, that I was still very cool about this great spiritual event. I had read books like *They Speak in Other Tongues*, which left me with the impression that this experience should make me walk on the mountaintops or sit on a cloud brimming over with love. I wondered if I had not got the right thing; maybe it was all vastly overrated, anyway. I went around Hong Kong trying to find someone who would talk to me about it, but no one would. Missionary friends said darkly, "Something very dangerous happened in China and there was a split between the groups." Even more surprising, the Pentecostal churches would not talk about it. I went to their services—they still retained the noise, the handclapping and the repeated *amens* and *hallelujahs*—but the gifts of the Spirit were absent. The Pentecostal missionaries explained that they had made a pact with the Evangelicals not to discuss these things because they could not agree about them. They agreed to talk only about Jesus. But I could see that the gifts were in the Bible; they came from God, so how could they be dangerous?[4]

As months passed, I began to dismiss the whole subject. This experience had not patently changed my Christian life; in fact, if anything, life became even more difficult about this time. I was still rushing around the Walled City, going to some kind of Christian meeting every night, trying with every ounce of my being to help people, but nobody seemed to have been helped. I felt cheated.

*Who do they think they are?* I thought when I first heard about the Willanses. An American couple, their young daughter, Suzanne, and companion Gail Castle had just arrived in Hong Kong and were going to start a prayer meeting. *What a cheek! Hong Kong doesn't need another prayer meeting. I'm already going to one of these every day of the week. Anyway, they've only just come—they should wait to see the church situation first.*

It was two years since I had left England—and a year since I had supposedly received the "gift of the Spirit." I felt that I was quite an authority on prayer meetings in the colony. But my clarinet pupil's mother, Clare Harding, urged me to go to the meeting, saying that it would be "charismatic." This new term described a meeting where they expected the various gifts of the Spirit—charisma—to be manifested.

"Well, I'll just go for a few weeks until I've learned all about it—then I'll go back to the other meetings," I told Clare. And so I was introduced to Rick and Jean Stone Willans.

"Do you pray in tongues, Jackie?" I was shocked by Jean's American forthrightness. No English person would be that direct.[5]

"Well, no actually," I replied. "I haven't found it that useful. I don't get anything out of it, so I've stopped." It was a relief to discuss it with someone.

But Jean would not be sympathetic. "That's very rude of you," she said. "It's not a gift of emotion—it's a gift of the Spirit. You shouldn't despise the gifts God has given you. The Bible says that he who prays in tongues will be built up spiritually, so never mind what you feel—do it."[6] Then she and Rick made me promise to pray daily in my heavenly language. They insisted that the Holy Spirit was given in power to the Early Church to make them effective witnesses to the risen Christ.[7]

Then, to my horror, they suggested that we pray together in tongues. I was not sure if this was all right, since the Bible said that people should not all speak aloud in tongues at the same time. They explained that St. Paul was referring to a public meeting where an outsider coming in would think everyone was crazy; we three would not be offending anyone and would be praying to God in the languages He gave us.[8]

I could not get out of it. We prayed, and I felt silly saying words I did not understand. I felt hot. And then, to my consternation, they stopped praying while I felt impelled to continue. I knew already that this gift, although holy, was under my control; I could stop or start at will.[9] I would have done anything

not to be praying out loud in a strange language in front of
strange Americans, but just as I thought I would die of self-
consciousness, God said to me, "Are you willing to be a fool for
My sake?"[10]

I gave in. "All right, Lord. This doesn't make sense to me,
but since You invented it, it must be a good gift, so I'll go ahead
in obedience and You teach me how to pray."

After we finished praying, Jean said she understood what I
had said; God had given her the interpretation. She translated.
It was beautiful; my heart was yearning for the Lord and calling
as from the depths of a valley stream to the mountain tops for
Him. I loved Him and worshiped Him and longed for Him to
use me.

It was a language so much more explicit and glorious than
any I could have formulated. I decided that if God helped me
to pray like that when I was praying in tongues, I would never
despise this gift again. I accepted that He was helping me to
pray perfectly.

Every day—as I had promised the Willanses—I prayed in the
language of the Spirit. Fifteen minutes by the clock. I still felt it
to be an exercise. Before praying in the Spirit, I said, "Lord, I don't
know how to pray, or whom to pray for. Will You pray through
me—and will You lead me to the people who want You?"[11] And I
would begin my 15-minute stint.

After about six weeks, I noticed something remarkable.
Those I talked to about Christ believed. I could not understand it at first and wondered how my Chinese friends had
so suddenly improved, or if I had stumbled on a splendid
new evangelistic technique. But I was saying the same things
as before.

It was some time before I realized what had changed. This
time, I was talking about Jesus to people who wanted to hear.
I had let God have a hand in my prayers, and it produced a
direct result. Instead of my deciding what I wanted to do for
God and asking His blessing, I was asking Him to do His will
through me as I prayed in the language He gave me.

Now I found that person after person wanted to receive Jesus. I could not be proud—I could only wonder that God let me be a small part of His work. And so the emotion came. It never came while I prayed, but when I saw the results of these prayers, I was literally delighted.

I began to get to know the Willanses better, and they became wonderful friends and counselors. The bonds of Christian conventions burst and I found, once more, the glorious freedom to live that we have in Christ Jesus. At my conversion, I had accepted that Jesus had died for me; now I began to see what miracles He was doing in the world today.

# THE TRIADS

H*ai bin do ah?* Where do you come from?" The slight, sal-
low-faced youth stared terrified as four members of the
famed 14K Triad advanced menacingly toward him. In
gang parlance, they were asking him to which black society he
belonged. He could not reply; he was trembling and his breath
came in short gasps.

"*M'gong?* Not talking then?" Ah Ping, the spokesman, jeered
at him and stepped closer until he was at kicking distance.
There was no escape—the boy and his tormentors all knew what
was coming. He was trapped down one of the Walled City alleys
with the wall behind and the gangsters in front. They taunted
him—teasing out his fear, advancing in ghastly slow motion.
They were enjoying their captive's terror, his cringing body.

The first blow came with amazing speed and ground into
the boy's ribs. Chinese boxers are skilled, their movements sup-
ple. Their kung-fu training affects a litheness and economy of
action that is precise and lethal. The victim fell to the ground as
more blows rained on his stomach, his chest, his groin. He
moaned, doubled up in agony, but still he did not speak. So they
drove him along the street and kicked him while he crawled and
then limped away. He would not be back. He had learned what
happened when you walked down enemy territory unprotected.

This made the Triads feel good. They were secure and superior in their own streets. They controlled what went on and who
was allowed through their turf. Before long, I found that the
room I had rented for the Youth Club was right in the middle of
the 14K patch.

I had just watched the sickening scene, but I did not yet know how inevitable this beating up was according to Triad tradition.

"Why did you do that?" I demanded. "Why? What has that boy done to you?" I suddenly felt rather unwell.

Ah Ping shrugged. "Probably nothing," he conceded, but the corners of his mouth turned down disdainfully. "He could not identify himself or show his reason for being here, so we got to teach him a lesson. He perhaps from our enemies the *Ging Yu*, and we got to let them know who's in power down here."

I was learning.

H. W. E. Heath, one of the former police chiefs in Hong Kong, wrote in 1960, "Triad activities have been noted in the official law and police reports of Hong Kong for the past one hundred and sixteen years. For the past one hundred and thirteen years special ordinances and related legislation have been created in attempts to deal with the problem. The Triad Societies are still with us."

In its earliest phases, the Triad Society was a Chinese secret society whose members were bound by oath to overthrow the foreign conquerors of their country and restore the ancient ruling house of China, the Ming Dynasty. Today, the historical Triad Society has degenerated into hundreds of separate Triad societies. All claim to be part of the Triad tradition, but in fact they are mainly criminal gangs who use the name and rituals as covers for their own evil purposes.

To join the original Triad Society, it was essential to go through certain rituals. These included learning poems, handshakes and hand signs and shedding and drinking blood. Sacrifices were laid down; when you entered the Triad Society, you swore to follow your "brother" forever. He became your *daih lo* or big brother; you became his *sai lo* or little brother, and you were then related forever. If you proved yourself, an aspiring Triad would ask to follow you, and you became his big brother. Thus, the Triad Society was a pyramid of relationships. Inside each gang there was a complicated hierarchy of ranks and duties. The officers had colorful names like Red Pole, White Paper Fan and Grass Sandal. At other times, these officers were known simply by their numbers—as 489, 438, 426 and 415. Ordinary members were called "49 boys."

All over Hong Kong the Triads inspired terror, which made it easier to run protection rackets. The Walled City was the perfect place for them; they took the fullest advantage of its uncertain sovereignty. Two main gangs operated there, divided geographically by a certain street. There was a tacit understanding between the groups regarding territory and business. The *Ging Yu* controlled all the heroin dens, both the selling points and the smoking dens. They also ran protection rackets and controlled prostitution east of Old Man Street.

Far more feared were the brothers of the 14K, which was a relative newcomer amongst the traditional Triad societies, having been formed in China in 1949. It derived its name from No. 14 Po Wah Street, Canton, where it was organized to support the Chinese Nationalistic cause. It was reputed to have 100,000 members worldwide at the time; 60,000 in Hong Kong alone. I understood that it controlled all opium *divans*, gambling, blue films, child brothels, illegal dog restaurants and protection rackets on the west side of the city.

It was highly decentralized, with each area gang leader looking after his particular patch. However, they could call on each other for help when needed; they all knew the main office bearers and referred to members of related gangs as "cousins." Within a matter of minutes, a Triad could call out a dozen brothers, and within hours several hundred could be ready for a fight.

Whereas the non-Triads slipped in and out of the place, praying not to be stopped, those committed to the 14K or the *Ging Yu* walked abroad only in their own territory. I used to pick my way over all the streets and made a point of learning every exit until I was more familiar with the place than the gangsters themselves, who were necessarily limited to one half of the city.

The Triads that I knew were certainly criminals, but to some extent they followed the old maxim that there is honor among thieves. In return for absolute obedience, the *daih lo* promised to look after his *sai lo*. If the little brother was imprisoned, the big brother made sure that inside prison he got food, drugs and protection. Not that all Triad members took drugs; drug taking was frowned on, because it lessened their usefulness. In fact, it was our shared concern for the addicts that would later place me at the same tea table as some of the Triad bosses.

It was no surprise to me when I learned that Christopher was about to be initiated into the 14K. How else could he walk on certain streets if he belonged to no gang? How else could he retaliate when wronged without a group of brothers to fight for him?

Christopher had been attending the Youth Club regularly, but he now carefully avoided me. Every time I tried to approach him, he disappeared into the maze. He had started to gamble and was hanging around well-known criminals. However, he had a conscience about this, and he did not want to let me see what he was doing. There came the day, though, when I trapped him. We met head-on when I was carrying my heavy piano accordion, which was large enough to prevent Christopher from passing me. We were in one of the tiny passages where retreat was impracticable; he was wedged in, and I asked him to carry the instrument for me to the repair shop.

As we walked, I talked to him in my pidgin Cantonese. I asked him, "Christopher, who do you think Jesus came into the world for?" He did not reply.

"Was it for rich or poor people?" I continued.

"That's easy—I know that one. He came for poor people." His schoolteachers would have been happy.

"But does He love good people or bad people?" I probed.

"Jesus loves good people, Miss Poon." It was a dismal catechism; he was hating this walk, this talk.

"You're wrong." Luckily, as he was carrying the accordion, I could wave my arms about. It helped to fill in the gaps in my vocabulary. "Do you know, if Jesus were alive today, He'd be here in the Walled City sitting on the orange boxes, talking to the pimps and prostitutes down there in the mud." You are not supposed to tell Chinese people that they are wrong because they will lose face, but I was longing for Christopher to understand. This was no time to be playing conventions. "That's where He spent a lot of His time. In the streets with well-known criminals—not waiting in a neat, clean church for the nice guys to turn up."

"Why did He do that?" Christopher asked incredulously. It sounded as if he really wanted to know.

"Because," I said slowly, "that is why He came—not to save the good people, but to save the bad ones—the lost ones—those who have done wrong."[1]

Christopher stopped suddenly. He was clearly overwhelmed by what he had heard. By this time, we had walked out of the Walled City, passing the street market where people were hawking everything from plastic slippers to pressed duck. He said he wanted to hear some more, so we left the accordion in the repair shop nearby and found a public bench by the traffic roundabout. I told him the story of Naaman, the army commander afflicted with leprosy,[2] and finished up by saying, "It's so simple—all you have to do is come to Jesus to be washed clean." I turned to Christopher to see if he understood.

The traffic was roaring past us; people were yelling as they always do in Hong Kong. Another plane came in to land, flying a few feet over our heads as it skimmed the flyover and thundered onto the runway. Christopher heard nothing; he had his eyes shut and he seemed to be talking quietly. He was not talking to me; he was admitting to Jesus how he had failed in his life and was asking Him to make him clean. Sitting by the dusty, noisy roadside, he became a Christian.

There were many problems in store for Christopher. The next Saturday, he came back to the Youth Club. Bravely, he stood up in front of the others and said that the week before he had not believed in Jesus; now he knew Him. The announcement was greeted at first with silence—it was so extraordinary a thing to say. Then came the jeers and taunts. Boys from bad homes did not become Christians; that was for good, educated, middle-class students. He was joking; he was mad.

Christopher was not. He now refused to carry on with his Triad initiation. He already had the book of poems, laws and ceremonial dialogue to be learned before he could be accepted. He sent it back. To make such a stand was both very firm and very courageous; such a thing had never happened before among those people. His decision was a breakthrough for me, too; now I knew that it was not true about there being a "cloud of unbelief" over Hong Kong. Jesus was alive in Hong Kong just as much as in England, and those who looked for Him could find Him.

The change in Christopher was remarkable. He worked so well at his factory that he was promoted to the rank of supervisor. Instead of gambling sessions with the Triads, he now spent his time at the Youth Club, and on Sundays he came to the evening service in the little Oiwah church.

As I continued praying in the Spirit in private, the results became apparent when more boys like Christopher made decisions to become Christians; we met together for Bible study and prayer anywhere we could—in the Youth Club room, in teahouses, in the streets or in my home. One day when we were praying, one of them had a message in tongues. We waited, and then Christopher began to sing the interpretation.[3] Astonishingly, this beautiful song came in English, which he hardly spoke. This is what he sang:

> Oh God, who saves me in the darkness,
> Give me strength and the power
> So I can walk in the Holy Spirit
> Fight against the devil with the Bible
> Talk to the sinners in the world
> Make them belong to Christ.

Another boy, Bobby, had the same interpretation, but in Chinese. He did not understand Christopher's English song, and so he did not know that what he spoke was a confirmation of God's message.

Although the Christian group was growing, not all of the Walled City boys were so clear about why I was there. Many of them came to the Youth Club for what they could get out of it. When we went on Saturday picnics or camps, I did not make them pay. I paid for the coach, rubber boats, football boots, roller skates, and even for the picnics. They were not grateful; they considered themselves underprivileged people and, imagining that I had a wealthy organization behind me, they wanted to squeeze me for anything that was going. They regarded this as their right and were demanding and aggressive. Such was true of Ah Ping.

During the months and years, I got to know Ah Ping very well. He came to the Youth Club a lot. He was often with us on walks and expeditions. I learned that he had been initiated into the Triads when he was only 12, four years before, and that he already had a great reputation as a fighter who had started to collect followers (*sai lo*) of his own.

One night when he was hanging around in the street outside, I came to the Youth Club room feeling very depressed and needing a kind word. He sensed that I was feeling a bit down and said, "You'd better go—you'd better leave this place, Poon Siu Jeh. You'd better go, because it's no good you working here. You should find a nice group of nice students to work with; you find some well-behaved school kids to preach to; they'll make nice Christians. We're no good—we never do what you want us to do." I listened without replying.

"Don't know why you stay here—you find us school places, and we don't go to school. You find us houses, and we muck them up. You find us jobs, and we lose them; we won't ever change. All we do is take—we take you for every penny you've got, and we kick you around. So why do you stick at it? What's the point?"

"Well, I stick around because that's what Jesus did for me," I replied. "I didn't want Jesus, but He didn't wait until I wanted Him. He didn't wait until I had promised to reform. He didn't wait until I got good. He died for me anyway. He died for me when I hated Him, and He never even told me off on the cross; He just said He loved me and forgave me.[4] This is the Jesus that came into the world and made dead people rise; this is the Jesus who came into the world and did miracles.[5] This is the Jesus who only ever did good, and He died for me. They said He was the Son of God, and He loves you, too, in the same way."

Ah Ping did not answer at first; then he said, "It couldn't be—nobody would love us like that. I mean, we . . ." his voice faltered, and then he continued, "I mean we have to rape and we fight, and we steal, and we stab. Nobody could love us like this."

"Well, Jesus did. He doesn't love the things you've done, but He loves you. Really, it doesn't make sense; but all the wrong things that you've done He said were His. When He died on the cross, Jesus pleaded guilty to your crimes.[6] That's really unfair, isn't it? He said that your stealing and your stabbing were His; if you give Him all the bad things you've done, He'll give you His new life, His righteousness.[7] It's sort of like giving Him your dirty clothes and getting back His clean ones."

Ah Ping was shattered. He could hardly believe that there was a God like that. He sat down there on the stone steps to the street and told Jesus that although he could not understand why He loved him, he was grateful. He asked Jesus to forgive him and change him.

Ah Ping was the first gangster from the fully initiated Triads to join the Christians. When he was only 14, a young bargirl had offered to "support" him in return for his protection. He had even sought my advice over it. Now his lifestyle changed dramatically. Each night, he brought his brothers to the clubroom and asked me to tell them about Jesus. More and more known crooks turned up to shake me by the hand or thump my arm muscle. The few remaining straight types, the students, left the club because they felt discriminated against. It must have been the only Christian club in Hong Kong where the good guys felt less welcome than the bad ones. However, I felt that there were dozens of places all over Hong Kong where the nice boys were catered to, so I let them go. It was not for some years that we were able to bring these two groups together and break down the wall of separation between them.

Some of my friends in Hong Kong met Ah Ping and invited him to tell his story in church. "Be careful," I warned him as we came out of the clubroom at midnight into the black street. "Satan doesn't like people talking about Jesus, so he'll probably have a go at you before Saturday. Go straight home tonight and don't stop along the way."

"All right, all right, Miss Poon," he said, nodding sweetly. But as soon as I had gone, he exploded. *Tchs. The Devil. Ha. What rubbish! I know these streets like the back of my hand. What, me worry?* And he wandered around instead of going home.

As if from nowhere, seven men jumped out of a black alley and attacked him. They were Chiu Chow gangsters, big for Chinese, and wild fighters. There was no reason for their attack, but that did not stop it from coming. Later Ah Ping told me, "As they came at me, I had two thoughts. First of all, *Huh, it's all Miss Poon's fault*; and then, *You're supposed to pray.*" So he prayed as the wooden bats beat him unconscious into the ground.

"Didn't do you much good praying, did it?" scoffed one of the club members when he heard the story.

"Yes, it did," retorted Ah Ping. "I'll tell you why. As soon as I began to pray, my father came down the street, and when the Chiu Chows saw him, they ran away. Otherwise, I would have been killed."

As it was, Ah Ping was left on the ground with a gash in his back and a hole in his throat. His father summoned help from his gang brothers from the 14K. They found him and took him to a doctor who gave his professional opinion that Ah Ping's injuries were so bad that he would not be able to walk or speak for at least two weeks.

Ah Ping's brothers determined to seek revenge on his behalf. They held a council in their gang pad and discussed tactics. "Okay, the Chiu Chows made it seven to one. We will take 50 to attack them. That's reasonable." Then they took long knives and choppers from their secret arms cache and told Ah Ping,

"Look, we know where one of these Chiu Chows lives. We are going to take him and his family members out of their house one by one and stab them. Right?"

Ah Ping indicated, through his injured throat, "No, I'm a Christian now and I don't want you to fight back." Then he gathered one or two Club members who were believers, found my room and asked them to pray with him.

All night they prayed for the gang who had attacked him. Ah Ping once told me that Triads were so touchy that they would threaten and even kill over trifles; once he had seen a boy wearing the same shirt as he was, so he fought him. He had come a long way since those days; as well as praying for his enemies, he also asked the other boys to lay their hands on him and pray for healing.

The next morning he was completely healed, and he could talk clearly. In fact, he spoke in church just two days later. He spoke of the change in his heart, how he had given up stealing, and how he had been healed. He also mentioned that he would no longer take the devil lightly. Now he *knew* that the devil was around.

Jesus said, "Blessed are the peacemakers,"[8] but gang fights are not easy to stop. This kind of problem was one that the new converts would have to face all too often.


I remember one Sunday evening inside Oiwah church. It was not a day off for most people in the Walled City; the fact that you could actually get to church was a source of pride to these marginally more prosperous Chinese folk. As I looked up from the organ keys, I could see some of the teachers from the Oiwah School, together with various hawkers, vegetable sellers and other traders. All looked to be solid, law-abiding, decent folk, serious and respectably dressed, although most were very poor. The fact that I troubled about the young tear-aways really rather appalled them. *This Westerner*, they thought, *simply doesn't understand how wicked these boys are.* They did not like having the

boys in church with them, whereas I sat there hoping and praying that some of them would come.

All at once, the little door swung open violently and the boys
arrived. The sight of their Teddy boy shirts and tight trousers
sent a ripple of fear through the congregation, who thought it
was a raid by the Triads. And this time, I too was a little surprised, because the boys were in a terrible state; normally scruffy,
this time they were caked with filth and blood, having come
straight to church after a terrible fight. Several of the boys had
dull red abrasions on their faces. One hunched over, limping
from a blow to the groin. Their clothes were torn and their eyes
were staring. However, they sat down and stayed quiet throughout the service. As soon as it was finished, I got up and hurried
to find out what had happened.

Apparently they had walked into a trap carefully set for
them. As the boys entered the local public lavatory outside the
Walled City to spruce up for church, a group of youths had leapt
out of the cubicles where they had been hiding and savagely
attacked them with bats.

Several were quite badly hurt; I took them out of the Walled
City, called a taxi and went off to the hospital with them. That
they should come and find me at church after such a terrible
fight pleased me very much. Naïvely, I thought it was wonderful.
*Praise God, they've come to church and they've come in here—they
haven't gone to their gang leaders; they've come to Christians.*

I was soon to find out that the rest of the congregation saw
the whole incident quite differently. They were outraged that
the boys should have dared to invade their church looking and
smelling so dreadfully. They did not accept that boys like that
could become Christians; they expected an inward change to be
followed by an outward change into shirts and ties and lace-up
shoes. And they were particularly upset that I had allowed the
boys to come into church immediately after partaking in violence. The elders were convinced that I was being used by a bunch
of unscrupulous rascals. In their experience, no one like that
had ever become a Christian. And when I asked that some of the

boys who had become Christians should be baptized, their answer was a straight "No." They told me very firmly that the boys should have a time of testing first. This ban on their baptisms meant that the boys could not take part in the breaking of bread ceremony, either.

At first, I continued to encourage the boys to come to the church, even though they were clearly not welcome. Then one day, a wise and older missionary, George Williamson, came to the Walled City; he watched what was going on and understood the whole situation immediately.

"Jackie," he said, "why do you make these boys come to church here?"

There was no escape; I had to give him answers. "Well, for two reasons really," I began rather hesitantly. "One reason is very negative. It's because I don't want to be criticized and I don't want everyone to think I'm doing my own thing." George smiled warmly; he knew how the older generation disapproved of women missionaries taking their own initiative.

"Second," I continued a little more confidently, "I think these boys need elder brothers and sisters and need the family of the church. In the same way, the church needs them. It is not healthy for us to be simply a young persons' group."

I felt that George, with his background, would be sure to agree with me. But he did not. "No, Jackie, your boys are not ready yet. You should look at it like this: They are like seedlings that you wouldn't transplant too young, because they'd die. At the moment, the boys can't take the knocks they are getting from the established Church. It's too soon to expect them to make allowances for the attitudes of these church people. You can't expect them to have that sort of grace." I felt amazed; he was asking me to go ahead and do my own thing. He continued, "Look on them as seedlings; take them away and care for them; tend them until they have grown up. Then they will be strong enough to stand and take the knocks. And then you can plant them and they can help the church to grow up. The church in Hong Kong isn't ready for them yet."

Therefore, instead of insisting that new young Christians join the church, I expanded our Bible study group; we met several times a week and were now open on Sunday mornings. The clubroom was used more and more and began to be well known among Triads even outside the Walled City as a splendid place to spend Saturday evenings. We had raucous singing sessions and ping-pong. If I insisted on a prayer, most of them would go outside and hoot in friendly fashion in the alley until I had got it over with. Then back they swarmed.

Without Dora Lee, I could never have coped. She had been head girl at St. Stephen's school and, together with other students, helped me with the kind of Chinese translation I could not manage, like translating from the Bible. She was an outstanding Christian, for years giving up most of her weekends in order to help the boys understand Christ.

Dora's help was valuable in other ways; she taught me much about how Chinese people think and react. The more I understood, the more I realized how English methods for telling the world about Jesus Christ and how to follow Him did not work out as practical possibilities on the other side of the world. Worthy members of the Christian Union talk about prayer in terms of getting up early and having a quiet time with God. But this sort of advice was quite impracticable for the boys I knew. They often lived in a house with 10 other people; it was never quiet, and no one had a bed to himself, let alone a room. They slept in the bed on a rotation system, some working while others rested. The idea of finding a quiet place to study their Bibles and contemplate the Almighty was a joke. But praying in a new language is essentially practical, because they could walk along any noisy Hong Kong street and no one would notice.

Many of them could not read, so my suggestions had to be workable. This I learned through a sad experience when one of the boys prayed that he desired to follow Jesus. In misguided fervor, I gave him a copy of St. John's Gospel, Scripture notes on St. John, and two booklets entitled, *Now You Are a Christian* and *The Way Ahead*. I did not see him for two years, and I felt hurt and

concerned for his spiritual well being. When I saw him again,
I asked why he had been avoiding me for so long. He looked
embarrassed.

"I wanted to know Jesus, and you gave me a library."

I reexamined some of my concepts about studying the Word
of God. The Early Christians certainly had no Bibles; they must
have learned another way. For those who could read, I suggested they take a few moments from their factory benches by
retreating to the toilets to read a few verses. Others found they
could memorize a few lines. I tried to see all the boys I knew as
often as I could, encouraging them to follow Christ's teachings.
They did make progress, but there was never enough time to see
everyone. My school duties curtailed my time and my inade-
quate Chinese meant that I found it pretty difficult to convey
spiritual truths. I needed more hours to study; practicing with
the boys was not enough when I did not understand the com-
plex structure of the language.

As the pressure grew worse, I began to pray about it. "Lord,
I've got too much to do. I need more time to spend with these
boys. And I can't do this if I have to spend much of the day teaching. You have promised to provide our daily bread; please let me
know if you will provide mine without my 'earning' it."

Three days later the phone rang; it was Clare Harding, the
friend who had introduced me to the Willanses. She came straight
to the point. "Jackie, I wanted you to know that when you leave St.
Stephen's, we want to offer you some money."

I was staggered; no one knew that I was even considering
such a move. "But hang on a bit," I gasped in reply, "who told you
I was leaving St. Stephen's? As it stands at the moment, I'm not."

Clare did not hesitate. "Yes, I know you aren't leaving right
now. But Neil and I have been praying together. And I wanted
you to know that if you were thinking of leaving, we'd like to
offer you HK $200 a month."

"Well, in any case, if I left it wouldn't be until July at the earliest, because I must continue teaching until the end of the
school year."

Clare replied, "The money can't be available until July anyway, but I just felt I had to ring and tell you now." It was mid-November.

Her call was a great encouragement. I felt that if God could tell someone who did not know I was even considering leaving my job to offer me a monthly check worth about US $33, it was nothing for Him to provide my whole living. Now, many years later, I realize that this was the point where I decided to live by faith.[9] But at that time, I had never even heard of the phrase, and I would have found it hard to tell anyone about my financial needs. I knew, surely, that if God wanted me to do this job, He would provide. It never worried me in the slightest as to how He would do it.

# BIG BROTHER IS WATCHING YOU

The telephone was ringing and ringing in my dreams. I struggled awake, clambered out of bed and lifted the receiver. It seemed to be the depths of the night; actually, the time was around 5 A.M. Ah Ping spoke in a quick, strained voice.

"Poon Siu Jeh, you've got to come quickly. Someone has broken into the club, and there is a terrible mess everywhere." He hung up.

Despite the sticky heat, I shivered as I hurriedly climbed into yesterday's clothes. I had moved by this time to the Kowloon side of Hong Kong and was sharing my apartment block with 8,000 other sardines. When I reached the street, it was still asleep and deserted. No buses were around that early, so I ran and ran.

My friend at the baker's stall was lifting a tray of hot pineapple buns out of his oven and carefully parking them on the pavement. At last, I found a cab that would take me to the Walled City. When I got there, I hurried again through the tortuous alleyways, the smells and the filth to the clubroom. I was ready to find a mess. The scene that greeted me was beyond my imagination. Benches, books, ping-pong bats and skateboards had been thrown around and smashed up. Far worse, the filth of the alleys had invaded our clean club. Someone had deliberately thrown sewage all over the floor and walls. Ah Ping had no need to explain anything; the destruction screamed its own message.

I wanted to sit down and cry. My pride crumbled to dust. I thought these boys were my people who trusted me as a friend; we had our problems, but really everything was fine. Then they threw feces all over my walls and showed what they honestly thought of me and the four-year-old club.

"All right, God," I said, "enough is enough. I don't mind working here forever, as long as they appreciate me. But if they don't want me or You, I don't have to stay here. I can be a Christian in Kensington and do normal things like normal people—dinner parties and discussion groups, apologetics and concerts. After all, I really don't want to stay down here for the rest of my life playing ping-pong. I mean, God, it's no joy for me to have a little room like this; I'm doing it for them. I'm willing to pour my life out for them, but if they don't want it, they need not have it. Let's close the room up." Resentment burned at me. "They'll soon miss the club if I close it up; they'll soon see what they've done was really harming themselves."

But at the same time, I also heard what Jesus had said: When people hit you, you should let them hit you again; when they persecute you, you should bless them.[1] There was another insistent passage about praising God in all your troubles.[2] But I did not want to do that—I wanted to howl and wallow in self-pity. I wanted my enemies to suffer too. I certainly did not feel like rejoicing or turning the other cheek.

So I spent the whole day sweeping up the place, muttering tearfully, "Praise God, praise God." I hunched over the bamboo brush and swiped the floor savagely—but less savagely as the day wore on and more sadly. "Praise God, praise God." I had fits of sobbing. The foundations of my world lay in ruins.

The next night, I opened the club as usual. For the first time, I was frightened—not of being beaten up, for God had always protected me from that—but of being rejected by the boys that I loved and ministered to. I did not know who had done it and why, and I stayed there in the club trembling all over. I was lonely and vulnerable.

A youth I had never seen before leaned against the club door. He jerked his head at me and spoke coolly, "Got any trouble?"

"No. No. It's fine, thank you very much," I replied hastily. "But why are you asking?" He sucked in his cheeks and thumbed his chest nonchalantly. "Got any trouble, you just let me know."

"I'm happy to hear that," I said. "But who are you? Who sent you?"

"Goko sent me," he replied abruptly.

I was shaken; I knew exactly who Goko was. He was the leader of one branch of the 14K and was reputed to have several thousand little brothers in the Walled City and surrounding areas. He controlled all the opium dens and vice in the area. The fact that this stranger had even used Goko's name to me was undoubtedly a compliment. It is both a term of endearment and respect, meaning, "my big brother." He was the Big Brother of the big brothers. One of the little brothers in my club had confided his name to me with awe; even 10 years later, gangsters were daunted that I knew his name, for it was only ever mentioned among themselves.

Although I knew Goko's name, I'd never met him. For some years I had sent him messages, but he had always refused to see me. The messages had been simple, like "Jesus loves you." I could understand why Goko did not want to see me, but not why he had gone to the trouble of sending me a guard for the club.

"Goko said if anyone bothers you or touches this place, we're gonna 'do' him," my protector continued. He demonstrated exactly how they intended to "do" him rather graphically as he picked up an imaginary dagger and thrust it low into a victim's belly.

"Thank you very much, how kind of you—I'm really most grateful," I said. "Would you mind telling Goko that I'm most appreciative of his offer and don't want to offend him, but that I don't accept it. Actually, Jesus is looking after us."

"*Yau moe gau chor.*" The Cantonese expression is the equivalent of "you must be cracked." The stranger was not at all impressed with my stand; his contemptuous expression showed that he thought he was talking to a crazy Westerner. Anyone who thought that Jesus was a fit protector here in the Walled City had to be deranged.

The following evening my protector returned, and the night after that as well. He clocked in every night just like a night watchman. I discovered that his name was Winson and that he was under orders to watch the club. I began to tell him about Jesus. He certainly did not want to hear what I told him, but as he was on guard duty, he had to stay. After a few nights of softening up, he began to talk about a friend of his who had an opium problem. I soon realized that this friend was Winson himself. So I told him that opium was no problem.

All you have to do with anyone who has an opium or a heroin problem or any other kind of addiction is to lock them in a room for a week. Certainly they suffer agonies during the process of coming off the drug—they may even lose their sanity—but they will also lose their physical dependence. However, the cure does not last; as soon as you unlock the door, they will go straight out to take whatever drug it is to which they are addicted, because their mind and their heart continue to crave it with a force they cannot possibly control themselves. Only Jesus, the Lord of life, can settle a person's heart inside and take away the craving.

I told Winson this many times. He always stood outside the club door, lounging in proprietary fashion. He would never condescend to come in, never interfere. He watched and listened to the boys' spirited renderings of the current "in" hymn. Then one night, late in the evening when the club was almost empty, I said, "Now, how about you coming inside and praising God."

"Okay," he said without hesitation.

I was stunned, for by this time I knew who Winson really was. His rank in the 14K Triad was number 426, which meant that he had the special rank of fight-fixer. His job was to fix the fights and choose the weapons, the location and the strategy. He was a very tough Triad indeed. And yet here he was standing inside my club praising God at the top of his voice. He was belting out, solo, "Give me oil in my lamp" as loudly as he could, and as he had no idea how to sing, it was an amazing noise—a wonderful burst of tuneless sound. Then he began to pray in Chinese—mercifully, he had never heard anyone praying before, so it came out quite spontaneously. I have never since listened to such a joyous prayer. I kept thinking, *Where did he get that from?* Although, of course, I knew.

It was an extraordinary session, for the next moment Winson began praising God in a new language. This was even more surprising, as he had never heard about the gift from me, nor to my knowledge had he heard anyone else speaking in tongues. After about half an hour, he stopped. The miracle had taken place; he and I knew that he was completely cured of his drug addiction. He had come through withdrawal as he prayed.

When his voice died away, I told him, "Praise the Lord; that is wonderful. Now what you have to do next is to lead your gang to make the same discovery for themselves. You can't follow your big brother Goko anymore. No man can have two Big Brothers. You have to follow Jesus or Goko. You cannot follow both."[3] So Winson went back to his gang leader Goko to tell him and the other gang leaders that he now believed in Jesus.

It was Ah Sor, at 18 already a seasoned jailbird, who told me later what had happened the night of the attack on the club. One of the boys had had some troubles, which he felt were all my fault. (These dropout kids had such a problem with authority that whenever anything went wrong in their lives they blamed the nearest establishment figure.) He had come round and started yelling and throwing things at the Youth Club windows. This incited his friends to action, and soon they were all on the rampage. Most of them had no idea what they were angry about; it was just mob violence.

Goko had a report within hours about this mayhem on his patch and was so displeased that he summoned the offenders to appear before him. He ordered them to return anything they had taken and to go back to the Youth Club the next night and behave.

"Can't do that," one of them replied. "We've broken up the place; she'll never welcome us back."

"Oh yes she will," Goko had said, "because Miss Poon is a Christian and she'll forgive you no matter how many times you offend. She'll open the door and welcome you back."

So they had come back, and Goko had sent Winson to see that his orders were carried out. I felt very small when I heard what he had said. Obviously he knew how Christians were supposed to behave, even though my inclination had been to do exactly the opposite.

Now that I knew Big Brother was watching, I was much encouraged in the direction the club had taken. Something of Jesus had got through, unaided by social programs and church services. Most of the hangers-on had by now disappeared, as they discovered that I was speaking the truth when I said there were no more funds apart from what I was putting in myself. There was no social advantage in being a member of our club; in fact, quite the reverse—most other churches definitely disapproved of this disorganized Youth Center. Social workers and youth counselors who visited me asked what the program was. I found this rather difficult to explain in terms of a schedule.

"Well, I open the club door at night and sometimes one person comes, sometimes 50. I make friends with them and talk. Sometimes we sing or pray; sometimes we go on an outing. I maybe sit all night with one who has no place to sleep or share a bowl of rice with a hungry one." Finally, I hit on an impressive phrase. "I'm doing unstructured youth work" was my reply to the social workers, who nodded earnestly and decided that this was the latest sociological technique already pioneered in forward-looking countries.

I had tried regular projects, but they were rarely successful, and I was frustrated in looking for helpers who would understand this. We had a football coach at one time who rented a playing field and had weekly training sessions. All the boys were crazy about football, and over 40 signed up for the activity. Twenty of them turned up for the first practice; the next week there were 10; the third week there were none at all.

The coach was most discouraged and wanted to quit and teach at the YMCA, where the youngsters were really keen. I tried to make him understand what had happened. The Walled

City boys lived such strange lives that they usually had no idea what day of the week it was. They slept by day and got up in the evening, as most of the vice operations they were associated with happened at nighttime. Sometimes they stayed up for 72 hours at a time or slept for two days. They stayed in gang pads, opium dens or wherever they could find a floor or staircase. The idea of football was most attractive, but actually getting there was another matter. They did mean to go, but they had absolutely no self-discipline. The third week of the course one of their brothers had got married, so they all went to the wedding feast. It never occurred to them to inform the instructor or me.

Had the instructor come back the following week, he would have found perhaps a couple of lads, and the next week four and the week after that maybe a dozen. Once they had the idea that the instructor was really concerned about them and would turn up even in a typhoon for one boy, they would have given him their loyalty and their friendship. Eventually, he would have built up a team for life.

Many people came to me and asked to help in the club. It sounded romantic and exciting to work in the Walled City, but few stuck it out more than a few weeks. If they held classes or games that were not well supported, they lost heart and never returned. I needed to find Christian workers who loved the people they were working with more than the activity through which they were trying to reach them.

Like the Walled City boys, I now slept by day and got up at night, at least in theory. In fact, since I had language lessons, court appearances, prison visits and other matters concerned with sorting out problems for them, it meant that I was also up by day. Every day, the only way I could get out of bed was by promising myself that I could come back and sleep later in the day. "I will. I really will," I would mutter as I struggled into consciousness, but I never did. Instead, I learned how to catnap, sleeping on buses and ferries.

One night, we went to the hills for a barbecue. It was the Autumn Moon Festival, and the boys had strung up paper lanterns all over the hillside. In the clear moonlight, I saw a large, rough-looking young tough sitting among us and stuffing himself with pork chops, beef steaks and chicken wings. As I had bought all these myself and had reckoned on them being sufficient for our entire coach load, I was quite mad at him. But while I watched, the other boys gave him their rations and seemed mesmerized by his every word. Ah Ping whispered that this was his own *daih lo*, the leader of his particular gang and of most of those present. He was actually the real brother of Goko and was the number two in the Walled City. As more and more of his "brothers" had been attending our club, Sai Di, curious and maybe a little jealous, had decided to come to this function himself. If he chose to, he had the power to run all the boys and the club itself, so there was a distinct possibility that this was a takeover bid.

"Would you mind coming for a talk?" I asked him and indicated a small patch of scrub just over the crest. He was amused at this request from a mere girl and made a great show of rising from his haunches and lumbering toward me amidst cat-calls and whistles. But when we were out of earshot, he dropped the macho attitude and listened quite seriously when I told him that the whole reason for the club was that I wanted them to know the love of Jesus.

His reply was an indictment and a confirmation. "I know," he said. "We've been watching you. Many missionaries come to Hong Kong to help us poor people. They put us in sociological boxes and analyze us. Then they take our pictures to shock the Westerners by our living conditions. Some men get famous because they've been here. But inside the Walled City, we usually get rid of them within six months." He spoke maliciously. "We find ways to discourage them until they have no heart to continue—had you been a man, we would have had you beaten long ago."

He added, "We couldn't care less if you have big buildings or small ones. You can be offering free rice, free schools, judo classes or needlework to us. It doesn't matter if you have a daily program or hymn-singing once a week. These things don't touch us because the people who run them have nothing to do with us. What we want to know is if you are concerned with us. Now you have been here for four years, and we have decided that maybe you mean what you say."

I did not sing in front of him, but there, on a hump in the Chinese mountains, my heart was bursting.


Now that the "rice Christians" had departed from our club, I found that those who remained were the ones who wanted to be friends and who eventually would become interested in spiritual things. Because they could not understand why I would actually be there if I had not been sent by an overseas church, they began to consider seriously the possibility that Jesus was real. One day, we were sitting on the benches in the clubroom when Ah Keung, known as the Walled City joker and a great friend of Ah Ping's, said, "Poon Siu Jeh, we sat up for the whole night last evening discussing you, and we came to one of two conclusions. Either the British government has sent you here as a spy, or what you say about Jesus must be true, because there can't be any other explanation. Nobody's going to spend their life with us down here unless they have to, or unless Jesus is real."

So Ah Keung became a believer too, and he proved to be a most "hot-hearted," enthusiastic Christian. I began to visit him and soon found out his fearful background. Ah Keung was one of six sons who lived with their father in the western district on Hong Kong Island. His mother had run away after the birth of the sixth boy and gone to live with a policeman. His father was a member of the powerful Wo Shing Wo Triad society that controlled that area, but after his friend was murdered in a gang fight, he decided to move to a new environment and chose a room in the Walled City. He worked as a *for-gei* in a gambling den doing *pin-mun*, meaning that he did odd jobs in the den, including collecting bets and pawning the gamblers' watches. As this was a night job, he never saw his sons during the day, and they were not brought up at all. When they woke, they ate their father's food, should there be any; and if not, they went to beg it from neighbors and street stalls.

As they grew older, the brothers became clever confidence tricksters. None of them went to school and, of course, they were all Triad members. The eldest three were imprisoned at the ages of 13, 14 and 15 for selling drugs; not only did they make money this way, but they also each became addicted. Later, the fifth and sixth brothers were also arrested for drug-related crimes, and the sixth had received a sentence of six months hard labor by the time he was 14. Ah Keung was the only brother who was never in prison, because he became a Christian just in time.

One night he rushed into the clubroom panting that I had to come to his home quickly. I ran down the street after him, dodging in and out of the prostitutes and around the gambling den where Ah Keung's father worked. I had to step with care here, for the entrance to Ah Keung's alleyway was very slimy. The gamblers used that alley to relieve themselves in the absence of toilets. It was 18 inches wide and led to a stone staircase that was crumbling and dripping with green slime. The atmosphere was evil.

Up the stairs, the door was open that night. The one-room dwelling was not large enough for all six plus their father to sleep, but since two or three of them were usually in prison at any one time, that was no great problem.

When I got there, I found the eldest brother injecting himself with heroin. On the floor there lay a man with stripes and bruises on every limb and a blood-soaked shirt and shorts. He had been beaten up savagely. I have never been brave at the sight of blood, as it makes me feel physically sick, but here I was faced with the job of cleaning him up and caring for him. My first reaction was to send him to hospital.

"We can't take him," they said in unison. "He's a gang member. He walked across someone else's territory, and they beat him up. If we take him to hospital, he'll be asked questions by the police. And then they'll find out he's a drug addict."

I had no alternative. I had to help, so I took their bucket of water and some filthy old bandages, went out and borrowed a shopkeeper's Mercurochrome, and began to clean the man up. Unexpectedly, I did not feel sick and faint; I was calm and happy. Jesus had said that He came to bind up the wounded, and that is exactly what they had asked me to do. As I washed away the sullen man's blood, I told him about this. I told him about Jesus' love and how he could know Him, too. He made no response, but I was sure he understood. He came back one day two years later.

After this incident, I became more involved with Ah Keung's family. I visited those in prison, tried to help them find jobs on their release, and found alternative homes for some of them. One night I was walking out of the city at about 2 A.M. when I overheard the second brother, Sai So, giving my telephone number to another addict.

"833179," he was saying as they ate their soup noodles at a makeshift table in the street. "Remember that number next time you are arrested. It doesn't matter what time of day or night you call. Miss Poon will come. It doesn't matter whether you've done the crime you're arrested for or not; she'll come. The only thing you must do is to tell the truth. You see, she's a Christian."

As I walked home, I knew that my labor in the Lord was not in vain.[4] Here I was privileged enough to see the fruits of some of those labors. Some of the vilest criminals in Hong Kong now knew that Jesus' name was truth.

As well as Ah Keung's brothers, most of the boys I knew were frequently arrested and sent to court. As I got to know them better, I sometimes believed their claims that they were innocent, because I checked their alibis myself. Of course most of them were criminals, but they were not always guilty of the crimes with which they were charged. It seemed to me quite wrong that they should either confess to crimes that they had not committed or deny crimes in which they were involved. I discovered that they regarded the whole business of arrests as a fatalistic game. And they felt that legal proceedings, carried out in a language that they could not understand, bore little relationship to the truth.

Several times while I was walking with Ah Ping outside the Walled City, he would say, "Whew, I've walked to the end of the street and I didn't get arrested." It was not that he had done anything—only that he had seen a couple of detectives who recognized him. Both the policemen and Ah Ping knew that he was fair game. If they wanted, they could stop him, search him and ask him a few questions. Or they could take him away and pin a crime on him. It happened frequently. Boys would sign "confessions," as they knew that they could not afford legal representation and that a guilty plea would earn a lighter sentence than a "not guilty" plea.

I began to plead with the boys to tell the truth and nothing but the truth in court. This led to my spending many, many hours in courts and magistracies. I shared the criminals' shame as I saw people pointing at me and saying, "There's that simple Christian sitting with those crooks." I knew the boys had done wrong things, and perhaps some of them were still involved in crime, but I was always willing to go and sit with them, guilty or not, as long as they spoke the truth. But the shame was awful, and it helped me to understand what an amazing sacrifice Christ had made when He not only publicly associated with us sinners but also took our wrong doings as His own.

One evening, I received a call from Mau Jai (a nickname meaning "Little Cat"). It was 7:45 P.M. and we had a roomful of St. Stephen's girls and Walled City boys who had just been praying together in my flat.

"Johnny's just been arrested. Get to the police station quickly," Mau Jai said.

"How do you know?" I asked. "And where are you?"

"Can't talk here—I tell you later," he said tersely.

On the way to the police station, I thought about Johnny, who was one of the most repulsive-looking drug addicts I knew. He was small and desperately thin, more a skeleton than a man.

"If that one can be saved—anyone can," I had said when I first saw him. He was a carpenter and earned quite a good wage, but he used the entire lot to smoke heroin. He was a Triad too, but useless to his gang.

When I arrived at the station, I asked to see Johnny but was told that he was not there.

"He must be here—he was arrested 45 minutes ago," I said. But the desk sergeant denied it.

"Why don't you go home and we'll telephone you if he appears," he suggested patronizingly.

"I'll stay until you produce him," I said and prepared to settle down for the night.

Two minutes later they indeed produced him, but I was too late. He had already confessed to a crime. He was charged with being in possession of a screwdriver with intent to break into a building a mile outside the Walled City. The time Johnny was alleged to have committed the crime was 8:15 P.M., but I knew this could not be true because Little Cat had phoned me half an hour before that. I went to look for him.

It transpired that Johnny and Little Cat had been taking drugs together in one of the largest dens in the Walled City when two detectives had come in and taken Johnny off. The detectives should not have been there; this was not their beat, but they knew well where the dens were, and addicts made easy pickings. The evil of the situation was that certain police, far from intending to stop this ugly business, actually had an arrangement with the vice bosses that they would ignore the dens in return for "tea" money.

The police made show raids, but several times I heard den watchers getting the tip-off from police who phoned to say that they were on their way. During the Walled City's heyday of crime, there was a syndicate payment from the vice and drug dealers that amounted to $100,000 daily. Although uniformed police rarely went inside apart from raiding parties, I was told that several plainclothes detectives were actually running some of the illegal businesses in league with the Triads. This made it extremely difficult to sort out the good guys from the bad guys, and I began to understand why the boys I knew were so muddled about right and wrong.

Johnny's family lived in a squalid flat just outside the Walled City. They were desperately poor, but they borrowed money and bailed him out. This was a mistake, because Johnny used the remand period of several weeks to take even more heroin until he had used up all the family money and pawned most of their belongings. I visited him and tried to persuade him to plead not guilty, as I knew that he was innocent of this particular charge.

Johnny was reluctant. "I can't deny the confession I've signed," he said. "The police said they'd arrest me for something else if I did. And I need to keep in with them."

Addicts claimed that they were often given heroin at the police station in return for their confessions. But Johnny had to learn to stick to the truth. I told him all about Jesus and how He always spoke the truth even though it cost Him His life. Then we prayed together. Johnny agreed that it would be right to tell the truth, but he said that it was too dangerous for him at that stage. He explained it all patiently: "If I do tell the truth in court, then that means I'm letting everyone know where the drug dens are. Worse still, I'm saying that the police themselves know where they are but that they are not doing anything about them. Both my friends and the police will want to get me for saying so in court after that."

I went on meeting with Johnny. When I say we prayed, it is not strictly true. I prayed and he listened. He thought I did not understand the danger he would be in when I continued to tell him that he should speak the truth. On the day of the trial, he had quite decided to go along with the police story and plead guilty, even though I had hired a solicitor to defend him. The solicitor cost me more than a month's living expenses, but I saw it as God's money, which I would use in His name. Just before Johnny went into the witness box, I showed him a Bible passage telling us not to be frightened when in court, for the Holy Spirit tells us what to say.[5]

Johnny told me afterward that when he stood up in court, he suddenly had an overwhelming conviction that he had to tell the truth even though he did not want to at all. What might have been a simple case lasting a few moments became a major battle lasting more than a week. There were long cross-examinations of the police evidence by our solicitor, but eventually the magistrate accepted it as the correct version and found Johnny guilty. The emotional strain of the week overcame me when he pronounced the verdict, and I burst into tears in court.

To see an English girl weeping for a Chinese criminal and drug addict was unusual; the prosecuting police inspector snapped his briefcase shut and came up to talk to me. He asked me why I was crying. "Because he didn't do it," I sobbed. "He isn't guilty."

"Well, he's got a record as long as your arm," said the inspector kindly. "In fact, he has 13 previous convictions. I shouldn't waste your sympathy on him."

"That's not the point," I replied. "He hasn't done this one."

"Well," said the prosecutor, "you know this is Hong Kong justice. Even if he hasn't done this one, he's done another crime. It's fair enough in the long run."

"That's not right," I insisted. "Jesus' name is truth, and we are called to tell the truth here in court."

By this time, the arresting detectives and their companions had gathered around. They knew that I knew they had been lying. They saw the tears streaming down my cheeks. They saw me as a fool, and they laughed. They laughed and they sneered as they left the court for a celebration meal. It was difficult not to feel bitter against them.

Johnny was sent to prison, and from there he was sent to a drug rehabilitation center. He was assigned a probation officer who summoned his mother, saying, "Don't let that Christian interfere with your lives—you're not Christians. You've got idols—you are idol worshipers." The officer was very rude and uncooperative, but I continued to visit Johnny.

The final verdict was yet to come. On appeal the chief justice overruled Johnny's conviction, and he was technically free. However, Johnny went back to using drugs, and later he went back to prison. Out of prison again, he returned to drugs once more and continued this terrible cycle.

But Johnny had never forgotten what had happened in court. I often used to go and visit him as he lay slumped on the chair that served as his bed. After about two years, he did finally believe in Jesus for himself. He became a Christian, went to a Christian drug rehabilitation center and was transformed. After graduating from there, he became a male nurse in a tuberculosis sanitarium, working on the addicts' ward.

Johnny's mother was overjoyed when he became a Christian. Every time I passed the market, she threw eggs and sausages at me. Not literally, but she sold these at her market stall and was so grateful that she showered gifts upon me. Another lady at a noodle stall did the same thing. I could hardly pass without a large bowl being thrust at me. Eventually I had to bypass her particular street, for my jeans were getting too tight.

This is to anticipate a few years, but out of that court case came other good results. It was the first case in which I had asked a solicitor to represent our boys, and many others followed. Each time, the police won the case. "Don't think that Western woman can help you," they would scoff in the interrogation room. "She has no power." But their actions belied their words. Several boys told me that they had been stopped by plainclothes men who asked them, "Are you from that place? Are you from that woman's club?" When they replied yes, the boys were not detained. The reason was that the police knew that if they charged one of our boys when he was innocent, they would be faced with a week's trial rather than a 10-minute hearing. Although they won the cases, this was too costly in time. It was one more sign to me that I was being watched, and that in this way, Jesus was preached.

Another result came 30 months later. It was Christmastime and I wanted very much to celebrate with a proper Christmas dinner for the boys, but we had no money. I thought they should have the best on Jesus' birthday, so having booked a restaurant, I prayed for funds. Suddenly the phone rang; it was my solicitor's office.

"We've been checking our records and we find we have to refund you 1,000 dollars," said a voice.

"No, you don't," I gasped. "You don't owe me anything."

"We've been checking through Johnny Ho's case, and we owe you 1,000 dollars in fees."

"Surely not," I said. "That was a correct payment; in fact, I know you took the case cheaply anyway."

"Our records show that there was an appeal, and that is paid by legal aid."

"Yes, I know that," I said, "but the original hearing was not on legal aid. We had to pay for that. Will you please check your books very carefully, because if you give me the money, I shall spend it."

They checked their books and they sent me the money. So on Johnny's trial money, we all had a wonderful Christmas dinner two and a half years later. God was watching over us, too.

# CHASING THE DRAGON

E merging from the dark city one night I was in a thoughtful mood; my lifestyle was extraordinary in the sense that
on no two days did I get up or sleep at the same time.
I prayed a lot as I walked, for I found that I needed to talk to God
all the time. That night, I reiterated a heartfelt prayer of thanks.
"Thank God I'm not married. Thank God I've been left free
to have time for other people's children." It would have been
awful to have to phone up a husband and say, "Put on the baked
beans, dear; I've been held up." I was sharing a flat with a girlfriend named Stephanie at this time and, mercifully, she never
worried what time I came home. It was well past midnight when
I climbed on to a minibus (known as a 14-man bus) on my way
home to Jordan Road.

My prayers were interrupted by the sight of a pathetic figure: a boy of about 15 who looked like a living skeleton. Huge,
hideous eye sockets were dark in a yellowish-grey face. This
child-ghoul sat down in front of me, and I tried to think where
I had seen him before. The bus lurched and grated through the
small hours while I searched my memory until I remembered
when I had first seen him.

It was five years earlier, when I had first begun to go to the
Walled City. There was a large teahouse outside, where this
small boy waited to open taxi-doors for a few cents tip. I noticed
that he did not even get to keep all of this, as there was an older
beggar, also in rags, who obviously controlled the pitch. The boy
looked desperately sick; clearly he was sleeping in the streets.
Since I could not then speak the language, I asked Chinese

friends to write me notes to him, offering to meet him at a particular place or clinic and get help for him. What I did not know
was that he had been a drug addict since the age of 10, when his
stepfather threw him out of his home. He had never kept any
rendezvous, but I had continued to pray for him.

So here he was again; I thanked God for bringing him back.
Now that I could speak Chinese, I had another chance to help
him. He got off the bus in Mongkok, a busy area full of bars,
ballrooms and dreary nightlife. I got off too and followed him.
He was carrying a filthy red plastic tooth mug that he used for
begging. I tapped him on the shoulder and introduced myself,
suggesting that we go to eat the seasonal rice dumpling, which
hung from the street stalls during the Dragon Boat festival.
The poor boy was terribly embarrassed. He hid his tooth mug
behind his back, and as we proceeded to the *daih paih dong*, the
street stall, he dropped it into a pile of rubbish.

He looked more and more uncomfortable as we ate; it was
clearly time for his next fix. His mind as well as his body was rotted by the amount of heroin he had consumed; he understood
nothing of what I was saying. There was no point in telling this
young boy named Ah Tsoi about Jesus, for he could not concen-
trate for long enough to take it in. I thought that if we could
find help for his addiction and his mind cleared, then I could
tell him.

For the next few weeks, I used to meet Ah Tsoi at all times
of the day and night. He never slept in the same place, and I
was frightened to lose him in case he was arrested. With track
marks all down the veins on both arms, he was an easy target
for arrest. Worse still, I discovered that he was holding people
up daily to pay for his habit—and he was doing this while on
probation, having already been in prison for drug offences.
Twice I forced him to begin keeping appointments with his
probation officer again.

I was obsessed with helping Ah Tsoi. The more I saw of this
pathetic character, the fonder of him I grew. Finally, Pastor
Chan agreed to take him into his Christian drug rehabilitation

center. I was overjoyed; this was the answer to my prayers. We were going to change Ah Tsoi's life. As he had a little time to wait before going to the center, I began to give him money. It was not much—only HK $5 a day. I felt a little uneasy about this, but he needed that minimum amount to support his habit. If I did not give it to him, he would have been forced to mug and steal, so I convinced myself that I was acting rightly. It was only for a few days, anyhow.

At last the day came for his departure to Pastor Chan's. I went out to the market and bought him a pair of shorts, a vest and a T-shirt, some underclothes, flip-flops and even swimming trunks, because Pastor Chan's center was by the sea. Finally, I bought him a toothbrush, flannel pajamas, new jeans and an extra shirt. I thought this was like what a mother would feel, and I felt very tender toward Ah Tsoi as I wrapped all these into a neat parcel ready for him to collect. I had asked him to come around to my flat to have a bath before he set off.

No Ah Tsoi. It was two hours after he should have arrived and there was no sign of him. Perhaps he was having a last fix somewhere. Then, just as I was wondering whether he would come at all, he arrived. He was filthy, but by now there was no time to bathe. Stephanie had a camera, and we wanted to take a picture of him before he went. He snarled at once. "I'm not going to be one of your film stars," he said. "No 'before and after' pictures of me. I'm not an exhibit." He went off in a very surly frame of mind, but I did see him safely into Pastor Chan's hands.

I went to bed and slept nearly 20 hours. For the first time in weeks, I could sleep easily. I was exhausted, but relieved. Thank God that Ah Tsoi was someone else's problem now. Pastor Chan could teach him about Jesus and help him to grow up. Now I could go on to find the next one . . .

I was awakened by a telephone call. Ah Tsoi had run away. He could not stand the pain of withdrawal and had tried to smoke his blanket to ease the craving. The others tried to persuade him to pray, but he refused and slipped away into the night. He went on to a neighboring village to steal blankets and money. The center staff tried to find him to persuade him to come back, but when they eventually caught up with him, he refused to return. There was nothing more they could do. That was the end of the matter.

It was as if a part of me had died. I felt completely shattered and lay down on the stone floor and wept. I cried all day, unable to move off the floor. As I lay there, I thought this was the end; I did not know what more I could have done. I had given Ah Tsoi everything I had. I had given him all my time, my love, my money, my food, and I had tried to tell him about Jesus. I had passed him to other Christians, but it had not worked. I had failed.

I did not feel angry at God but very disappointed and perplexed by the whole episode. I could not understand why He let me get involved with Ah Tsoi in the first place if it was not going to work out. At last I gathered strength to pray. "No more of those, please, God; no more drug addicts, because I can't bear it. I had almost enough love for one person, and I gave him all of it. It wasn't enough, and I don't think I've got any more."

Next morning, I got onto a bus to go to my Chinese lesson. Hong Kong buses do not allow one the luxury of choosing a seat; I was wedged in with the other 40-odd standing passengers when, out of the corner of my eye, I saw a mentally handicapped boy. I did not want to look at him, so I turned around. And there I was, facing another drug addict. I could only shut my eyes and pretend that they were not there. It would not hurt if I could not see them . . .

"God, I'm not looking because I don't want to go through all that pain again," I prayed. "I did believe that You would help, but it didn't succeed. Why not?" I thought back to the time when I was walking through the Walled City and first learning about addicts. In one street there were over 100 people openly smoking heroin; every single street seemed to have its emaciated wrecks. "It would be worth my whole life if You would use me to help just one of them," I had prayed.

Slowly, as I recovered from the Ah Tsoi ordeal, I saw more clearly my mistakes in dealing with him. I had tried to give him everything I had; I had even prayed to God to save him, although in reality I was trying to save him myself. I wanted Ah Tsoi off drugs, but he was not desperate enough to want it for himself—especially when I subsidized his habit.

I had not dared to take Ah Tsoi off drugs and through withdrawal myself. (This was before I had seen Winson come off opium miraculously.) I was convinced that he needed expert care, and when the expert care I fixed up did not work, I was shattered.

Later, Pastor Chan took me to tea. He had bravely walked a lone path in Hong Kong by opening a farm for rehabilitating addicts in the New Territories. Without medical assistance, he brought them through withdrawal. Then they continued to heal and grow strong in Christ because he gave them 18 months of discipline with love.

Many of his graduates became church workers and counselors in government and voluntary agencies. While the government-supported drug centers had impressive statistics, I had never met any addicts who had been through them and stayed off drugs; Pastor Chan's men were the only ones I had ever known personally who were still drug-free. He had slowly built up his program through experience and heartbreak, so it was very comforting when he said, "Miss Pullinger, you will make a very good worker because you care."

Social workers are taught not to be involved with their cases, but I knew that had I not been so close to the people concerned, I could not have stayed. Ah Tsoi's failure taught me that I was not brave or nice enough to take on such a job simply because it was a worthwhile project. I could not imagine how drug workers could tackle their depressing task without God and I had a deep respect for them, but I knew that my own resources had run out. Despite my prayers for no more addicts, however, it was not the end of my dealings with them, but merely the beginning. I found that I could care for them again with God's love.

As my acquaintance with the Triads grew, it seemed as if every other one was on drugs because they were so cheap and easy to obtain. The heroin at that time was undiluted with additives and was extremely potent. In fact, the U.S. government warned its servicemen visiting Hong Kong on their "rest and recreation" trips from Vietnam that if they injected what seemed to be a normal dose, they could overdose and die.

One night, I visited a heroin den. It was in a large tin shed on the outskirts of the city, but it operated with the knowledge of the police. It was a filthy place with long low rough tables at which were seated what appeared to be effigies. I felt I had invaded a devil's banquet, a weird and silent meal. Each table was ruled over by a *pahng-jue*, a host. For 50 cents, he provided the screws of toilet paper, the tinfoil and the cardboard funnels necessary for chasing the dragon. Few Chinese addicts injected heroin; they only did so when their physical need was greater than their resources. They were afraid of overdosing—they could remember the days when each morning the corpses of dead addicts were piled by the single toilet ready for collection . . .

Among the 50-odd bodies sucking in their horrid delight sat a boy in his early teens. His skin was pale and waxen, and his strength had died. His girlfriend, who looked about 14, sat beside him and supported him in her arms as he inhaled his poison. It was a peculiarly intimate pose, and I was touched until I remembered that this girl had to sell her body to support her man. I looked at the others present, knowing that every man there would have to pay for his habit this way unless he stole or pawned his family's belongings. It was a degrading scene, but I was fascinated and attracted. I felt the pull of the drug that every potential addict knows and which defies logic. He knows it kills; he knows it leads to addiction and depravity. He knows all the arguments with his head, but he still has to try it. And having tried once, he has to continue until he is part of the mystique that drew him.

Every addict has a love-hate relationship with his drug. His mind despises it and its hold over him. His body longs for it when deprived for too long and cheats his mind into seeing it as a salvation. No one ever knows when he crosses the line from "playing" with drugs to being dependent on them. One novice vomits the first time and tries again to see whether it improves. Another feels little effect and imagines that he can take it again quite safely. He starts with a small dose, but what satisfies at first is soon not enough and he needs to take more to prevent withdrawal pains. He takes bigger doses more and more often until he is arrested or dies.

I felt the pull of the drug. It was attractive. It was demonic.

When Winson came into the Youth Club and was set free from his opium addiction, God showed me that the battle with this dragon could be won. At that moment, I believed that Winson's experience should be possible for others if they were converted and filled with God's power. Very soon after, Ah Ping told me that his addicted friend wanted to come to our annual summer camp, and I welcomed him readily.

Ah Ming was a powerful Triad member from Hong Kong Island, a cousin to this branch of the 14K. We met on the ferry that was taking us to Lamma Island for the camp, but Ah Ming avoided shaking hands or talking to me—he was coming on his own terms.

A couple of English students, Tim and Nick, were to join us a few days later. But for the first two days of the camp, I had no men helpers, so I prayed, "Please, God, send the right boys to the camp, and keep the wrong ones away."

Our campsite was at the top of a mountain, serene and beautiful. The only distressing factor in our one-hour walk up the hill was the 30-pound sack of rice, which I had to carry most of the way. The boys thought this was women's work, and anyway, they were there to play, not work. Years later they became more helpful and protective, but I was still very much on trial at this point.

The camp program was very strict, with work details and bedtimes carefully arranged, but it proved difficult to effect by myself. I slept with the few girls in tents and the boys slept in an enormous dormitory; I could not go in to search their belongings or to turn out the lights. I realized that most of those 30 were Triad members, and I began to feel uneasy. Still, I had prayed that prayer about keeping the wrong ones out . . .

Ah Ming appeared outside the boys' dormitory and saw me sitting out there in the dark with my hurricane lamp. He had not expected that. "Hmm. I do—er—I do like looking at the stars," he improvised.

"Yes," I agreed, "so do I. They're beautiful, aren't they?"

We sat there for maybe three hours in very polite conversation. He was obviously longing to go off and take his drugs. Finally, I could not sit it out any longer. So I went to bed, and Ah Ming went to the other side of the mountain to take his heroin.

I had prayed that God would keep the wrong ones away, so I had to deduce that the boys who had come were sent by God, but taking drugs on a Christian camp was not quite what I had in mind. The missionaries had advised me that the way to build a church was to work on one boy at a time. When he was a Christian and doing well, then you could work on another one until the house was full. I had done it completely backward, however, and had landed with a dormitory full of gangsters. Who was running whom I was not sure. I began to think that the missionaries were right.

Two days later, Ah Ming was *in extremis*, having run out of his drug supply. He sent a brother to me who announced that there was an urgent matter that three of them had to attend to, so they would be leaving. I intended to argue this, but since the rest of us were having morning service, they escaped.

I sent Nick to chase after them; he was an enormous six-footer. That he could not speak a word of Chinese was greatly to his advantage, for the wily addicts had invented a very good explanation as to why their departure was imperative.

Fortunately, Nick could not understand them, so as they continued to walk he continued to follow.

They walked over three hills. All they could hear was this Englishman repeating, "You must come back, you must come back, you must come back" and "Jesus loves you, Jesus loves you." But no way were three sick addicts going to turn around and come back. The craving for heroin was so strong that they would have climbed 100 mountains—or even killed someone—in order to get the ferry back to their supply.

Meanwhile, back at the camp we were praying for their return.

Without knowing why they did so, the three fleeing boys stopped dead. Then they lit cigarettes and began to retrace their steps. When they reappeared with Nick on top of our mountain, they looked very sheepish; they could not explain this prodigal turnabout even to themselves. However, when I suggested to Ah Ming that we chat for a while, he nodded as if he had been expecting this all along . . .

It was pouring with rain, and we were forced to seek shelter in one of our two-man army tents. Poor Ah Ming did not want a lecture. He was feeling intense discomfort, but he could not leave the tent because the downpour had reached monsoon intensity. "I'm sorry, Ah Ming," I began. "I know you're feeling lousy, but I'd like to show you something that will help you." In the earth I drew three crosses.

"I know this sounds silly, but I want you to imagine that you could actually see all the wrong things that a man has done. We'll use this *lap-sap* [rubbish] to represent them." I collected up some bottle tops, dirt and waste paper lying around. "Now when Jesus was crucified, two men were nailed on either side of Him; they were thieves, probably murderers."[1] I placed a heap of litter on the outside crosses, leaving Jesus' cross empty. "Do you know why the middle one has no *lap-sap*?" I asked Ah Ming. He looked rather bored and replied, "Yeah, Jesus never did no wrong, so He got no sins on Him."

I became a storyteller, pointing to the crosses. "So You're the Christ, eh?" mocked this man. "Prove it. Call on Your henchmen to save you now. Come on then. You save Yourself, and save us too while You're at it." He was dying himself, but he still had plenty of spit.

"You shouldn't say that," objected that thief on the right cross. "We done wrong—we oughta die. This man ain't done nothing," and he turned to Jesus saying, "Lord, remember me when You get to Your Kingdom."

"Today you will be with Me together in paradise," answered Jesus.[2] While I said this, I lifted the heap of dirt off the right cross and placed it all on Jesus.

"You feel like throwing up now?" I noticed Ah Ming looked gray and trembly. "Well, Jesus felt like you do only even worse, because as well as taking that man's sins, He took all the sins and all the pains the whole world ever felt on Himself, so that we could be free of our sin and pain."[3]

For some time we both stared at the ground and the message drawn there. Then I said, "The thief on that side is forgiven and now can live with God, but why not the other one? Weren't they equally bad?"

"One believed and the other didn't," replied Ah Ming.

"That's all you have to do. I know you don't understand, but if you are willing to give all of your pain to Him, Jesus can take it away right now. He's God's Son, and that's why He died. Are you willing?"

Ah Ming was not very willing. His eyes were running and he kept sniffing as he clutched his stomach. It was still raining outside; he was stuck in this tent in great distress. At last he could not stand it any longer.

"Suppose," he said resignedly, "suppose I—er—well, suppose I try."

It was enough.

He then prayed clearly, asking Jesus to take away his pain if He were God. He asked for his wrong things to be taken away, too, so that he could start his life again. It stopped raining.

Outside, I found my English friends. They joined me in the tent, and we laid our hands on Ah Ming's head, telling him that

Jesus would give him healing and power. When we prayed, Ah Ming too received the gift of the Holy Spirit, and we all prayed together for a while.

A week later when we returned from the camp, Ah Ming told me how God had answered those prayers in an extraordinary way. He had gone to bed feeling confused after praying and was not at all sure what had happened. As he slept he had a strange dream. He dreamed that he was lying on a wooden bunk in a mountain hut. It was blowing a gale outside; through the sounds of the wind, he heard a knocking at the door. As he was alone in the hut in a terrible state of drug withdrawal, he did not answer it. The knocking came a second time, so he went to the window to see who it was. There he saw a man carrying a candle, which he thought very odd on a rainy mountain, but being in a foul temper he went back to bed. The third time the knocking came, Ah Ming thought, *Poor man, he doesn't have anywhere else to go.* He went to the door and opened it, and then he lay down again. The man, who seemed oddly familiar, came into the hut and over to the bunk bed, where he put down the candlestick.

He asked Ah Ming to sit up and then gently put his hands on his head. The withdrawal pains disappeared; he never had any pain again. "I knew He was a healer," said Ah Ming, reveling in his release from drugs.


A whistle was blowing. Early each morning, I insisted that the boys do a version of physical jerks before breakfast. They all tumbled out of bed. Ah Ping noticed that although Ah Ming had risen, he was groping around on the bunk. He asked Ah Ming what he was doing.

"I'm looking for the candle wax," replied Ah Ming. "I'm looking for the candle wax." The dream had been so real that he was sure that Jesus really had been there. After that, he joined in the morning exercises with great vigor, surprising all his friends who knew that addicts going through withdrawal could not usually do pushups. Later that day, he was baptized in the sea. When we all returned to the mainland, he looked fit and very happy.

Ah Ming did not actually do any work himself but had a job at one of the dockyards, where he used to lie in a cabin all day while his younger brothers fed him heroin. On his first day back at work, he sat on the ferry and prayed while crossing the harbor. He prayed so hard that he did not notice when his neighboring passengers stole his flip-flops as a joke. Undaunted, he carried on to work and walked through the dockyard gates shoeless. When he saw a gang of rival Triads armed for a fight with bottles and knives coming toward him, he instinctively took up the nearest weapons—two heavy iron poles—and waded into the attack.

What I had not known when I prayed that God would send only the "right ones" to the camp was that Ah Ming had come to our camp especially to plan his strategy for this gang war. He had given his orders to some of his brothers at the camp, and now seeing him going into the attack, they ran to various street stalls and drew out meat choppers and melon knives to be used in the battle.

Suddenly Ah Ming thought, *Help! I was praying about peace on the boat this morning. I can't fight.* He dropped his poles, sat down in the road and began to pray again.

A few minutes later, he looked up to see his enemies surrounding him; they were all looking down at him curiously. "What are you doing?" their leader asked.

"I'm praying. I'm a Christian now—would you like to hear about it?" They nodded, dumbfounded, so Ah Ming told them what had happened to him. They were so impressed that several came to see me later and began to attend meetings.


In this way, our Youth Club grew bigger and bigger as those who became Christians brought their friends. I had not yet met the renowned Goko, but his large chop-eating brother came in frequently to sing. Some weeks after the camp, we were praying in the clubroom when one of the boys had a vision. Since all the boys who believed in Christ had received the power of the Spirit with the gift of tongues, they were not surprised when God caused wonders to happen.

The vision was of us in procession walking down the street singing and dancing. Only 12 were willing to go. The rest made excuses. "Poon Siu Jeh, we live here," they said. As I imagined myself prancing around my parents' village in England, I could sympathize.

One of our favorite songs in the club was "Silver and Gold Have I None," which went like this: ·

> Silver and gold have I none
> But such as I have give I thee
> In the name of Jesus Christ
> Of Nazareth, rise up and walk.
> Walking and leaping and praising God,
> Walking and leaping and praising God,
> In the name of Jesus Christ
> Of Nazareth rise up and walk.

I took my accordion. We had one guitarist and a couple of tambourines; the rest of the 12 followed in single file. The street was too narrow for two people, but when we reached the "leaping and dancing and praising" refrain, we all managed to jump around a bit.

It is the only time I can remember during that era when so many vice businesses stopped without there being a police raid. At the blue film theatre and the gambling dens, the patrons rushed to the doorways to see what was happening. One of Ah Keung's brothers, asleep in an illegal casino, heard the singing and woke up with a start, believing himself to have dropped off during our Sunday morning service. Many people had seen Christians handing out bits of paper before (the addicts used to smoke them), but never before had they witnessed singing and dancing in the streets of the Walled City.

Passing by the opium dens, we came to the two largest
heroin dens, where Ah Ming, who had assumed leadership of
the procession, stopped and, quite unbidden, began to preach.
Inside the den, a tall young Chinese named Ah Mo had just finished injecting himself. He had already discovered that "Miss
White" (one of the nicknames for heroin or white powder) did
not keep her promises. He had hardly gained a moment of
enjoyment from her—for no sooner had he taken his fix than he
had to think about obtaining money for his next appointment
with the lying lady. Ah Mo was wondering where to do his next
robbery when he heard singing outside the heroin shed.
Emerging from one gloom into the next, he was amazed to see
his friend Ah Ming telling people in the street how Jesus had
changed his life.

It was obvious to Ah Mo that something very wonderful
had indeed taken place, for barely three weeks previously he
and Ah Ming had been squatting side by side taking heroin
together in that very same den. Forgetting his projected robbery, he joined the end of the procession and followed it until
it wound back to the clubroom some 30 minutes later. There,
he came in and listened with wonder as the boys told him how
Jesus could change him. But he shook his head and asked to
speak to me privately.

"I can't be a Christian, Miss Poon. I killed my wife." He told
me the tragic tale of his rise to fame in the Triads as a muscle-
man. He used to throw people out of nightclubs and bars in a
more glamorous district of Kowloon. He had soon become
powerful enough to employ his own bouncers and eventually
controlled a little empire. He lived with a ballroom "hostess,"
but he had a great macho image of himself and enjoyed three
other mistresses at the same time. When he was arrested, his
hostess visited him in prison, taking him drugs and money. She
really loved him. Although he promised to be faithful, he continued to visit the others after he was released.

She was so miserable that she too began to take drugs and,
near death, was rushed to hospital to have her stomach pumped.

To placate her, Ah Mo rented a white wedding dress for her and a morning dress for himself, and they had a mock wedding picture taken in a bridal studio. They sent the pictures to their relations in China. But Ah Mo did not give up his lechery, and so his girl overdosed a second time. The third time she overdosed, she could not be saved. She died in the hospital.

Ah Mo was wracked with guilt; he lost interest in his bouncing business and punished himself with drugs.

As he stood before me, all bones and rags, it was hard to imagine that this man had inspired such a fatal passion. But when I told him that he could find forgiveness in Christ, his eyes grew hopeful, and I caught a glimpse of the handsome man he was. He prayed to receive Jesus and left the club in a daze. Some of his cronies were in the passage outside; seeing his face they laughed, "He's got religion; he's got religion."

"But I didn't mind," Ah Mo told me later, "because my heart felt light."

I had assumed that because Winson and Ah Ming were cured miraculously of their addictions, anyone who believed in Jesus would automatically be delivered. Ah Mo was not. He continued to take drugs although I told him that this was not consistent with being a Christian.

I asked Pastor Chan to take him into his center, but he had to wait several weeks before there was a place. I was puzzled as to why God did not save him instantly as He had saved the others.

"Praise God," Ah Mo announced when he joined our Sunday service some days later. "I haven't had to rob or steal this week to pay for my heroin habit. I've got a job."

When I discovered what that job was, I found myself unable to praise God for it at all. He was employed by one of the dens as a *tin-man-toi* (weatherman). Each night from midnight until 8 A.M., he sat in the street of the illegal dentists guarding one of the entrances to the Walled City. In his cigarette pack was concealed an electric plug. Should he spot a police raiding party, narcotics bureau spy or an alien Triad, his duty was to fix the plug into a socket built into the crude wall. This set off an

alarm bell in the various vice and drug dens so that by the time
any intruder approached, business had stopped and they were
ready to repel invaders.

For these labors, Ah Mo was paid HK $15 a day—enough for
his heroin requirement, but not enough for rice.

Each day, I found Ah Mo and took him a little food. I had
learned my lesson about not giving money. He slept in an alley
behind the Kowloon City public lavatory, paying HK $15 a
month for this privilege to another street sleeper who was the
self-appointed "king" of the street. Most days I sat and prayed
with him, although he was usually half asleep when I left my
offering in a plastic bag.

I was thankful that the drug den watching did not continue for long. I could not justify it morally, nor could I suggest
an alternative. Ah Mo eventually went to the center, came off
drugs and, in one month, gained 20 pounds in weight. One
more dragon bit the dust.

I continued to send messages to Goko after Winson's miraculous cure. I wrote notes, sending them with various *sai lo*;
I called in at gambling dens and left my name; I spoke to the look-
out man outside Goko's favorite opium den; I talked to his wife.
Eventually he agreed to see me—as the accumulation of messages suggested that I had an important matter to discuss.

Winson was dispatched with an invitation inviting me to
tea at the Fairy Restaurant outside the city. It was a Chinese cafe
selling Western food and usually out of my price range. As I made
my way past the street letter-writers ponderously scribing their
missives, I wondered what Goko would be like. I knew that he
was tall and big and had been a great football player before his
deterioration through opium. I had heard how he lay all day in
his own den while his younger brothers fed him with opium.
This dependence was in sharp contrast with the power he
wielded and the dread his name inspired. He had carefully
brainwashed his followers: Heroin was forbidden, but opium
was merely the continuation of an old social custom no more
harmful than drinking brandy after a meal. He was an older

Triad boss and prided himself on keeping the rules, such as being responsible for the funeral arrangements of a murdered gang member and assuming financial care for his dependants.

Goko recognized me first, as I was the only Westerner to enter the restaurant. He was in his mid-30s, respectably dressed, sitting alone. He courteously gestured to me to sit down. Looking him fully in the face for the first time, I could see that the opium had drawn lines of dissipation on his strong features. He seemed to have shrunk within his large frame like an old man. He smiled at me and showed teeth rotted and stained with fumes from his opium pipe. While I was with him, he smoked cigarettes continuously, puffing and inhaling too frequently.

Politely, the ruthless leader of corruption asked me what I would like to order. I drank coffee, he drank Horlicks, and we shared pineapple buns.

We carried on conversation-class pleasantries until I blurted, "I wish you wouldn't be so polite; please, let's stop pretending. You and I have nothing in common. Why are you being so kind to me?"

Goko paused. "I believe you care about my brothers like I do." He was not using idle words; he was famous for the care he took of his followers.

"Yes, I do care about them," I agreed, "but you and I can have no union. I hate everything you stand for, and I hate what you do."

It was strange, but now (as in future meetings), the more bluntly I spoke the more Goko responded. He dropped the polite frills and began to speak straight.

"Poon Siu Jeh, you and I both understand power. I use this way," he clenched his fist, "and you use this way," he pointed to his heart. "You have a power that I don't have. If my brothers get hooked on drugs, I have them beaten up. I don't want them on heroin, and I've found I can't make them quit. But I've watched you. And I believe Jesus can." He paused to light a cigarette while I marveled at the significance of what he had said.

"So," he continued, "I've decided to give the addicts to you."

"No," I replied quickly, "you can't do that. I know what you want to do. You want Jesus to get them off drugs, and then you want them back to work to fight for you. But Christians can't serve two bosses; they have to follow either Christ or you. I believe you love your brothers, but you and I are walking different paths and can have no meeting point. I have no intention of helping your brothers off drugs only for you to take them back. They will certainly go back to heroin if they follow you."

Goko stared down at the tablecloth covered with crumbs from the pineapple buns. He looked up slowly.

"All right, then. I give up my right to those who want to follow Jesus."

I could hardly take in what he had said. The Triads never released their members; once you became a Triad, you remained a Triad for life. Even the Hong Kong law courts accepted that Triad membership was binding forever. To try to leave was to invite savage punishment or even death. There were stories of rebellious members who had their cheeks raked or were quietly stabbed one unsuspecting night. Yet here was Goko volunteering to hand over some of his brothers. Never before had I heard of such an offer . . . he interrupted my thoughts: "I'll tell you what I'll do; I'll give you all my rotten brothers and I'll keep all the good ones for myself."

"Fine," I said. "Jesus came for the rotten ones anyhow."

So that was our strange pact, and from that time onward, Goko sent me addicts to cure. When he heard what happened to Johnny, he said, "I'm watching. If he lasts five years, I will have to believe for myself.

# GROWING PAINS

Winson was in difficulties. He came to me full of excitement. "Poon Siu Jeh, I have to praise the Lord," he said. "I was in the opium den last night and someone invited me to have some free opium. I did want to, but I prayed and God gave me strength, so I did not take it. Instead I knelt down and sang songs about Jesus for everyone to hear."

I was furious with him. "That's not 'praise the Lord,' Winson; it is tempting Him. It's not clever of you to ask for protection in a drug den—you shouldn't be there in the first place."

The problem was not easily resolved. I found out that Winson had no other place to sleep. At the time he was converted and freed from his drug addiction, he was living in this opium den, which was a favorite haunt of his 14K brothers.

I had told him to leave his gang and follow Jesus, but it was the same in practical terms as patting him on the back with a "Go, I wish you well; keep yourself warm and well fed"[1] and doing nothing about his physical needs. Although they had become Christians, both Winson and Ah Ping were still involved with the Triads by the very fact of living in the Walled City. They faced a dilemma when a brother was attacked. Their instinct was to defend him, as they had been raised in an atmosphere where loyalty to a brother excused violence to the point of murder. It was very hard for them to turn away from those they had grown up with and cared for. I also felt that even if they themselves no longer took an active part in crime, their very presence gave tacit approval to Triad affairs.

Ah Ming likewise encountered difficulties. "Before I became a Christian, I was well-known for my command. If I said, 'go,' my followers went; if I said, 'stab,' they would stab. I didn't have to think at all; I was without pity."

He reminded me of the centurion Jesus had met. "But now," Ah Ming continued, "when they come to me with grievances, I have to stop and think. I can't tell them to fight, because I'm a Christian. For the first time in my life, I consider the feelings of attacked victims. When my brothers see me hesitate, they lose respect for me, and this hurts me." Behind his fear of losing face, he was growing a conscience, a sensation alien in the Triad world.

As I walked around the Walled City, I kept on running into ex-addicts and Triads who had expressed a serious desire to change. Clearly they had to be removed from their evil environment, but like Winson, they had no other place to live. They could not survive the constant temptations with their meager spiritual knowledge. So I hunted for homes and Christian hostels only to find that all of them were for the respectable Chinese—tenants were required to have a job or to attend school, two pastoral references, a month's rent in advance, plus a deposit. Since none of the just-converted gangsters I knew had any one of these qualifications, they were effectively excluded.

To every Westerner I knew, I had at some time or another attempted to have one of my boys live in that person's house. (Chinese families never had any extra room, having enough problems housing their own relations.) Yet this was not satisfactory in Winson's case, as he needed more watching and discipline than an English family could give. Besides, most people found it a strain after a while having a gangster, albeit a converted one, living in the *amah*'s room.

Mary Taylor burst into tears when she first saw our flat in Lung Kong Road. True, the walls were crumbling, there was a hole in the roof, we only had night soil buckets in lieu of a lavatory, and there was no electricity, but in my opinion it was a godsend. I really could not see why my old school friend was so upset, because we had prayed about getting a place into which I could shepherd my sheep. As far as I was concerned, this was it.

I found my flat when enquiring at a street stall just outside the Walled City whether there were any apartments available in the vicinity. A very well-dressed lady who was shopping there took me straight away to this derelict place. By Chinese standards it was enormous, having more than 900 square feet inside, and stairs leading up to a roof, which had been partly covered with corrugated iron to make an extra room. She offered it to me at a very reasonable rent, saying that she had kept it vacant for a year, waiting for Christians to occupy it. She herself was a Buddhist.

I was so excited when I saw it that I could only see the possibilities. Mary, being more pragmatic, could only see its drawbacks; she may have been right, for it needed an incredible amount of work to make it habitable. Walled City boys helped in the renovation by lending their skills and non-skills. It is doubtful if this method was really cheaper than employing professionals, as they were keen on soft drinks and meal breaks in exchange for their services.

On the principle that work is done more quickly if one is on the spot, Mary and I moved in amongst a heap of rubble, no lights and a dubious water system, camping in one room while partitions came down and ceilings went up around us. Our greatest asset was the roof garden—once we had exchanged the heaps of old bicycle frames and bedsteads for begonias, cacti and climbing vines. These were carefully arranged so that we would not be overlooked by the Mahjong School opposite us, which catered to off-duty policemen who were very amused to see us sunbathing.

I needed to decide whether to share my house with girls or boys, since so many of each were homeless. If I took boys into my home—which I thought rather unsuitable in my single state—it would necessarily rule out the girls, as I could not mix them. But the decision was made for me when Ah Ping and Ah Keung had to leave the temporary home I had found for them and had nowhere else to go except back into the Walled City or Lung Kong Road.

Our new family was then joined by Joseph, the original Youth Club president. Winson left his den for us, and we arranged for Ah Ming to live with friends. We were forming a Christian community and helping the boys to grow up in Christ. I felt how nice and neat it was with this one here and that one there.

However, I still had much to learn. I did far too many jobs. I cooked for the boys, fed them, clothed them, cleaned the house and got them to work or school. I was also opening the Walled City room nearly every evening and visiting vice dens and brothels whenever there was a contact. When at last I got to bed, I was frequently awakened by drug addicts ringing on the doorbell, wanting to hear about Jesus. Prostitutes rang me from police stations, detectives appeared on the doorstep seeking information, and prison or probation officers referred cases to me, as ours was one of the very few places in the colony that housed delinquent boys. I did not fancy the idea of meeting a policeman in my nightgown, so from that time I adopted the habit of sleeping in my clothes. I was always ready to dash out of the house in an emergency.

One such event occurred when a young man phoned me at 4 A.M. to say that he had had an argument with his wife and that she had fallen out of the top bunk in their resettlement room. He had run away in panic but asked if I would please go to his home and check to see if she were dead or not.

Our flat eventually became mixed after all. Another night there was a knock on the door and when I opened it, there stood a little teenage girl holding a baby on one arm and an enormous suitcase on the other. Behind her crouched her younger brother and two little sisters. "Poon Siu Jeh," she whispered, "we've come to live with you."

I had first come to know these children some three years previously and had many dealings with them since. Their addicted father had not only harmed himself but had also caused his family dreadful suffering. The history of the Chung family was appalling. They all lived on a double bed. There was no space for anything else in the room, since it was only the roof of someone else's shack and had to be reached by a wooden staircase.

Their own roof was a plastic tarpaulin that sagged in the middle when it rained; every now and again they prodded it with a pole and emptied the rain into buckets to prevent it from flooding their little room. The children learned to walk on this bed; they slept on it, cooked on it, played and did their home-work on it. All five of them were painfully shy, and when I went to visit the family, they turned to the wall, pretending that they were not there. There was nowhere else to hide.

I never saw them eat anything except white rice, which they boiled to a porridge known as *congee*. This was because their miserable father spent all his earnings on heroin and never gave his family any support at all. The only income came from Mrs. Chung, a tiny little 30-year-old who carried water buckets for a living. She brought these buckets from the water pumps out-side the Walled City, carried them down the narrow streets on a pole, and then upstairs to people's houses. She received 5 cents each time for this service, but lost even that income after she got rheumatism in her legs and could no longer walk with the heavy buckets.

Although she was expecting a sixth child to be born into her foodless slum, Mrs. Chung was always smiling. She had asked to receive Jesus into her heart and she, I and some of the Christian boys from the Youth Club often prayed together, which brought her great joy. We used to take her dried bacon, salted fish and oil so that the family had more nourishment to put on the rice. Had we given her money, her husband, who came back occa-sionally, would have stolen it for his heroin. We took the chil-dren (who were aged from 6 to 11) toys for Christmas, and we paid their school fees. Even then the children had to work in factories to keep buying the rice.

I referred this case to the social welfare department, asking for compassionate resettlement and some kind of financial aid, as I could not afford the money to support them all indefinitely. The officials in the enquiry office were unhelpful. Mrs. Chung could not read, so she did not even know which floor to go to; and because they had told her to fill in forms before she could see a social worker, she had not even reached the queue that began the process of receiving help.

The next time she went, I went with her and sat all day waiting to see the caseworker. I suggested that she classify herself as separated, as Mr. Chung rarely came home and did not contribute to the family income anyway. I was shown out brusquely while Mrs. Chung was interviewed. When I visited the family again, this poor little lady told me that she had gone back to the office to sign for aid and that a letter would be coming. Four months later there was still no letter, although she remained optimistic that it would come. Eventually, I checked with the welfare department, who looked up the family's files. I was told, "This family does not qualify for aid."

"If that family doesn't qualify for aid, then I'm sure no one does," I replied. "I've never seen anyone so poor, and they have a newborn baby." Mrs. Chung had had to walk back home from the clinic on the day she gave birth to her sixth child. "Would you please explain your assessment?" I asked.

Apparently the welfare authorities had asked Mrs. Chung's husband to go to the office to provide a statement about his income. He told them, "I earn HK $600 a month, out of which I give my wife HK $400." This was a complete lie, but it would be great loss of face for a Chinese man to admit that he could not support his family. The misinformation was carefully written down, and then the welfare officer asked Mrs. Chung to sign her husband's statement. She did not know what it said. She thought she was signing to receive help, so she made her mark.

"Couldn't you see that he was on drugs?" I said to the officers. "His word can't be trusted." I was so upset that I was aggressive.

"He told us he was completely drug-free," they replied defensively.

"Don't you know what an addict looks like? That's as plain an example as I've ever seen. He has heroin staring out of his eyes." The officials, who had learned their procedures out of books, labeled me a troublemaker, but they reversed the decision and Mrs. Chung received some financial help at last.

We then helped the family to move out of the Walled City. My boys hired a lorry and we moved the double bed, only to find barrels and barrels of clothes stored underneath. The family had previously been in contact with another welfare organization that had donated a dozen barrels of clothing sent from overseas for the "refugees." The barrels were full of articles such as soiled sequined evening dresses, but Mrs. Chung had been so keen to have possessions that she would not throw anything away. We bought 150 hangers and strung them up in the family's new room, which was otherwise completely bare. Then we began the unpacking; the barrels were crawling with cockroaches. Whole nests of them had been living there for years and emerged to take up quarters in the new home. When only half the barrels had been unpacked, each hanger had about three gray, crawling, moldy items on it. There were six fat English ladies' winter coats, which had rotted and stank.

There were scores of unsuitable and unwearable garments, so I put great heaps of them by the trashcan around the corner of the building. The next day I came back to find that the eldest girl, Ah Ling, had gone and fetched them all back—they were the only security she had.

About the time we moved into the Lung Kong flat, Mrs. Chung told me with simple acceptance that she had been ordered to go out and get a job, as the government could not support drug addicts' wives indefinitely. She told them she was not well, but they refused further help. Two weeks after hearing this decree, she died. She had had a cough for a long time, and although it was difficult for her to get to a doctor, she had visited a clinic several times. A bottle of medicine was all that had been given to her.

I felt partly to blame for her death. I had known that she had been coughing, but I had never taken the trouble to accompany

her to the doctor, and she had not had her tuberculosis diag-
nosed. She had sought help from professionals; we had all
kept her waiting, and she had died a death that might have
been prevented.

After the funeral, I continued to visit and support the children who were now being exploited by their father. He took
the 13-year-old daughter away from school and sent her to
work in a factory. For a pitiful wage of HK $100 a month she
sewed collars on dresses; she had to give her father all the
money. When the Youth Club went on outings, we would take
all the children with us, which was when they suggested coming to live at my house. I flatly refused this as a possibility and
told them that under the law they belonged to their father.
One month after my refusal, they packed all their belongings
and ran away from home, to me.

They were a pathetic sight huddled in my doorway. They
had complete trust that I would take them in. It did not seem
very suitable; my house was already sleeping boys on the floor,
but I had no option when I discovered that Ah Ling was being
molested by her father. She showed me the bruises on her legs,
so I took her to hospital and then allocated bunks for the little
ones. They were so withdrawn that it was a long time before any
of them would speak to me. However, I soon discovered that
our boys, themselves rejected, were really good with the children and loved playing with the baby.

So the family in our house grew and was further augmented
by constant appearances from Mrs. Chan, whom I had come to
know some months earlier through her son, Pin Kwong. He was
a vicious addict of 19 who had no intention of changing his ways
and who collected money by holding up victims at knifepoint in
the public toilet. I often asked him about his widowed mother,
but he refused to allow me to visit her, saying, "She is an old idol
worshiper. She won't want to hear from a Christian."

When Pin Kwong was arrested and put in prison for the
fifth time, I sought out his mother and found her lying on a little bed in her Walled City room. She had decided to die, because

her son had been arrested yet once more. She had no husband or family; Pin Kwong was all her life. Chinese women are very proud of their sons, but Pin Kwong was rotten and took away any money she ever had, so she had no more will to live. He had not wanted me to visit her for fear that I would discover that he had been exploiting her for the little amount she could collect selling vegetable herbs in the market. When we found her, she had already lain there for some days without eating and was very weak. The boys went out and bought chicken essence and bones to boil for soup, and we set about restoring the elderly lady. While we fed her, we told her about the Father who had given her His most precious possession, His only Son, because He loved her.[2]

Mrs. Chan was a simple woman who had never been to school. She had never heard of Christ before and could not follow long sentences. We laid our hands on her and prayed out loud, asking God to teach her in a way she could comprehend. After the prayer she looked up, grinning from ear to ear, saying that when we prayed she had been healed of "sickness of the lungs" and could breathe clearly for the first time in years. Her illness never returned.

That night, she dreamed that a man in a long white robe came to her and, holding out His arms, asked her to come to Him and be baptized. Since that time she was quite radiant, and when I moved into Lung Kong Road, she was delighted. We gave her a key to the new home and she pottered in and out, happily cleaning everything in sight, cooking meals and introducing all her local market vendor friends, who would sell us provisions cheaply. Bestowing on me a signal of honor, she became my *kai ma* and I her *kai neui*, meaning godmother and goddaughter. She adored her new family and bossily clucked around us all.

Because she could not read a word, I had the boys teach her Bible verses. It took her a week to learn, "Jesus declared, 'I am the bread of life.'"[3] This had to be near to her heart, as she had formed a passion for the toaster and now downed marmalade sandwiches in a most un-Chinese manner.

Three years earlier than this, when Dora first started to help me in the Walled City, she had come one evening to translate for a Bible study. It was one of those times when only one of the boys turned up; the others had forgotten completely. I was feeling cross that I had used up an unreasonable amount of time collecting and chasing them up for meetings. It was one of the very rare occasions when I really wished to be back in England, where Christians at least knew what day of the week it was. I did not voice these thoughts, but as we prayed, God gave a message in tongues to the one boy present. Dora had an interpretation of the message.

"No one who has left house or brothers or sisters or mother or father or children or lands for me and the gospel will fail to receive a hundred times as many in this life of houses, brothers, sisters, mothers, children and lands, and in the age to come, eternal life."[4] I had heard these words before, but it was not until Dora's interpretation that I really listened. Hurriedly, I looked up the verses in St. Mark's Gospel, to find that it did say we would receive in this life a hundred times as much as we had left. I had only ever remembered the eternal life part, and that was for after death. So that evening I claimed the promise, "God, I'd like a hundred homes, a hundred brothers and sisters—a hundred mothers and children, too."

Now in the flat in Lung Kong, I counted up and found that among the Walled City boys and students, I had at least 100 Christian brothers and sisters. I was living in my sixth home—with many others opened to me—and the children were adding up. Because I had been a bit short on the mothers, Mrs. Chan appeared, too. She joined a lovely church full of old ladies outside the Walled City and looked after the potential "mothers" I sent her.

More mothers in God came along. One day I was visited by a young man assisting his granny from a nearby resettlement block. She looked very frail and her head was bandaged, partially concealing an ugly gash on her temple. "I want to be baptized," she squeaked.

I was immediately suspicious. "It means nothing to be baptized if you have not believed in Jesus. If you would like to hear about Him, I will be glad to tell you, but if it's the bit of paper you require, I cannot help you. We do not give certificates in our church. There are many others that do, and I'm sure they will be glad to help."

It turned out that having fallen down and cracked her head, this granny was afraid to die without a burial spot. There was a great shortage of these in Hong Kong, and a thriving black market demanded outrageous sums. However, as a member of a Christian church, she could get a reasonable piece of consecrated real estate, and this is what the old lady was after. I took her to Mrs. Chan, who became friends with her and led her to Christ. The old granny had a true conversion, was baptized, and died six months later with a place reserved in heaven.

I had no idea it would be so much hard work caring for the boys in my house. All the books I had ever read about criminals becoming Christians stopped short at their conversion, giving a strong impression that they lived happily ever after. Mine was a basic mistake—I thought that "if anyone is in Christ he is a new man," whereas the meaning of the text is "a new creation."[5] Although the gangsters had become Christians, they were like newborn babies and had a lot to learn. Their ignorance of normal living was appalling. Some of them, such as Mau Jai (Little Cat), who had been in the drug den when Johnny was arrested, had lived on the streets since they were five years old.

Mau Jai had not been allowed to sleep at home because his father had two wives, and the second one, "Little Mother," was out of favor, so her children were banned from the home. They had no normal childhood; deprived of this, they grew up quickly in craft and cunning. Since they were used to being up all night, they could not understand why they should shut their eyes at 12 P.M. They got up when they awoke, and if they did not wake up in the morning, then that was that. If they did not feel like going to work, they did not go. They associated any rules I made with prison, which was the only other kind of authority they had known, and were careless in keeping those rules.

In Lung Kong Road boys came and went. I sometimes had the suspicion that they were running me rather than vice versa, but I did not want to admit it. For example, Ah Hung came to us on release from prison, sent by the authorities and supposedly drug-free. It turned out that he took heroin the very day he was released, and he must have continued to take it throughout his stay with us. It was therefore not surprising that he soon lost his job as a skilled jade craftsman and disappeared from our flat.

One day, he turned up high on heroin to confess to having taken part in a recent robbery in which a policeman had been wounded. We persuaded him to give himself up, but 10 minutes later he ran away. Since he had spoken of a gun, I rang the police and had six carloads of detectives screeching through the harbor tunnel and up to the flat, waving revolvers, as they thought he was still there. Embarrassed, we tried to smile at crowding neighbors as if nothing unusual were happening. They all thought us extremely unfriendly not to divulge the details. A series of detectives greedily ate our meals and kept a watch on the house for 24 hours. One pair skipped half of their night shift to find a better class of food, leaving us a nightspot telephone number where they might be reached in case of further developments.

It all turned out to be a hoax. Ah Hung appeared a day later to own up that he had not taken part in the crime. I did not believe him, and so I took him off to the police to confess. This was the best thing that could have happened to Ah Hung, because, according to information that the police later received, there was no way he could have been party to this robbery. He was jeered at for making up such a story under the influence of drink and heroin. But it was exactly what was needed to force his drug taking into the open and bring him to the point of truly seeking help.

The Walled City boys clearly needed discipline, and I was quite unable to give enough. Part of my difficulty was that I had reached the boys through being their friend and equal and it was hard to make the transition into being their teacher or pastor. I had become so involved with them that I was not firm enough, so they came in at all hours of the night and morning, left me to do all the drudgery of the housework, and were not growing up as I had hoped. Since I was out most of the night myself, it was difficult to check up on what they were doing. I began to pray that God would send someone else to look after the house so that I would be free to get back on the streets.

To ease the pressure on me, I asked two Chinese young Christian men to join us and to help run the house to free me for other work. This was not a success, however. They wanted a salary that I could not promise; they wanted to be addressed as "teacher"; and they felt that any kind of manual work was beneath them, since they were church workers. When I rose in the morning, I asked them if they had woken up the other boys and prepared the breakfast. They replied that they were too busy having their "quiet times," that is, times for praying and reading the Bible. Their idea of the teaching role was to hold a Bible study with the boys and preach at them for one and a half hours. I discovered that this was how they had been taught to conduct Christian work—having meetings, having a title and preaching was as much as they understood. They had not learned about Jesus washing His disciples' feet.

To help both myself and the boys, I often took them to the Willanses' meetings, which they loved. The meetings were always translated into Chinese so that they could fully join in and meet Christians from other countries and backgrounds. Because of this, many people prayed for us; but sadly, no one wanted to be further involved. One day, Jean Willans firmly spoke to me, "If you have to work with these boys, all right, Jackie, but you don't have to *live* with them. At least have somewhere where you can escape from them and regain your strength in peace." I did not understand this attitude; in fact, I could not understand why the whole world did not want to work in the Walled City. If someone passing through Hong Kong said he was praying about finding work, I always thought, *You don't have to pray any longer. Can't you see the Walled City? There it is.* I did not want to be anywhere else, yet

I felt defensive about my work, exhausted but unable to escape the maternal obligations to my children.

Yet despite the confusion in my disorderly home, I learned that God would often use very young believers to encourage me and the others. All those who became Christians received the power of the Spirit at the same time they believed, just as Winson and Ah Ming had. We encouraged them to share spiritual gifts when meeting together, so they knew clearly that having these gifts was no cause for pride but a way of helping one another. One night we were praying when one of those boys had a prophecy; he said that God had given him the words to speak. "Go and pick the cabbages, and quickly catch the bus." It sounded a startling message. My Cantonese still had some gaps, and it took a few minutes' search through a dictionary before I found the correct translation. "The harvest is ready; go out and work to gather it in."[6] There and then we went into the streets and talked to the street sleepers around our alley. One man, impressed to see people of his own background changed and starting a new life, prayed with us and later came off drugs in our house.

I was also much heartened by the boys another time when I arrived home exhausted and deeply worried about the situation in the house. Mary had left; the two youth workers had departed. I was feeling quite unable to manage the many converts plus a succession of boys referred by prison workers. I wondered if people in other countries could have the problems with new Christians that I did, because I certainly did not read about them.

"Please find me a nice, encouraging Bible verse," I asked the boys, feeling too tired to give them a teaching lesson. After thumbing through the Bible for some minutes, the most encouraging thing any one of them could find was a very depressing text from Revelation. "Enough of that," I decided. "Let's pray instead."

As we were praying, I had a message in tongues, and one of the boys interpreted it immediately. He had only been to school for a couple of years in his life. He could not read the Bible, and he had only believed in Jesus for a few days before this event. But his interpretation was a clear, direct quotation from the psalms:

> Those who sow in tears
> Will reap with songs of joy
> He who goes out weeping,
> Carrying seed to sow,
> Will return with songs of joy,
> Carrying sheaves with him.
> Unless the Lord builds the house,
> Its builders labor in vain . . .
> In vain you rise early
> And stay up late,
> Toiling for food to eat—
> For he grants sleep to those he loves.[7]

These spiritual babes through the working of the Holy Spirit were able to say exactly the right words to me at that time. Thus ministered to, I could not agree with those who considered spiritual gifts merely an optional extra. It was no wonder that St. Paul exhorted us to desire these gifts, for their purpose is to edify one another and thus glorify God.[8]

I knew that God would provide for me, but as the family in Lung Kong Road grew, I was amazed to see our income grow, too.[9] Ever since I had stopped teaching full-time, I found that I received all that I needed. I was able to pay for the rent, the Youth Club room and my language lessons. Sometimes a check would arrive in the post. Sometimes a friend would give exactly the same amount as I had been praying for. When I wanted to buy a rubber boat for a swimming expedition with the boys, a friend sent the right sum from England without knowing the need. Now, while we never had enough money to pay for the next week's food or rent, we always had enough for each day. This was exhilarating for the boys, who felt they had a real part in God's work when they prayed each morning for their daily bread. Sometimes an anonymous sack of rice would appear on the doorstep; on one occasion, it was a coffee table.

Every Sunday after the morning meeting, we invited many people to lunch with us all at Lung Kong Road. A number of guests needed the good meal, so it was sad when one Sunday I had to tell the boys that we had no money for food.

"Boil the rice anyway, and we'll pray for something to put on top," I said. Ten minutes before lunch, a panting and sweating visitor arrived carrying tins of food and fresh bean sprouts. His Kowloon Bible class had made a collection for us on the spur of the moment and sent him with their gifts. The young man, William, enjoyed being an answer to prayer just as much as the 30 of us enjoyed the huge meal only 10 minutes later. It was an exciting way of life.

I committed many follies during these days, but God honored the spirit in which I did them. One evening, I had the flu and was sitting at home feeling blurry, when in marched Geui Jai. He was a famous kung-fu fighter, having been the champion and renowned expert amongst the 14K Walled City brothers. He was one of the few who had received any education at all; he was clever, and his English was good. He was also now a wreck of a drug addict, fallen both in status and usefulness to the gang. I often found him sleeping in the streets or staircases near my home, because both his parents and his Triad brothers had kicked him out.

"Could you please lend me your typewriter, Miss Poon?" he asked me earnestly. "You see, I can get paid a little money if I help somebody with his Chinese translation and type a letter. This will give me enough money for my heroin today. So I won't have to steal it, or hold someone up."

I knew that he was hoping to quit drugs, but the flu must have impaired my judgment. I let him take the typewriter on condition that he brought it back the same evening.

Later that night, he telephoned me. "Miss Poon, I am sorry, but I can't give it back quite yet, because I have been asked to do another job. Isn't that good? I have to type out 200 invitations for a Lunar New Year party; please, how do you spell 'lunar'?"

This all sounded quite credible to me, until I put the phone down and thought about it. How ridiculous—no one in Hong Kong types their letters 200 times; it is so quick and easy to get them printed. Of course he had pawned it, and that was the last I would see of my typewriter.

Some of the other boys from the Walled City found out what Geui Jai had done and were very angry. They threatened to beat him up and hounded him, although I told them, "Never mind, all right, he has made a fool of me and I lost my typewriter, but so what? Jesus lost His life; a typewriter is nothing in comparison. I was willing to take the risk because I wanted to help him, and it's my fault, not his. Just forget about it." But I heard that he had to go on the run for some time and that all the gangsters were angry with him.

Three months later, God produced the first positive result. My typewriter appeared in the bookcase in my flat. I did not know how it had got there, so I questioned Ah Ping as to what happened. He finally admitted that Goko, when he heard what Geui Jai had done, had been so upset that he had sent his men after him. They found him and then demanded that he hand over the pawn ticket. Then Goko had gone to the pawnshop and paid his own money to redeem my typewriter. He then sent it back without a message.

Once more I sent an urgent demand to Goko, for I wanted to thank him for what he had done. Once more we had a tea party. In this incongruous setting, I talked to the powerful gang boss who ran illegal businesses with one hand and protected a missionary with the other.

"Thank you very much for the typewriter," I said, avoiding his name, for I felt that I could hardly address him as my brother, which his name implied.

"*Moe yeh, moe yeh*. It was nothing, nothing at all," he replied, looking very embarrassed.

"You have touched my heart deeply," I continued. "So I would like to explain something to you."

Goko was puffing cigarettes furiously, lighting one before finishing another and then stubbing it out again after a few gasps. "Geui Jai is a bad boy—he should not have done that to you," he said.

"But you had no reason to redeem my typewriter yourself," I continued. "I am not your friend, I am against you, and I have come here because I want to destroy what you stand for." Then I told him something of what Christ had done when He redeemed us with His own blood, buying back our lives with His own life while we were still His enemies.[10] Goko listened and looked almost shy. Avoiding my eyes, he paid the bill with a HK $500 note and fled. But he had listened to the story of redemption.

The second result was that Geui Jai's guilty conscience made him vulnerable. Once more during my wanderings, I fell across the faded fighter sleeping on the pavements and staircases. He saw the change in Winson and Ah Ming, and he was envious. His desire to be a new person grew until the day he prayed with us, went into Pastor Chan's center, and exchanged his syringe for a cross.

Those gangsters who had hounded Geui Jai could not dismiss what happened to him. He not only came off drugs but also went to Bible school for some years and became a pastor.

Looking back at the experiences of those years in Lung Kong Road, I have mixed emotions. It was a time of learning and of growing up. Often, I was in awful confusion. I find it easiest to express what I feel in the words of St. John: "A woman giving birth to a child has pain because her time has come; but when her baby is born she forgets the anguish because of her joy that a child is born into the world."[11]

The pains of that time can be forgotten, for they gave birth to many children and to a partnership with the Willanses. These things brought me great joy.

# TRY JESUS

J ean Stone Willans is a glamorous, vivacious lady.
She has the gift of being able to "speak in tongues,"
and she has just published the most lighthearted,
entertaining book about religion that has ever been written. The book is *The Acts of the Little Green Apples* and
describes the adventures of the Willans family—her husband, Rick, and daughter, Suzanne—after they came to
the Far East. Mrs. Willans doesn't practice religion, she
lives it. Also she seems to have established a way of
communicating with God. This, she claims, is available
to everyone; some people take advantage of it; some
don't. The stand Jean Stone Willans takes is that if God
is asking her to do His work, then He should make sure
she is able to do so. Time and time again He does.

So wrote the *Hong Kong Standard* in July 1973, describing
Jean's hilarious book. I could echo its enthusiasm, for by this
time Jean and Rick had become my very close friends and spiritual advisers. They taught me that God's good things were to
be enjoyed, which surprised me, as I had been brought up to
believe that missionaries should always have the least of everything and that it was virtuous to live in rags. The Willanses had
been through times of great poverty, but certainly they did not
expect that God wished them to live like that forever. When
they had beautiful possessions they took real pleasure in them,
but they were equally ready to give everything away if so directed. Maybe that is why they were such fun to be with—they had
learned to be content whatever the circumstances. They were
also the only people I knew with whom I could simply sit, pray

all night, watch television, have a drink, play charades, or go out to a gourmet dinner—although I did know others with whom I could do one or two of those things . . .

We had discovered by this time that there was a remarkable similarity in our journeys to Hong Kong, since Jean and Rick too were called to the East through a dream and a prophecy. Their work in Hong Kong was in a completely different sphere, but meeting one of my boys changed this.

One day I was in Causeway Bay Magistracy listening to a case when I spotted David squatting in the dock. He was a friend of Ah Ming's whom I had met on the beach at Winson's baptism the previous year. David had planned to plead not guilty to his charges; however, when he saw me, he suddenly had a pang of conscience, began to pray, and pleaded guilty. After hearing his case, the judge decided to let him off, and David came out of the courtroom in a daze. "Coffee?" I suggested as we walked out. In deference to my choice, he and his colleagues bypassed the chicken's feet, entrails and other delicacies displayed in restaurant windows and joined me at a coffee shop. David announced that he was ready to follow Jesus completely. Having seen the mess he had just emerged from in court, I thought we should inform his gang boss that he would be leaving the Triads, as it would be so much better if he could make a complete break with the criminal world.

"Who is your *daih lo*, David?" I asked. He looked terrified and shifted about on his plastic seat.

"He won't want to see you."

"But what is his name?" I persisted.

"His nickname is 'Jesus,'" David said out of the side of his mouth, hoping that the others sitting there had not heard him reveal all. "But he won't want to see you."

"Why don't you ask him? If you're going to be a Christian, you can't follow two different leaders called Jesus. You must decide which one."

"Okay," said David. "I'll try to find him," and he went to the telephone. While we waited, David's friends ate pink ice cream while I drank more cups of coffee. At last David came back, looking surprised.

"He'll see you. You are to go to Block 20 of Chaiwan Resettlement Estate at midnight tonight and find the noodle stall. Someone will meet you there and take you to Jesus. But you must take 100 dollars."

"Why the 100 dollars?" I asked curiously.

"Well, nobody in Chaiwan knows you, Miss Poon," David replied. "It's not as if it was the Walled City, where you are protected. Chaiwan is a very dangerous area at night, and you might get mugged. If you have 100 dollars, they will take it and leave you alone; but if you have nothing, they will be angry and beat you up."

"Don't be silly," I reasoned. "I haven't got 10 dollars, let alone 100. I'm not taking money. If I am on God's business, then He will look after me. And anyway, if it would help you to understand how much God loves you, then I wouldn't mind dying. I have nothing to lose."

David looked at me incredulously for a moment and then said, "You're crazy! You're mad!" But he glanced at his friends and said, "We never met anyone who would die for us before."

I arrived by minibus at 11:30 P.M. and spent a little time looking around Chaiwan. This enormous area at one end of Hong Kong Island consisted of resettlement blocks where tens of thousands of people were housed by the government. Each family had one room to live, eat and sleep in, with communal toilets and showers at the end of each floor. The street level was humming with life—and at night—as hundreds of people sat on fold-up seats eating their *siu yeh* (bedtime snacks) at the shacks and portable noodle carts, which abounded.

Midnight came. I was waiting at the Block 20 noodle stall, which turned out to be down a narrow, dark corridor. Refuse had been tipped into the gutter below and there was a runnel of little gray noodles swimming past my sandals. I was so absorbed in the noodle race that I did not see my guide approach.

"What do you want?" The curly-haired Cantonese lolled against the wall and spoke through the cigarette stuck to his lips.

"Take me to your leader," I replied, clutching my huge evangelical Bible firmly.

"Who do you want to see?" He was testing me.

"I want to see Jesus."

"Why do you want to see Jesus?"

"I want to tell him about my Jesus."

The man looked amused and then laughed to himself. "Are you *sure* you want to see Jesus?" He meant to sound sinister, but it all felt like part of a bad film to me.

"I'm sure."

"What do you want to talk about?"

"I want to tell him about my Jesus," I repeated.

The man changed legs and shut his eyes, and then with a camp gesture thumbed himself as he grimaced—"You're talking to him." It was a very ham B movie.

"Jesus" and I sat in a cafe while I opened my big Bible and told him about my Jesus. Something happened while we were sitting there. He understood what I was saying. He simply understood it all. It was almost as if the Holy Spirit had come down over our formica table. He sat there with the tears streaming down his cheeks, quite oblivious of his surroundings, including the pretty waitress. He prayed, asked Jesus into his life and was baptized in the Spirit in the midst of our coffee cups.

It was about 3 A.M. when I left Chaiwan to catch a van back to Kowloon City and my neglected flat. Just before the van left, I remembered my discipleship training.

"Oh, by the way, you are supposed to tell at least one other person that you have believed in Christ today." I sped off after having fixed an appointment with him for the next day.

When I saw "Jesus" the next afternoon at a friend's apartment, I hardly recognized him. He looked bright and keen, unlike the seedy villain of last night's movie.

"Did you tell one person that you believed last night?" I asked eagerly.

"No, I didn't," he replied. Disappointment gonged in my heart. But he continued, "I told my whole gang. We stayed up until 6 in the morning looking at the verses you underlined in the Bible, and now they all want to believe, too."

The prostitute kissed Jesus' feet and poured perfume on them. The demon-possessed man who was healed sat dressed and in his right mind at Jesus' feet. The woman who had been bleeding for 12 years touched His cloak, and when it was discovered that her bleeding had stopped, fell at His feet trembling.[1] There are as many descriptions of encounters with Jesus as there are Christians, but no one who has not made that encounter for himself will ever understand the wonder. I wanted to jump, sing, dance and join in the celebration that was going on in heaven in front of the angels—big bold braying brass and spiced woodwind striving with millions of desks of strings in a wonderful symphony of praise . . .

However, I was still in Hong Kong and very much on Earth, and standing before me the clear-eyed Triad looked expectant. He had brought a *sai lo*, Sai Keung, with him, who had been there at the dawn discussion. Sai Keung did not want to discuss any more; he wanted to know how he could receive the power of Jesus like his *daih lo*, so he too received Jesus and the gift of His Spirit. I always told the boys that as they believed, Christ would give them the gift of a new tongue to help them pray, but I no longer expected it to happen automatically as in Winson's case. These new believers accepted easily that if they were going to follow a powerful God it would be quite in character for Him to give them a new language to help them talk to Him. Every single one received this gift, so there was no confusion about some being more spiritual than others. To avoid problems, whenever possible I avoided laying hands on a young man myself but encouraged other Christian boys to do this so that they would know that the gift came from God Himself and that even young Christians could pray with others to receive.

Sai Keung looked radiant. He was a short, stocky individual who was not given to long speeches, but he warmly encouraged me to go back to Chaiwan the next night to talk with the others.

I went back the next night and many nights afterward. We met in the back of a photograph shop or in the concrete park, and the number of enquiries increased dramatically. We had Bible studies at noodle stores, prayer meetings in camera shops, and evangelistic meetings on tenement staircases. Some of the Chaiwan gang joined the Lung Kong Road home and others joined the Willanses' meetings. The work was expanding beyond the borders of the Walled City to reach people in other areas.

As was my custom, I asked "Jesus" (now renamed "Christian") to introduce me to his own big brother. I had the usual response.

"He won't want to talk to you. He's much too important. He controls many different areas besides Chaiwan and has hundreds of followers. If we want to speak to him, we don't even know where to find him. Sometimes we don't see him for weeks. He's too busy. Forget it."

I learned that this emperor among gang leaders was named Ah Kei. I agreed that I would not try to force a meeting with him, but Christian was under instructions to pray for him, and Jean and Rick also put in overtime on his behalf. We all had a feeling that Ah Kei was to be an important part of our ministry. I carried around sets of Bibles, ready for any emergency.

The time was 12:15 A.M., the location a Chaiwan street stall, the cast Miss Poon, Christian and the Chaiwan believers. The fluorescent lamps cast a hard pool of light against the blackness of the night. Ah Kei emerged from the shadows. He was in a belligerent mood.

"Poon Siu Jeh," he challenged—although no one had introduced us—"if you can convert me, I'll give you 1,000 disciples." He enjoyed thus throwing down the gauntlet; indeed, it was almost as if we were preparing for a duel as he stood there in his black leather gloves, sneering.

"I can't convert you, Ah Kei," I replied. It was obvious whom I was talking to by the awed reaction of our seconds. "If you believe in Jesus, then that is your decision. And you cannot tell your *sai los* to believe in Jesus; they will have to decide this for themselves."

We were in for a long night. Ah Kei had heard rumors of what had been happening in Chaiwan. If there was going to be a revival, he wanted to control it. Sitting down at our table, he ordered dishes and dishes of expensive food and drink. He scattered his largesse, conspicuously inviting all around him to eat. He would make sure that we all knew how many hundreds of dollars he spent—how generous he was. He ate nothing himself and cared little if I were hungry or not; this was an exhibition.

I showed him pictures of Ah Mo looking fat and healthy now that he was off drugs. Ah Kei knew him well, as they used to deal together. He became rather thoughtful, and after the meal he invited me to accompany him alone to a secret destination where he had something to show me.

We began to walk toward the shantytown area, whose vice Ah Kei controlled. He was carrying his mackintosh slung over one shoulder. Turning to me suddenly, he said, "Poon Siu Jeh, do you look down on drug addicts?"

I thought that a difficult question to answer without appearing condescending.

"No, I don't, Ah Kei, because they are the people Jesus came into the world for."

"Are you willing to be friends with one?" he asked, and both he and I knew to which one he was referring.

"Actually, the people in the Walled City criticize me because I am more willing to be friends with an addict than with someone who thinks his life is all right," I replied.

By this time we had come to an unlighted path that led through the shanty shacks. We walked on in silence until Ah Kei stopped by the outside of a tin hut. The darkness outside gave no hint of the brilliant lighting inside, and when Ah Kei pushed through the blackout material curtain, I found myself staring at dozens of surprised gamblers. The door watchers came up to us. Although this was one of Ah Kei's own dens, they were obviously worried by the presence of a strange Western lady at three in the morning. Ah Kei held up his hand for silence; there was a hush.

"Don't be afraid," he said. "She doesn't look down on us; she's a Christian and has come to tell us about Jesus." He then gave me the floor and invited me to preach.

Afterward, he took me into his opium den next door. Inside the den was a terrible spectacle—there were little gray and yellow old men lying on a low platform covered with grime and slime. There were half empty cups of green tea and large spittoons filled with sordid saliva and sediment. The men lay like giant stick insects, more limbs than body, and half of them were insensible. The "weatherman" sitting at the door looked very alarmed until Ah Kei spoke. He repeated what he had said before: "Don't be afraid. She doesn't look down upon us. She's a Christian. She's come to tell us about Jesus."

All those who were actually conscious listened carefully to what I had to say, and when I left, I gave them a pile of my Chinese Bibles and translations of *The Cross and the Switchblade*.

To have spoken about Jesus in two of these dens was amazing in itself, but after this Ah Kei became a determined evangelist; he insisted that together we visit more of his empire of drug, vice and gambling dens. We traveled from Chaiwan to Shaukiwan and then visited Lyemun, Kwun Tong and Ngautaukok. In each place he introduced me as a Christian, and each time I was heard with respect. It was an amazing journey into vice. I scattered Chinese Bibles as I went.

In one of those dens, they brought me a man doubled up with pain. His face was contorted with suffering.

"Poon Siu Jeh, are you a doctor? Are you a nurse? Do you have any money? Can you take him to hospital? He is in agony." They thought every Westerner was either rich or medically trained.

"No, I'm not a doctor or a nurse and I don't have any money to take him to hospital—but I tell you what I can do. I'll pray for him," I said. They sniggered at this, but they agreed to find us a little room at the back where it was quiet. Then they stood around waiting curiously to see what I was going to do.

"I'll pray for him on one condition," I announced. "No one is to laugh, because I'm going to talk to the living God." Complete silence.

I laid my hands on the sick man and prayed for him in Jesus' name. His stomach immediately relaxed and he got up, looking surprised. He had been completely healed. Everyone else looked a bit surprised, too; one of them asked, "Is this the living God—the One you've been telling us about?" They began to believe, because they saw through His works of power who Jesus was.

At the end of the evening—it was nearly morning—I gave Ah Kei a Bible and wrote in it, "To Ah Kei, my friend; I pray one day you'll be my brother." He might have laughed inwardly, *Huh? Brother! Some hope,* but he thanked me politely—he was still handing out favors. He had no intention of reading it. It was in fact strange that I had given him a Bible at all, knowing how such men hated to read.

For the next three months, I followed Ah Kei around. He had a wife and family, but he used to sleep wherever he found himself late at night—often on a staircase. He got so high on drugs one night that he even read two pages of *The Cross and the Switchblade,* two pages of *Run Baby Run,* and then two pages of the Bible in turn for two days. He began to confide in me and told me how much he regretted marrying so young—he already had three children under five. My sympathy was rather with his wife for having a young family and a husband who never came home.

Sometimes Ah Kei would sleep for three days at a time. At other times, he would not sleep at all. During these binges, he would go through a fantastic amount of money. He was being fed drugs all the time by his gang members. God told me which staircase he was sleeping on and after a while, each time I found him, he had a hunted look. "Oh, it's not you again! I mean, how did you know I was here?"

Meanwhile, I had armies of Christians all around Hong Kong praying for him; this had to have an effect. One day when I caught up with him, he said, "God's been talking to me."

"What do you mean, God's been talking to you?" I asked crossly. I was annoyed, because I thought he was joking.

"Yes, God has been talking to me," he insisted. "I've been reading in the Bible and it says He gives special grace to people like me." He almost preened himself at "special grace."

"What do you mean by special grace?" I enquired.

"It says in the Bible that if you've sinned the most you get forgiven the most."[2] He sounded so privileged that I almost felt jealous, but he was completely serious about this discovery and was ready to ask for the special grace. We were in a hut next door to the gambling den that he had originally taken me to. Ah Kei sat down on the floor, and I sat down in the darkness too, hoping I had avoided the cockroaches. We prayed together for the first time, and Ah Kei asked Jesus to take his life and make him a new person. He believed that Jesus died for him, but at that point he had very little sense of sin and was still rather proud of his past.

I rushed across the harbor to Mei Foo, where Jean and Rick were living. I knew they would be delighted to meet Ah Kei after praying for him so long and even more pleased that he had become a Christian.

We had a party, a grand celebration of Ah Kei's first birthday. Sarah, the Willanses' Australian friend, and their daughter, Suzy, were also there and shared in our gladness. We usually prayed at parties, and as Ah Kei had not yet received the gift of the Spirit, we told him that God gives this power to all who follow Him. All of us sitting around began to pray together in the Spirit, and when Ah Kei heard this, he suddenly fell forward onto his knees with a terrible thump. Afterward, he told us that when he heard the tongues he was knocked down by the awareness of his past life of robbery, drug pushing and selling girls into prostitution. As he gained this terrible sense of his own sin, he felt that he could no longer sit in front of God. He had to kneel; and he began to pray in tongues. It was a near impossible sight of a Triad boss on his knees; in Chinese culture, it is the most servile of positions—and a gang leader lowered himself to no one.

As he continued to pray in tongues, the Willanses' parrot, Sydney, triumphantly extricated himself from his cage and, flying across the room, alighted on Ah Kei's head. For some time afterward Ah Kei was rather confused about the Holy Spirit and doves, since his had been a heaven-sent parrot. That same night we took a taxi to a beach, where Rick baptized Ah Kei in the sea.

During the weeks before his conversion when I was getting to know him, Ah Kei and I sometimes settled down to read the Bible in a wooden shack at 3 A.M. or so. He told me that he would not believe in Jesus in a hurry because if he built a house quickly it would fall down just as fast. But the night he was baptized, he began to put his life in order immediately. He went home to his wife for the first time in many months. She looked as if she would like to believe Ah Kei had changed, but she had such a deep distrust of her husband that she was afraid it would all turn out a forlorn hope.

Ah Bing had married Ah Kei seven years previously. Their courtship could not have started more badly; Ah Kei met her at a party and seduced her in order to sell her as a prostitute. But he fell in love with her and decided to keep her instead, which was only temporarily to her advantage. Years of neglect then reduced this once pretty girl to a careless sloven who kept their tiny resettlement room in a filthy state.

In a way Ah Bing was right to be cynical, for when Ah Kei decided to build his Christian house, it demanded too great a cost. He not only relinquished his vast illegal income and control over men with no alternative source of cash to care for his family, but he also had to face coming off opium and heroin.

Ah Kei did not immediately come off drugs, and I did not know what to do about it. Some addicts who became Christians were delivered instantly, while others went to Pastor Chan's center to withdraw, where there was a greater amount of

after-care. Ah Kei applied to this center and others, but he was
refused admittance because there was no place available. What
could I say to him: "Pray, Ah Kei, and you'll get off drugs miraculously"? I could say, "Pray, and perhaps you will cut down
gradually." That would be compromise. I could try, "Pray, and
maybe God will give you money for your heroin." But surely
God did not support drug habits.

I could not take Ah Kei into my house, for it was already
full of boys who either were supposed to have quit heroin
already or who had come out of prison officially drug-free.
I wondered what was happening in that house sometimes—
some of the residents behaved very strangely—and I certainly
did not want to mix in an open drug-taker with them. So
instead, I encouraged Ah Kei with a weak, "God will work it out,"
and hoped that he would get into a withdrawal center sooner
or later.

Just before Christmas, I was awakened by a telephone call at
4:30 A.M. I never liked to sound as though I had just woken up.
If I had just woken up, my solution was to clear my throat and
practice saying, "Good morning—good morning!" very bright-
ly so that by the time I picked up the receiver, I sounded like the
bird of the dawn.

Ah Kei was in no mood for sunrise salutations. He had rung
to say goodbye.

"Thank you, Poon Siu Jeh, for these past nine months of
Jesus talk, your care and consideration. But my gang brothers
were right all along. I can't be saved."

"Yes, you can, Ah Kei. Anything is possible with God." I
meant it sincerely, but my words sounded weak to my own ears.

"It's no good. I can't be a Christian anymore."

"What do you mean you can't be a Christian?"

"I can't afford it. I've given up running the gangs; I've given
up running the girls, the gambling and the drugs. Now I have
nothing left to live on. I can't afford to be a Christian. Thank you
very much, Miss Poon, for everything you have done; I'll never
forget you, but I will not be seeing you again. It just didn't work."

I tried desperately to reason with him. I dragged up every argument I could think of—I hunted around for suitable texts. We could not lose him. If I could keep him talking, maybe the trouble would all go away. But Ah Kei's voice sounded harder and harder, and he was impossible to reach. He was far colder than before he had become a Christian, and he started to speak cruelly and bitterly. I could hear him carrying on a simultaneous argument with someone at the other end, and then he said he was going out to find Ah Chuen to kill him.

"Ah Kei, you can't kill people. You're a Christian." He was long past listening to my pathetic interjections. He was high on heroin, and having furiously informed me that he would shortly be forced to do a couple of robberies to raise some money, he hung up.

I stared at the phone in the gloom. I really could not believe what I had heard. I did not want to accept the fact that someone who had believed in Christ could contemplate murder. I quickly rang up Jean and Rick. They knew that both Ah Kei and I had a talent for the dramatic, but they soon listened with deep concern.

"You've got to get up and pray. I think Ah Kei is going out to murder someone, and he's planned a couple of robberies." There are not many people I could tell to do this at that time of night. The Willanses prayed.

I prayed despairingly all through the Christmas celebrations. I cried all through the Christmas carols. *Joy to the world?* I thought tragically. *It doesn't look very joyful to me.* Because I was grieved for Ah Kei, I was also a little angry with God.

*Lord, I really believed You were the answer. How can it be that he knew You and then didn't want You? You didn't do everything You were supposed to either, Lord, did You? I mean, Ah Kei believed in You and others did too, and look at them now. There are a load of addicts and spiritual cripples lying around the streets being a reproach to Christ. People look at them and mock, "What a God— He started a miracle but it didn't last; it was something that came and went."*

I hunted for any Christian who could reassure me that when Christ began a good work in someone, He would carry it to completion.[3] I believed this was true, but it certainly did not look as if God were doing His part right then.

Some days later, Ah Kei turned up on my doorstep. "I don't know why I've come—I was just passing—but anyway, goodbye."

"Wait a moment," I said. "What about the robberies?"

"Well," said Ah Kei looking rather sheepish, "my wife got the pillow cases all ready, hoods for our armed robbery, slits cut in them so we could see through. The first time we got everybody together, we found that one of my own gang had given the game away. So we couldn't do it. Then the second time we were sitting in the car all prepared with knives. We were ready to drive off, but I just did not feel like doing a robbery that day, so we didn't go."

He had also been unable to find Ah Chuen the night he had telephoned me. I thought it was time we now did something positive about Ah Kei's future.

"Right," I said. "We are now going to see the Willanses; you have got to talk to them. It's time someone was firm with you."

We left the house, and on the way Ah Kei bought a gift of oranges wrapped in pink paper. He presented it to Jean and Rick, and we all ate dinner together. As usual Jean was extremely hospitable, but I could see that she was becoming more and more annoyed at a situation in which a true believer was not coming off drugs.

"Do you have any problems?" she asked him while I translated.

"Oh, no, no problems," he said airily and then added, "well, just one; I'm still on heroin."

"When we were in Indonesia and had no money," Jean continued firmly, "we prayed and it simply appeared before us. If you are really serious about Jesus, He will do anything you ask."

"I'm serious," nodded Ah Kei.

"Well, would you like to stay here and withdraw from heroin?" Jean asked. I was amazed; this was what I had hoped for and longed for but never dared to suggest, as I knew how precious the peace of her home was to Jean. She herself had never meant to suggest it either, but concern for Ah Kei's future and the Spirit of God worked together in her to bring out an invitation that surprised her.

"I agree," said Ah Kei. He opened up his jacket, took out some red paper packets of heroin and flushed them down the lavatory bowl.

Next, Ah Kei made some dramatic gestures. First, we went back to his resettlement home, where he tore down the idols his mother kept and threw them out of the room. Then he reached under the bed and dragged out a box containing several weeks' supply of heroin. He washed it all down the lavatory while we watched. Finally, we took him back to the Willanses' flat in the Mei Foo district, where he climbed into bed.

Jean called a Christian doctor and asked what to expect from a 10-year addict with a 100-dollar-a-day habit. The doctor said that without medication Ah Kei would suffer agonies, accompanied by chills, fever, vomiting, diarrhea and intense stomach cramps. He might roll on the floor with pain and become violent to the point of attacking his helpers. He did not advise it, but if Jean insisted on her course of action, he would come around and administer a substitute drug, methadone.

"We will try Jesus," said Jean, refusing his offer, and so began the experiment.

I spent three sleepless nights sitting with Ah Kei; I expected all the terrible side effects that had been forecast, but he slept like a baby. At the end of three days, I looked haggard and unkempt and he looked wonderful. When he did awake, if he experienced any twinge of pain, we would quickly urge him to pray in tongues, and the pain would miraculously disappear. Now we knew without a shadow of doubt that praying in the Spirit was the answer for painless withdrawal from heroin. Ah Kei was able to eat well and ordered cheese sandwiches, which he swallowed voraciously.

After four days, Ah Kei's wife came round to see him. She tried to persuade him to go home, as he was cured. We opposed this firmly; he still needed care and a drug-free environment. Fortunately, he was suddenly seized by withdrawal effects—sensations of terrible cold followed by feelings of tremendous heat. As Ah Kei had once before tried unsuccessfully to withdraw from heroin in China, he knew how terrible the pains could be. We all went back to praying in the Spirit to obtain relief, and as we worshiped God, the pains left him. Again, God had delivered him. On the fifth day, Ah Kei knew he was free from heroin, but he still badly wanted to smoke; he did not want to give up cigarettes. Rick insisted that if he did not free himself from tobacco addiction as well, he would not be free. Ah Kei was very unhappy about this, and on the seventh day he persuaded the Willanses' Buddhist maid to give him a couple of filter tips. Almost immediately he felt the pains he should have felt during his heroin withdrawal. All of us redoubled our prayer effort. And once he was willing to agree to Rick's demand, the pain disappeared.

Throughout his withdrawal period and for the next few months, I was commuting between my own house and Mei Foo, because the miracle of Ah Kei's healing was repeated with several of his friends. Jean took Ah Kei to the Hilton to get his hair cut; there he ran into his old friend Wahchai, whom he had introduced into the crime rackets years earlier. Ah Kei persuaded him to come back to the Willanses' flat, and we had an impromptu meeting. During the meeting I had a message in tongues, but there was no interpretation. As St. Paul says, there has to be an interpretation every time someone has a message in tongues,[4] so we waited and waited, but no one spoke. Finally, Wahchai admitted that he had received an interpretation but had been afraid to speak; he could not believe that God would use him because he was still on drugs, even though he had recently been converted and received the gift of the Spirit. As he told us the interpretation of my message, he began to weep uncontrollably. After that, it was only a matter of sitting with him while he had a painless withdrawal from heroin. As with Ah Kei, whenever he had pains, he began to pray in the Spirit and so felt better.

At the following Thursday night prayer meeting, yet another boy who had accepted Jesus asked for the power of Christ to free him from his addiction. After the prayer meeting was over, I suggested that he come off drugs that very night. By this time the Willanses' flat was full, so we rented a room for him in one of the apartment houses generally used as a brothel, and I sat up with him all night praying. For the next four days, other boys in our group sat and prayed with him until he had completely withdrawn. We took two hourly shifts all day and night, quite confusing the proprietors of the "hotel" who were used to quite a different kind of clientele. Then, when he was clear, he went and spent a week in the Willanses' flat to complete his rehabilitation.

Two weeks later, Ah Kei decided to go off and spend a week in China. A whole group of us went to see him off at the railway station; when he arrived at the Chinese border, the Chinese security guards wanted to know who the people were who had seen him off at the Kowloon station. He replied that there was an American (Rick), an English girl (me) and his Chinese friends. "Who," they asked, "were the Westerners?"

"Ah, they are the people who told me about Jesus Christ," he replied cheerfully.

"All right, answer us this," the guards replied. "Who are better, Chinese people or Westerners?"

Ah Kei replied, "Well, being Chinese I naturally think Chinese are better, but these Westerners are Christians, and so they are very good. In fact, I find I like them very much." At this point the guards, who may have belonged to some kind of special security branch, revealed that they knew exactly who Ah Kei was. They knew he often tried to smuggle drugs across the border and that he was a leader in the Triad groups.

"Why are you not trying to smuggle drugs this time?" they demanded. "Who are these Westerners? What are their names? How did you get involved with them?" The questioning was relentless.

Ah Kei was completely frank with his questioners. He explained that he was off heroin because the Westerners had told him about Jesus and had prayed with him. He explained that he had left his Triad gang and given up criminal activities—instead, he was starting work in an office in March. The security men refused to believe him, saying that he could not have come off drugs—the Chinese opium wars had proved that no one could escape from addiction. Ah Kei insisted that he had been free from drugs for the past six weeks and that now he believed in Jesus Christ, he was a new person. The security men asked if he had achieved this result with medicine. He explained that he had used no medicines; the whole cure had been affected with Jesus and the Bible.

At this, the security men bristled and said that it was impossible; clearly the Westerners were exploiting him. This was Ah Kei's cue to launch into a full-scale testimony of what Christ had done for him. He talked for nearly an hour; the security men listened in quite a friendly way to the news and then allowed him to cross the border into China, carrying with him his Bible. When Ah Kei arrived at his village, he discovered one Christian Chinese girl who did not know much about the Scriptures because she had never had a Bible. Ah Kei gave his Bible to her, and the word spread.

Once Ah Kei had become a Christian, he began to tell the good news to all his family, who one by one accepted it. Ah Bing's father was so pleased to see the change in his son-in-law that he too became a Christian and was baptized with the Spirit. The dinner he gave us all to celebrate this was truly memorable: quail eggs with strips of breast of chicken, beef with mushrooms, stuffed boneless roast duck, corn soup, braised duck's feet with another type of mushroom, boneless pork fried in sweet soy sauce, steamed fish, sweet peanut soup, and pastries. Afterward, the father rose to his feet and announced, "Once I was young and now I am old, but never before have I seen a bad man become a good man."

# THE HOUSES OF STEPHEN

Text of a testimony by Daniel, written from my house in Lung Kong Road:

Before I introduce myself, I thank our Lord Jesus for rescuing me from my past and for giving me a new wonderful life in Him. My Chinese name is Ah Lam, and my English name is Daniel. I don't mind which name you choose to call me by.

The reason I mentioned thanking our Lord Jesus is because I was a very bad person. I remember about 10 years ago when I was just 14 years old I left school and joined a Triad gang. The reason I joined was because I wanted to be respected, known and feared, and I felt that being a Triad member would give me all this. So I dropped out from the normal way of life and began living in the underground (underworld, I mean). One year later I was arrested and charged with armed robbery— I was sentenced to a Training Center for young offenders for a period of 9 months to 3 years.

At the time I really regretted what I did, and I felt sorry and miserable. I decided then to change, to turn over a new leaf, to live a decent life as soon as I left prison. But on my discharge, instead of living a decent life as I planned I became worse, got deeper into crime, and went around with my old friends, back to the same places. I felt a big emptiness inside me. I wanted to forget everything and so I turned to big *H* (heroin).

I was heavily addicted. I tried to get off drugs a couple of times but never made it. It was by a stroke of luck—or more likely fate—that I came to know Jesus, and I repented and accepted Him as my Savior. I felt different—how can I explain it? (Words would never be able to justify my feeling.) It was as if I was released from something, as if a heavy burden was lifted from my shoulder. I felt free, wonderful. It was really a beautiful experience that I'll never forget, and I can truly say I have never looked back or had cause to look back since that day. He has given me so much and I have learned so much from Him—like patience, humbleness and love— and I am learning more every day. It is a very exciting life, and I thank Jesus for making all this possible.

I hope and pray you will be able to have the same experience as I have had. Only then you will fully understand what my testimony is all about.

May God bless you,

Ah Lam

This was written by one of the criminals who flocked to see me or the Willanses after hearing what had happened to Ah Kei. Word quickly spread along the addict grapevine that if they were willing to believe in Jesus, they would receive some kind of power that enabled them to kick drugs painlessly. Addicts queued up to be admitted to Jean and Rick's house.

I tried to avoid taking them into my Lung Kong Road house. It was so near the Walled City that in 30 seconds or so a desperate addict could find an unlimited supply of heroin or opium. Also, it was possible for addicts to jump off our roof into the next-door flat, and knowing this made them feel less safe in our care. In Jean and Rick's flat, we gave them no option of escape. There was a secure double lock on the door, the windows were barred, and there was at least one person on watch 24 hours of the day.

A young man brought to my house by a priest said, "I've seen what happens to addicts when they go to Miss Pullinger and I would like to try, but I'm a bit worried about the Jesus bit."

The priest replied, "Don't worry about that! Jackie won't push it." He could not have been more wrong—if we did not "push" Jesus, we had nothing to offer the junkie. If he could not pray, he would only suffer agonies through withdrawal. Medication only postponed the pain. I had once seen six strong boys sitting on top of Little Cat when he was trying to kick drugs on his own. Little Cat was a small boy, but when the need for drugs came on him, he was suddenly strong enough to overthrow those six and run half-crazed.

However, we never had to face the problem of the junkies being unwilling to believe in Jesus; they did not come to us until they were ready to believe, as they knew the way we worked. Their numbers grew until Jean and Rick's house was always more than full. Several times I was obliged to hire a room in a brothel, where there were washing facilities, a plentiful supply of Chinese tea and locks on the doors. There were drawbacks with this arrangement, however, beginning with registration . . .

Obviously, we needed a place solely for the addicts to come off drugs and stay afterward so that they could grow up as Christians. Most of them had been seriously disturbed people before they became addicted, and they needed and demanded constant attention.

Involvement with Ah Kit, one of Ah Kei's relatives, brought our need for a secure house to a head. Having been off drugs for only a few days, he decided that he would like to control his own life again and left the Willanses' house. All of us prayed that he would end up in a place where he could not continue his life of drugs and crime and that he would return to Jesus. This prayer was answered impressively—Ah Kit was arrested and put behind bars. He underwent a real change of heart and genuinely repented in prison. As he waited for his case to come to court, he began to pray and talk to his cellmates about Christ. He was charged with armed robbery.

At the trial, the judge commented that Ah Kit had an appalling record and well deserved a long sentence. However, he heard Jean's account of Ah Kit's change of heart, and taking into account her willingness to care for him, the judge released him into our care for 18 months.

The judge's clerk, the court officers and the prison officers looked aghast. The judge had actually done the impossible in legal terms by releasing a man who had been arrested on such a charge. We knew differently, as two rows of us were sitting in court praying. We took Ah Kit home to Mei Foo. On our way out, we overheard the prison wardens asking one another whether it was not more powerful to have a God than a lawyer.

Ah Kit began to slowly grow up as a Christian. He loved staying in the Willanses' house, but he demanded 24-hour attention. After a life of neglect he yearned for love—to him, this was having someone talking to him all the time and being given exactly the same presents as Suzy, the Willanses' daughter. Should Jean turn to talk to someone else or settle down to do her own letter writing, he felt rejected.

This caused such a strain on the family that one day Jean found 17-year-old Suzy packing her bags. "Either the addicts go or I go," she said—and she meant it. She was a serious Christian, but no family could survive that pressure for long. The time had come to find a new place that had a home atmosphere, plenty of love and a 24-hour surveillance by workers who were committed to looking after the boys full-time.

I was visiting my family in England when the Willanses telegrammed the news. They had found it! Someone reading Jean's book had been so inspired that he made a sum of money available for renting a flat, which was to be especially devoted to helping drug addicts who wanted to start a new life in Christ.

"Society of Stephen" was the name chosen by the Willanses' prayer group in Hong Kong to publish literature. The organization was later registered in the United States as a church and recognized by the federal government. As more and more criminals were being helped by the combined efforts of the Willanses and myself, we needed an official body through which we could operate when dealing with rent laws, court cases and other official matters. So we became known throughout the addict subculture as "Stephen" and by the rest of the world as "SOS." We called the new flat "Stephen's Third House," mine having been the first and Mei Foo the second.

The first full-time worker was Diane Edwards, an American from Hawaii. She was a former Maryknoll nun who had spent five years in Hong Kong and spoke fluent Cantonese; she had been baptized in the Spirit several years before at the Willanses' meetings. We sent a telegram to her in Hawaii that read, "PLEASE COME—STOP—HELP NEW DRUG CENTER—STOP—WE LOVE YOU." Diane, knowing that she would receive no salary but that we would share everything we had with her, arrived in Hong Kong within a week.

We began with one resident, but within a few weeks we had increased to six, and more were clamoring for admission. As each boy arrived, the miracle was repeated: He came to Christ and came off drugs painlessly when he prayed in the language of the Spirit. Ah Kei and his family moved in to assist Diane in running the house as it expanded even further.

By Christmas, there were 17 people in the tiny apartment, with 4 boys sleeping on the floor. We began to pray for yet another place, a fourth house, by the New Year to accommodate those who were waiting to come in. It was so hard to refuse them admission when we knew how simple it was to come off drugs with Jesus' power.

The Saturday meetings at the Willanses' flat grew so large that they had to move to a larger place on Hong Kong Island near Third House. Sometimes 150 people—including ministers, professors, priests and nuns—would gather together with our Triads and ex-junkies. At the New Year's Eve meeting, we prayed a prayer of faith that God would give us the new house by the New Year and thanked Him in advance for it. We had no inkling of where that place would be at that moment.

After the meeting was over at 10:30 P.M., an English friend asked me why we were still praying and had not yet rented the new house.

"We either need the promise of some rent money, the gift of a flat or assurance from God that we should sign a lease without actually having any money," I said.

"I put the money in a special account for you two weeks ago," he announced.

So we sent a couple of boys straight out to look for places. They came back immediately, having found a neighboring flat empty, and we settled the rent with the apartment watchman by 11:30 P.M. And we did all this in Hong Kong, which is surely one of the most difficult places in the world to find accommodation of any sort. We sealed the deal by seeing in the New Year with a prayer meeting in the new house. It was the most memorable watchnight service of my life.

Through praying with Ah Kei and the other addicts, I now knew that one did not have to wait until God "accidentally" delivered junkies. I saw that a man, provided he was willing, could be freed through the power that Christ gave him as he prayed in the words of His Spirit. We never forced the addict to pray when going through withdrawal; it is impossible that anyone can ever be forced to pray. We simply reduced the alternatives to nil, or rather to one alternative—of suffering.

One time, a very well-known syndicate operator from Shep Kip Mei had prayed a prayer of faith in Christ and had been filled with the Spirit just before entering one of the houses, but he refused to pray when his withdrawal pains started. On the second day, he packed his bags and announced that he was leaving. I refused to allow it because I believed that he had been sincere when he said that he wanted to follow Christ and come off drugs. When he rebelled, I knew that it was only the heroin talking.

"You can't keep me here, you have no right," the Triad leader objected. He was not used to being crossed.

"Yes, I can," I replied. "You asked us to help you start a new life, and that is what we will do. We would be selling you short if we allowed you to leave as soon as you felt pain."

"I'm leaving." He was adamant and moved purposefully toward the door where I was standing.

"You will feel much better if you pray."

"I've decided I don't want to follow Jesus after all. You can't stop me. I'm leaving."

"Well, you can choose one of four ways," I told him, and then began counting them on my fingers. "You can knock me out and steal the keys, you can jump off the roof, you can stay here and suffer, or you can stay here and pray. But you are not leaving without my permission. You will have to step across me first."

I watched him weighing up the alternatives. A powerful man such as he did not use violence on women; it was beneath his dignity. He knew he would be killed if he jumped off the roof, so he stayed and sulked in his bedroom. The awful suffering drove him under his *mintoi*, and finally he was so desperate that he prayed. As soon as he began to pray, the pain went away, and he slept peacefully.

The next time he was threatened with pain, he prayed. For a couple of days he was too stubborn to admit to us that it worked. But when the withdrawal period was quite through, he allowed himself to confess that he had prayed by himself in tongues and was now prepared to do so with other people.

Few of the junkies apart from Walled City boys had had any exposure to Christianity before coming off drugs. Far from being a hindrance, this actually helped them. Now they would arrive saying, "I have heard how Ah Kei [or some other friend] has changed. He says it is Jesus who did it. I think Ah Kei is the meanest addict I know. If Jesus can change that one, He can change me too."

Their faith did not depend on any understanding of theological concepts but on seeing Jesus working in others and on their willingness to let Him work in their lives. Each time they prayed, their prayers were answered, and their faith grew as they were healed.

Those who explained this extraordinary spiritual happening as an example of "mind over matter" had to be ignorant of the facts. A drug addict facing withdrawal has a mind already half dead through continual drug abuse and is deeply fearful of pain. Most of our boys began to understand Jesus with their minds only after they had already experienced Him in their lives and bodies. Understanding of the Savior, the cross, forgiveness and redemption came some time after they had already obtained the benefits of these truths.

With four houses to run, plus the Youth Club in the Walled City and the meetings at Chaiwan, we needed more and more full-time help. Doreen Cadney, an English nurse, came to assist, and Gail Castle came back from the United States. Several volunteers from Hong Kong and England helped for short periods, and then Sarah Searcy gave up her paying job to be responsible for running the houses.

In another sense, the work became easier and easier because the boys who had come off drugs themselves were very good at helping the "new boys." They happily cooked meals and did housework, and they had endless patience. They sat with the new arrivals, encouraging them to pray and praying with them. Having recently been through withdrawal, their faith was high. The other boys listened to them with some respect when they said, "It works—once you begin to pray, the pain goes. Just ask Jesus and pray in the Spirit."

It was a balmy time. Boys arrived to get off drugs almost daily. Having seen the change in them, many "decent" people were so impressed that they began to believe, too. One High Court Judge even bought our Christmas dinner after coming into contact with boys who had become Christians.

People came to my flat at all hours with problems and went away as Christians baptized in the Spirit. We held Sunday morning meetings in Lung Kong Road that were jammed with students, Walled City boys, ex-junkies and visitors who had come to ask for healing or counsel. Sometimes I could not manage to see them all until 6 P.M., so I would ask the other

Christians there to talk and pray with them.

For many years I had tried to do all the jobs and ministries by myself because there had been no other help available, but now we all began to share the task. Now I began to understand the meaning of the Body of Christ for the first time, as each person fulfilled a different function in the overall work to which we had been called. I found I was not indispensable after all, especially in the running of the houses, which Jean managed with fairness, extraordinary spiritual discernment and a great talent for fun.

We learned that it was a long-term job to turn an addict into a responsible member of society. In my Lung Kong Road experiment, I had tried to get the boys into a job or school as soon as possible. The first question visitors asked was always, "Are they working now?" The experience we gained there at Lung Kong Road made us sure that even though the boys were physically fit, they still had to learn much before they were ready to walk alone.

Many had been on the streets for years—their habit was to lie and con in difficult situations. We wanted to keep them very close to a Christian family with plenty of love and strict discipline until their habit was to act in a Christian way. At first we thought three months with a clear routine and teaching would be enough, but then we saw that they would need at least six months for their thinking to change—until they actually forgot their former pattern of cheating, stealing and blackmailing. Later on, we recommended a year as the minimum time to stay in the houses; we preferred two years.

No boy who wanted to follow Christ was ever asked to leave. Those who wanted to come off drugs were told that because they had made a free decision to follow Jesus and come into our houses, we would not permit them to leave before staying 10 days. After that period, when they were completely drug-free, they had the option of leaving or staying on to learn about Jesus. Of course, we did not recommend a stay as short as 10 days— indeed, if we thought a boy was not completely ready to stay a year, we would suggest he reconsider coming to join us. Following Christ would be a lifelong decision, and if the brand-new believer did not have the basic commitment to change, Christ could not change him.

Routine established itself, although it was never rigid; the boys found security in this and began to settle. Once they knew that we would not allow them to go back home, to their old district, or indeed anywhere at all unless accompanied by one of our helpers, they calmed down and began to enjoy an ordered life. Each day they prayed together and alone, went to the market, cooked and did household chores.

Members of the church gave a Bible study and coaching lessons in Chinese reading and English. Most days, the boys played a sport such as football and used the opportunity to tell others about Christ. The football field was next door to a methadone center, where addicts were provided with substitute drugs by the government. Our team of strong, healthy boys was so outstanding that many of the addicts hanging around the center came to hear how Christ could save them from addiction.

The people in the market soon noticed our boys too, and several came to the Saturday meetings curious to meet this Jesus who got junkies more bothered about the price of bean curd than heroin. The donation of a rotary floor polisher and cleaner led us to form a "Stephen Cleaning Company," and teams of boys went to wax and clean flats. This provided an opportunity for spreading the gospel through shining deeds as well as through words. It was also an occasion to judge how well a boy could work.

There was never a better supervisor for our floor working jobs than Tony, who dressed in neat tennis whites, watched over the other workers, and ran the company like a military operation. Tony was used to power. We had first met a couple of years before. I was eating shrimp dumplings in noodle soup at the Lung Kong Road street stall. He wondered why a Westerner would be eating at a food stall, especially at that time of night and with a group of notorious criminals to boot. His friend

introduced us, and when he came up to the house, he was clearly impressed. Later, he went to another church and said that it
made him feel good but also that it was all rather like a fairy
tale that he could not quite grasp.

Tony's own life had been far from a fairy tale. He was born
during the Second World War in Havana, Cuba. He was the
eldest son, and when he was eight years old, he was sent by his
father to China to be a helper for his childless first wife. He lived
miserably with "Big Mother" in Peking until the city fell to the
communists. "Little Mother," his real mother, wrote from Havana
imploring him to return, but for a penniless eight-year-old boy
without friends, this was impossible.

Tony was selected for training as a Red Guard; the government thought that he would make a good spy because of his foreign looks. Eventually, when he was 14, he did escape from Big
Mother and resourcefully traveled across China to the Hong
Kong border with a friend. On the way his friend was drowned,
but Tony ploughed on and finally successfully crossed into
Hong Kong.

Tony had no money to pay for school fees when he arrived,
so he shone shoes and picked pockets to survive. Inevitably, he
met up with the Triads, who trained him to rob with violence.
He began to take heroin at age 16 and soon graduated from chasing the dragon to injecting the drug directly into his veins. He
said that heroin became his wife, his friends and his life. He felt
no one cared about him and, because of the traumatic experiences of his childhood, formed a hard shell of bitterness around
him so that no one could touch or hurt him. This earned him
the reputation of a lone wolf among his gang brothers. Even
they feared this ruthless leader who had gained so much power.
Eventually, Tony and two others formed a new branch of the
14K. They were involved in blackmail, fighting and even killing,
both to survive and to maintain their supremacy in particular
districts.

Ah Kei telephoned me urgently one night begging me to look
for Tony, who was in desperate trouble. It was around Chinese

New Year, the coldest time of year, so I buttoned up tightly in order to pay a nocturnal visit to Diamond Village, the headquarters of Tony's territory.

I found Tony sitting in a teahouse with his coat collar turned up against the cold. He was shivering. Flanking him were two henchmen; obviously they were addicts too, judging from their gaunt bodies. But as I looked at Tony's face, it was not its drug-induced degeneration that shocked me, but another expression altogether. He was going to die. He was resigned to it.

I did not know then how he intended it to occur, but it was appalling to realize that he had it planned. He began to tell me what was going on, and as I listened I looked around at the congealed spittoons in the teahouse. The scene was a reflection of the sordid kingdom that he was preparing to relinquish.

He told a story of wars and unfinished gang business. He told a tale of coming out of jail to discover that the rival group had attempted to take over his territory. They had stolen his possessions and, knowing his passion for music, they had taken his guitar, broken it in two and left it in the mud. It was an act that demanded retaliation, and Tony knew the dreary course of events to come.

He was really weary of fighting but had no option but to plan a revenge attack. However, some vague memory of something sweeter nagged at him until he decided to appease the memory by selling his 10-by-6-foot hut and donating the proceeds to the Society of Stephen. He was not surprised to see me in his village, for he had sent for me in order to make this grand gesture. However, before I arrived, the other gang had burned down his house after dragging his clothes through the dust one by one. He showed me the site, and I saw the guitar strings splayed rudely over the ground.

"Miss Poon, I want to give the Church the deeds to this piece of ground," he offered.

"We don't want your land, Tony, we want your life," I replied.

"I will arrange for you to collect the documents so that you can use the land for a church," he continued.

"We don't want to build a church building, Tony; we'd like to help you build your life."

We walked down the dark path that wound through the village shacks, and I saw how the inhabitants watched him. He was the king of the village who had been feared and respected. They all knew of the attack and were waiting to see him take revenge. It was expected of him. He could never walk the streets again as their leader unless there was a reciprocal fight. So he had decided to kill or be killed. Either way, he would end up dying; it mattered little to his tired self.

He was still muttering about the land papers when I said, "God has chosen you, Tony. Come with us." He refused, so I repeated, "He has chosen to save you. He wants you. Come with us."

I hailed a taxi and was only half in it, saying, "God wants your life tonight, Tony. Come with us," when he climbed in beside me and sat down. He did not understand what he was doing, but it was the last time he saw his village for several years. He never said goodbye to his gang brothers. He never went back to fetch a thing.

Up in my Lung Kong Road flat, the boys were awake and ready to welcome Tony. They asked him if he, too, wanted to receive Jesus. He was afraid of God, but he kept remembering, "God has chosen you, God has chosen you" and nodded as they told him how he could be forgiven and receive a new life. Later, he wrote this testimony:

They prayed for me, and I accepted Jesus as my Lord and I received the baptism of the Spirit. At first I felt very cold, but when I was filled with the Spirit a surprising thing happened—I felt my heart burning within me, and my whole body grew warm and I wept. I had not cried since I was a child. I sat shamelessly weeping in front of everyone, and I knew that I had truly been "born again."[1]

They took me to Stephen's Third House to come off heroin. I had tried many times to come off drugs. The pain had always been greater than I could bear. The first time I went to prison I had to come off "cold turkey" and it was so terrible that I broke out of prison into barbed wire, and I bear the scars to this day. From that day on, I always had heroin hidden on my person so that I was never caught without it. But this time it was different. My brothers in Jesus prayed for me, and I also prayed in tongues and the pain disappeared. Two months later I went to live with Mr. and Mrs. Willans, who run the houses. My own parents cannot be traced, but Mr. and Mrs. Willans are now my parents.

I have witnessed God moving in many areas of my life since that time. I not only went with my new mother and father to China, but in 1976 I visited America and England with them and joined them in speaking in a number of churches and on radio and television. What an amazing thing for me, a former Red Pole fighter in the 14K Triad society, an ex-convict and heroin addict, to be given a special waiver to visit the United States of America. And the Home Secretary himself cleared my travel to England when everyone said it was impossible.

I have since been trained in a first-class hairdressing school to be a hair stylist. I work in a leading salon in Hong Kong and live with my parents in a nice apartment. It is truly astonishing and shows that my Lord Jesus is very powerful. But the greatest thing He has done for me is to change my heart, and now I no longer follow sin, because I follow Him.

It would have been ideal if each one of the boys could have become a special son in a family where he was cared for and loved. Tony's unusual background made him a special case, however, and it was wonderful to see him grow and change. He had lost his life and so found it.[2]

The other boys in the houses were growing up too, although it was sad to see some leave before we thought them ready to take on the outside world. The strongest influence over them was their parents who, once they ascertained that their son was drug-free, started whining about money and family responsibilities. For a boy with a dozen years of street habits, it was too much to take on the burden of supporting a family after only a few weeks off drugs. He soon realized his need to stay really close to God's family. Some went back to drugs and then begged to come back to the house. We allowed them to do so if they seemed really serious about changing.

Siu Ming did not have parental pressures. He was an orphan, and so mercifully escaped a greedy blackmailing mother. His mother had died when he was seven, and he lived with his younger sister and gambling father in a small hut on a hillside. The shack was dark and infested with rats, cockroaches and snakes. The only light came from a hole in the wall covered by a board that the family had propped up with a stick. As with many Hong Kong families, they all slept in one bed and had no kitchen, bathroom, electricity or running water. They burned oil lamps for lights and built a fire for cooking.

Siu Ming and his sister used to sit on a rock by the door of the hut, waiting for their father to come home at night. If he carried something, they knew that he had won and there would be supper. If his hands were empty, it meant that he had lost and they would have nothing to eat that night. They were too poor to go to school, so Siu Ming sold newspapers for a living. He never learned to read or write.

At 15, he joined a Triad society. His father was angry and scolded him so frequently that Siu Ming left home. A year later, his sister found him to tell him that their father had died. Now they had no one left, and Siu Ming began to take heroin in his misery. His sister pleaded with him to stop, but he was hooked. Instead of listening to her, he beat her. Then he left home again, this time forever.

As selling newspapers did not bring in enough money to buy heroin, Siu Ming had to rob and steal to get drugs. He was caught twice, and the second time he was sent to a rehabilitation center. He left there after five months and went back to drugs again. He was later readmitted to the center, came out for a holiday, and was immediately arrested once more. This time he went to prison. He came out feeling bitter toward the world and went straight back to heroin.

Sui Ming's probation officer said that he was without hope. He had even broken his probation order and was liable to have a warrant out for his arrest. However, knowing that ordering this warrant would only begin the cycle of imprisonment again, the probation officer decided to give Siu Ming one last chance and told him to find the Society of Stephen. He wrote my name and address in Chinese on a piece of paper and Siu Ming set off for my house, thinking that he was visiting a Chinese lady. He had no idea that we had anything to do with a church, but he must have been desperate for any help at all, as he bothered to cross the harbor and find Lung Kong Road.

He hid his surprise at meeting a Western woman quite well, but when I told him that Jesus really loved him, he looked undecided as to whether to accept this. Eventually he concluded, "It's either jail or Jesus," and took Jesus. Some of the former gang members living there at that time prayed with him, and he began to speak quietly in a language he did not know. We then took him back across the harbor to Third House so that he could withdraw from heroin.

Some of the boys who were smart enough to pray immediately never had the slightest twinge. Others, like Siu Ming, waited until they were *in extremis* before learning that God did not want them to suffer at all. Siu Ming refused to pray, which was understandable, since his experience of praying was limited to the session in my house only a few hours earlier. He was in agony with withdrawal pains and did not know how to make a prayer, even had he felt like it.

At last he said he could bear no more and in desperation agreed to pray in tongues. He did not have to think what words to say—God's Spirit gave them. He said he felt wonderful, and 10 minutes later he was asleep. He slept right through a day and when he awoke, he had a real confidence that Jesus did love him. Through this experience, he learned to pray in the Spirit and was freed from heroin painlessly. Although this miracle had been repeated each time with each of the boys, they all knew that it was especially for Siu Ming.

Siu Ming was so quiet and seemed to have so little charac- ter that for the first few months he lived with us we hardly noticed him. On trips to the beach or football field, there was always the nightmare of counting heads and hoping that none of the boys had slunk off to smoke in the bathroom. Siu Ming was the one we always forgot to count, because he was such a nonentity. But as the year progressed, he began to grow into a person who was kind, trustworthy, hardworking and, most important, spiritual. He learned to read and write through the daily Bible studies and was often found praying by himself. Eventually his ministry of serving the brothers and Christ was evident; he was ordained a deacon in the church and became a helper to all the new boys who arrived.

We also had some older men living in the houses, a fact that was often obscured because we continued to refer loosely to all the inmates as "boys." Ah Lun and Mr. Wong arrived separate- ly at Lung Kong Road, but on the same day. They had both heard from other addicts about our houses and demanded to be admitted immediately. Ah Lun was running a little heroin den from his cubicle in a resettlement estate. He had been in prison 18 times and only existed to eat and to take heroin. Mr. Wong claimed to have been a general in Chiang Kai Shek's army. (This may have been true, but I met many nationalist sol- diers who all claimed the same thing, and I came to suppose that it was an army composed entirely of generals.) Mr. Wong also said that he had been to many different churches in Hong Kong and that ours was the first one in which Jesus was sitting.

I tried to palm off the two old men. Ah Lun was almost 60, and Mr. Wong was in his 50s. They did not seem suitable for mixing with our younger boys. But every day for some weeks they appeared at my stone steps, waiting to be let in. I could not leave them there and deny them the opportunity to accept

Christ . . . I could not send them back to heroin dens once
they had accepted Christ . . .

So the two old men came to live with us, too, and fitted in
extremely well, making a more balanced family. God was adding
fathers to me at last. Of course there were problems too, as Ah
Lun turned out to have the habits of a packrat and kept an enormous supply of extraneous objects under, in and on top of his
bunk bed. He stored toilet paper, English books, cushions, a vast
array of apparel, extra mattresses and just plain junk. He also
kept a supply of Jean's books for himself, although he could not
read a word of English. However, it made it easy when anyone in
the house needed something unusual.

Mr. Wong thought himself superior to the others because of
his position. He had never been a Triad—he had been an army
officer waiting for Taiwan to regain China. When this did not
happen, he turned to drugs and became as addicted as all the
others. Although his rehabilitation would have seemed to be
easier than Ah Lun's, he in fact had the same basic problem as
all the boys: pride. Mr. Wong used dreadfully flowery Christian
language that he had picked up from the other churches he had
visited. He was very preachy; he became self-righteous and easily provoked; he was contentious and a pain in the neck.

After coming off drugs Mr. Wong thought that he did not
need Jesus' help anymore and stopped praying. Sarah, who was
in charge of his house, had a way of discovering these things.
So she told Mr. Wong to pray every morning and night in
tongues as well as to pray at least half an hour during his private devotions. His attitude immediately began to change, and
he remarked later, "My heart of stone is melting and God is giving me one of flesh."[3] Yet his manner did not change.

Many of the boys were healed of other diseases when they
prayed to be released from heroin. One boy had chronic asthma
and tuberculosis when he was admitted, and the others were
afraid to sleep in the same room. But after two days, his asthma
completely disappeared and his tuberculosis reading was clear
(we insisted that he finish his course of medicine anyway).

Also, Ah Lun had an enormously enlarged liver when he arrived, but he too was healed and remained normal.

As long as they were on drugs, the addicts were not aware of other ailments, but we soon discovered any that still remained after the withdrawal period. Teeth were the most common problem. None of us seemed to have the knack of praying for teeth, so we spent a small fortune in dentists' bills and false teeth. Mr. Wong had to have every single one extracted, as the heroin had rotted them so badly.

Mercifully, the British army made their facilities available to us for severe cases, and Mr. Wong went into the military hospital to have all his teeth out. He grinned throughout his stay there and had no pain, which he "tried to exthplain to the British doctor was because of the Holy Thpirit." The army completed the job by donating the proceeds of their carol singing to us, thereby providing the funds to buy Mr. Wong a complete new set of dazzling dentures.

This was not the first time the army had assisted the Houses of Stephen. They had helped me with my first house and often made available campsites and coaches for outings. We found this mutually beneficial, as many army friends became Christians through these contacts. If there were any who didn't, it was certainly not the fault of the boys who would say in their enthusiastic English to a red-faced soldier, "Have you believed in Jesus yet?" and before he could formulate a polite brush-off, volunteer their aid: "We will pray with you now if you like!"

One of the most hot-hearted among these evangelists was 33-year-old Ah Fung. He did not come from the poverty-stricken background of most of our boys but from a very wealthy family. He had completed several years of secondary education and considered himself a thinker. His uncle who had looked after him belonged to the socially exclusive Jockey Club and counted his member's card together with his American Social Security number and Mercedes Benz as his most prized possessions.

Despite these advantages, Ah Fung was underprivileged. His father had died and his mother had long since disappeared.

He was heavily addicted to heroin and needed a means to support his habit. His uncle gave him a lot of money, which only gave him greater chances to indulge his habit. Eventually, even the money his uncle gave him was not enough. He lied, cheated, stole and did anything else necessary to get enough money for drugs. He soon learned that prison sentences were lighter for living off immoral earnings, and turned to pimping.

When his uncle found out about his nephew's addiction, he made Ah Fung live at home for two months under strict supervision. Ah Fung agreed to this voluntary imprisonment but insisted that they never bother him at night; he claimed that if he was woken, he could not get back to sleep again. Secure in the knowledge that he would not be disturbed, he made a dummy figure for his bed and every night would slip out of the house unnoticed. Having found his nightly fix, he would then slip back into the house.

It finally dawned on the family after two months that Ah Fung was still hooked, and they threw him out. Unhappily, he cheated his uncle and himself, because he really did want to get off drugs. He sought professional treatment; later, he made the sad claim that he had been in every drug treatment center in Hong Kong. He even went to Taiwan and Australia in an attempt to live and work, but he was still addicted.

When I met Ah Fung, he had been in prison six times, was spending HK $180 a day on heroin and seemed a hopeless case. He came to my Walled City room. "Miss Pullinger, what are the procedures required for entering the Society of Stephen?" he asked. It reminded me of the old woman looking for a burial spot. "Where do I have to register, how long do I have to wait, and how much does it cost?"

"Well, Ah Fung, it's not quite like that," I answered. "You see, we are not a drug treatment center. We are a group of Christians who are concerned that your whole life should change. If you simply want to get off drugs, I can recommend a center. They will keep you for a few months and then you can leave—and go back to drugs if you like. But we don't want you at all unless you are really serious about changing and are prepared to stay at least one year."

Ah Fung nodded; he would agree to anything. Some of the boys sitting in the clubroom told him enthusiastically about Jesus Christ: His life, His death and His resurrection. Ah Fung nodded dumbly and agreed to pray with them.

The next day, we took him into Third House. He arrived tanked up, having smoked the entire "withdrawal" money that he had conned off his landlady, stating that we charged. On the second day he felt the twinges, which indicated he was beginning to go through withdrawal. He refused to pray and demanded to leave. His pains grew worse. He still refused to pray.

Jean and Rick were sitting down to dinner in their Kotewall Road flat when an urgent phone call came from one of the helpers who said that Ah Fung was still obstinate, shouting and struggling to escape. Rick went down to the boys' house and spoke strongly to Ah Fung as a father. He told him that whatever happened he would not be allowed to leave for eight more days and that he was ashamed of his behavior.

The voice of authority calmed Ah Fung, and he prayed with Rick. When Rick laid hands on his head, he said that he felt a glow all over and that Ah Fung's pains subsided. He and Rick prayed together in the Spirit until he fell asleep.

The next morning when he awoke, he felt the pains coming back and remembered what had happened the day before. *It might work again*, he thought to himself. Looking around to make sure no one was watching, he laid his hands upon his own head. Nothing happened. He decided to pray instead. And it was when he prayed that he was delivered.

So Ah Fung learned that it was not Rick but Jesus who had healing hands. He stayed not one year but two in our houses and became very helpful and responsible with the other boys. He was just one of the 75 boys we took in during the first 20 months. Each had his fascinating story, and all, without exception, came off heroin without pain and trauma.

The boys all knew the reality of a living Lord and the power of His Spirit; those who followed Him were evidence of an incredible transformation. Ah Fung himself quoted the Chinese proverb, "It is easier to alter the features of the country than to change one's disposition." He recognized a God who could move mountains.

# ENTERTAINING ANGELS

They might have been 20 years old; they might even have been 60. There was no way of telling. They had given up all pretence of trying to look pretty or attractive. Their heads hung down as they squatted or propped themselves up against the wall and waited for customers.

The prostitute who had bought Maria as a baby was preparing to retire. Now she either stood outside the blue film theater, urging the voyeurs to sample the juvenile delights promised upstairs, or sat by the cubicles where the young girls were contained and counted up the money.

Maria was 13, and when her stepmother wanted her to begin work in the Walled City brothels, she rebelled. It was not that she found sleeping with different men morally repugnant, but the idea of having to sleep with old men for a fee did not attract her. Having been raised in a brothel, she thought it merely a way of earning a living and was indifferent to its social disadvantages. She was a very attractive, perky child with beautifully clear olive skin and expressive eyes, which she soon learned to use to her advantage. However, she was looking for love and attention and enjoyed flirting with the boys she met at the Youth Club during its early days. So she ran away.

Maria became a ballroom girl at a ballroom in Kowloon, there being little alternative for a teenage Chinese girl on her own. A ballroom girl was a much higher class of prostitute; indeed, she did not think of herself as a prostitute but more as a hostess. Men paid for every dance they had with her; if a man chose to buy all her dances he could, and he would have to pay a further fee to take her home for the night. Every ballroom girl had a protector, or "ponce," who collected her earnings. Should the girl wish to change her man, a transfer fee of several thousand dollars had to be paid—either by the girl or by her new protector.

I did not know where Maria was; all I could find out was that she had run away from the Walled City. She could have gone to any of the hundreds of ballrooms or brothels throughout Hong Kong and Kowloon . . . the longer she was missing, the more I worried. Eventually, one Sunday afternoon after praying about her, I wandered off up the Jordan Road, asking God to lead me to where she was. *Walk straight on. Do not turn to the left or to the right.* It was the first occasion since I had been baptized in the Spirit that I had experienced another of the spiritual gifts: the word of knowledge.[1] I did not hear a voice or see a white cloud, but I knew quite surely where God wanted me to go.

I walked ahead, crossed the main road and then understood just as clearly: *Stop here.* I was standing outside of a tall multi-apartment block that had many flats with windows boarded up, posing as "massage parlors," "music halls" or "hotels." At this point, completely denying the knowledge I had been given, I said, "Lord, this is a silly game. I'm not playing spiritual detective anymore," and went home.

A few days later, I dreamed of Maria and saw clearly the room she was living in and the man she was living with. I woke up crying, for I did not know how to find her and tell her that I cared about her. The only way for me to discover her whereabouts was through the Triad network; because of their control of the vice rackets, they were usually able to locate missing girls within days.

I did not need to resort to black society methods, however, for a few months later Maria telephoned me herself. She said that she had been trying to contact me for ages too, but that she did not dare go back to the Walled City and did not know my new telephone number. She gave me directions on the phone, and I went to visit her. It was the same block outside of which I had stopped on that Sunday afternoon months earlier. It was the same room I had dreamed of, except that around the walls and on the ceiling there were many mirrors.

After that, I visited Maria every Sunday afternoon; she told me how she loved her man and how she was in debt to her ballroom. Ballroom girls were issued with beautiful dresses and taught to dance, but the ballroom took the cost out of their future wages. Because of these debts, a ballroom girl could not leave her ballroom without paying quite a large sum. Maria was trapped. She felt that one way out of the trap was to become pregnant, so she became pregnant by her protector, but then had the baby aborted. She became pregnant a second time and went to live with her protector's mother; after the baby was born, she got a job in a factory. But her protector's family, friends and even her protector himself looked down on her because she had been a ballroom girl. Eventually, the lack of friendliness made her feel that it was not worth being a good girl and working hard in a factory, so she decided that she might as well go back to the ballroom.

Her baby girl stayed with the granny; she was called Jack-yan, after me. I put savings into the bank for the baby's schooling, but sadly Maria and her protector spent the money on themselves, as they had no ability to think of the future.

Maria found a new protector, but she still was not content and became more and more unhappy. Every night she danced and danced; to keep going she used pep pills, and when the dance hall closed, she could not sleep as she was far too revved up. She went off to the gambling dens with the other girls and the inevitable happened—she ran into debt and was forced to borrow money from a loan shark. Many loan sharks in Hong Kong charge 20 percent interest daily; soon she was hopelessly insolvent. The loan shark then demanded that she become a "snake"—his property as a prostitute for two years—while he kept all her earnings to pay off her debts.

Maria rang me up in a panic, and her voice was high with terror. To be forced to be a snake was for her the ultimate humiliation; as a ballroom girl she was independent in a way, but now she was to be a prisoner to a ruthless man who would extract every penny she earned. She wanted me to produce HK $1,500 to save her from this fate, but I did not even have HK $15. My greatest concern, however, was whether she was sincere; she had prayed to receive Christ in the past but had not made any serious effort to follow Him. I had no intention of paying money to a girl who was not serious about changing her life, for she would just soon end up in the same mess again. But clearly I had to go and see her, and I decided to take Ah Ping with me; he had been in her world, and I needed his worldly discernment to know if she was exploiting me.

Together, we prayed about it. When I reviewed my material assets, I thought of the only thing I had in the world of any financial value: a very precious and favorite oboe. I had played it for years in the Hong Kong Philharmonic Orchestra and, like all oboists, regarded it as a personal friend—handpicked and almost irreplaceable. Knowing nothing of my secret riches, Ah Ping had an interpretation of a message in tongues. He said, "The Lord Jesus Christ gave up His most precious possession for you, even His very life. Why do you store up your treasures on Earth; you should rather store up treasure in heaven."[2]

If Jesus had given up His life, what was an oboe in comparison? What could I say?

"All right, Maria," I told her. "I will pay the money on two conditions. The first is that you let me hand over the cash in person; the second is that you leave this kind of life. I'll help you find a job, a room, anything you like—but if you remain here, you will soon be in trouble again."

"They will never agree to deal with you," argued Maria. "Michael is a very exacting money lender and very particular about his debts." However, she had no choice, and so set up a meeting in a tearoom on Jordan Road for two nights later at half past midnight.

I sadly sold my oboe and filled a brown business envelope with fifteen HK $100 notes. I arrived at the restaurant and chose a central table, where Maria and I drank coffee while we waited for Michael the sharp-toothed loan shark.

Squealing tires heralded the arrival of the collecting agents. Michael had not come himself but had sent four men, who slouched into the room Chicago-style while their engine growled outside. Barely glancing at us, they picked up the envelope and, after checking the contents in the manner of a gambler checking a deck of cards, walked out again without speaking.

I was very disappointed. They had played the scene too quickly. They were about to go through the door when I called out, "Hey, wait!" One of them looked back, raised his eyebrows, and said disdainfully, "What do you want?"

"I want to see Michael," I replied.

"What do you want to see him about then, huh?" The spokesman sounded extremely condescending.

"I have got a very important message for him."

"Well, you can give us the message."

"No," I replied. "I have to give this message to him in person."

"What is it?"

"It is a very personal message; I must tell him myself. How can I find him?"

Slightly to my surprise, they gave me his telephone number; even more surprising, when I rang him up he agreed to see me. I was summoned to a skyscraper in a smart part of Kowloon; Michael's nightclub was on the twenty-first floor. It was clearly very exclusive; the doorman let me in with a golden key at least three feet long after having vetted me through a spy hole. I was expected. Inside were thick carpets and soft lighting, and everywhere there were enormous teddy bears—on the bar, on the tables, around the walls. Each table had a telephone connected with the cubicles upstairs; the members sat with their drinks downstairs, and when they wanted a girl, they dialed her number. This, then, was the club that Maria would have had to work in had not the money been paid. I sat at one of the downstairs tables and waited . . . and waited.

Various minions were sent to offer me drinks; I was assiduously attended to. Eventually Michael himself deigned to grant me my interview. He was a real smoothie; he looked very pleasant and well groomed as he sat down opposite me. He spoke with glib eloquence about the terrible problems of living in Hong Kong and how without this loan business he could not afford to send his 11 brothers and sisters to school. As it was, he was able to support all his family, including his mother, on the proceeds. Indeed, he felt that he actually had a service to provide to the community; when parents lost their children, they often asked Michael to help, and for a fee he could usually find missing children within 48 hours. He knew all the clubs, bars and ballrooms and could trace them through his Triad contacts.

After completing his self-justification, he began to attack.

"You are a fool. You have lost that money. You may have thought you were doing something very noble by paying for that girl, but I know her and know that she is not going to change. She is going to get back to the same thing . . . Do not think she is going to be grateful to you or change her life in any way. You have just seen the end of that money. You have been tricked into making a completely wasted gesture."

"That doesn't really matter," I said. "I'll tell you why I did it. Have you heard about Jesus?"

He had heard some of the Bible stories.

I explained, "Jesus is the One who did all those miracles. He was the one perfect man who has ever lived; He only did good, healed people and raised them from the dead, but His enemies put Him on a cross and killed Him. He died for my sake, but He did not wait until I was good before He died for me. He never said He would die for me only if I changed. While I ignored Him, He laid down His life for me, and even as He was dying, He still said He forgave me. That is what Jesus did for me and that is what I want Maria to understand." I stopped, uncertain if he had understood my English but aware that he was too proud to speak Chinese.

"She won't change; she will go back to her old ways. It was a wasted gesture," he repeated.

"I would rather be a fool and lose the money. After all, what's losing the money? Jesus lost a life. I would rather be a fool and lose money than be a cynic and see her go to hell. Now she has a chance of a new life, whether she wants to take it or not. It is up to her now. I cannot change her life, but she has the opportunity; Jesus made that opportunity."

Michael opened his mouth to reply, but no sound came. He had been struck dumb. His mouth opened and shut and his lips formed words, but his throat was paralyzed by emotion. Minutes passed; still he could not speak. His eyes filled with tears. Finally, with his eyes turned away, he croaked, "I have nothing to say." And then he was silent.

I never saw Michael again, but I was joined in the lift by one of the club employees, whom Michael had granted permission to come after me.

"Can I talk to you?" he asked. I was surprised and a little nervous of his motives, but he went on, "I want to hear about being a Christian. Can you tell me where there is a place I can go?" It was three in the morning and there was nowhere nearby where we could talk except a bar, so we sat there for the rest of the night, our coffee cups on either side of an open Bible.

By this time I had started to take boys into my house and obviously could not invite Maria to share it, even if she were willing to come. We had already discovered that helping such girls was much more difficult than helping the boys, as very few of them wanted a new life. Many had no feeling of doing wrong; they knew that society officially disapproved of their profession but felt that the stigma attached was well worth the freedom they gained. They were free to enjoy themselves, make money and escape the drudgery and anonymity of the Chinese housewife.

Most young girls retained their illusions for some time. They loved their boyfriends romantically and willingly supported them, and only realized that they were being exploited several years later. By that time, they knew no other life and discovered that they had not bought freedom at all but were captives to the game. There were no homes for retired prostitutes, and no pensions, either. A girl had to become hard and either attach herself to a wealthy man or trick her protector so that she could amass money for the years when she would no longer be desirable or serviceable.

Even if a girl genuinely desired to change her lifestyle, the men she supported would naturally resist, and there might be as many as seven or eight of them. Some girls would have liked to leave but were in debt to the club where they worked and feared their pimps. During my visits to Maria's ballroom, I met many such girls. Long before they admitted their desperation, even to themselves, they were popping pills in the girls' restroom while I chatted with them.

One evening, I received a phone call at Lung Kong Road from Frederick, one of the Walled City Club boys.

"Poon Siu Jeh," he spoke very quietly. "I have a friend who has been beaten up for trying to leave the Triads. This person is desperate and has nowhere to go to escape. Can we come to your house?"

"Fine, Fred. What about tomorrow morning?" I answered. I liked the idea of the church being a sanctuary.

"Too dangerous," he said. "My friend cannot risk being seen by the gangs. We will come when it is dark."

The following evening, I opened the door to receive my smuggled fugitive and saw with a shock that Fred had delivered a girl. Because of the lack of gender in Chinese speech, I had naturally assumed that it was a boy running from the Triads. Actually, she looked more like a beanpole than a girl; she was emaciated and had arms and legs like stalks. Her eyes were dark and bruised. Hurriedly, I let her in and tried to talk to her, but she would not utter a word that evening or for some time to come. Nods and headshakes sufficed for her conversational needs. Her name was Angel.

Frederick told me that she had been employed as a prostitute by a gang in Mong Kok. This was because her mother had no room for her in their resettlement room. Several members of the family were already sleeping in the passage, so the mother gave Angel to the man who asked for her, saying that she hoped they would marry. She knew that he was already married, but she convinced herself that marriage was not out of the question and that the partnership would be economically advantageous.

It did not work out that way. Instead of the man providing for her, Angel found herself not only supporting him but also four or five others. Every night she was sent to a brothel, where she worked. Some of the brothels employed boys as young as 14 to "watch" the girls. The boys sat and played cards, looked at television or ate; they were there to make sure the girls worked proper hours and did not escape. They had no need to use force. One night Angel did not turn up for work, and when she returned to the Mong Kok flat she was beaten up by her boyfriend. He told her that he would beat her to death if she did not go to work in the future.

Angel did not want to be beaten anymore; neither did she want to continue this work, but she had nowhere to go instead. If she went home, her boyfriend would find her; if she rented a room, the Triads could locate her within 48 hours. She had no friends except other bar girls who would also be with their men. The only other person she knew was Frederick, so she went to him. He had nowhere to conceal her, so she came to us.

Angel looked 17 but was actually 25 and rather simple-minded. After a few days she understood enough to accept that Jesus loved her, not because she would go out and earn Him money, but because He loved her as she was and forgave her. So she became a Christian, and we saw some kind of animation light up her vacant eyes.

Although she had started a new life, poor Angel could obviously never be free to walk around in Hong Kong while the situation remained as it was. This was unfinished business, and gang law required a settlement. There had to be a *gong-sou,* or talk-out, to decide on a separation fee before Angel was officially transferred. Otherwise, if she were seen in the street, the gang could snatch her back, disfigure her, throw acid at her or start a gang war against us.

I arranged with Angel that we should meet her former boyfriend. I phoned him and chose the Hong Kong Hotel Coffee Shop, because it had several entrances and exits and we could not be trapped. It was also public enough to prevent Angel's men from abducting her without attracting attention. I also rang the police and told them that we were having this kind of talk there and, whereas it obviously did not warrant anyone coming down to make arrests, it would be helpful if someone were around keeping an eye open. They kindly agreed.

One of the Lung Kong Road boys accompanied Angel and me to the hotel, where we found a whole table of Triads sitting with the boyfriend. As the discussion progressed, I gradually became aware that dotted around the coffee shop were several more tables occupied by their gang brothers. They watched us and directed questioning glances at Angel's boyfriend. I guessed that these dozen or more men were all there because they could only imagine that Angel had fled to another Triad. I could see that I was not making much of an impression.

I left Angel to do the talking, until I realized that she was not discussing anything at all but agreeing with everything her ponce said. It was a habit of years, and I could see us leaving the hotel and getting into separate taxis while she meekly went back to being a whore. I entered the conversation but the boyfriend was adamant; he would not release her. He then became quite maudlin and disgusting as he tried to convince both me and himself that he really loved and missed Angel.

"A very strange way you have of showing your love," I retorted, "sending her out to do this job and expecting her to support you. I think you are just sorry about losing your income."

"I am not willing to give her up. She is rightfully mine. She was given by her parents," he persisted.

"Angel has no chance of any kind of life with you—you cannot even marry her," I said. "She wants to break away and start a new life. She has come to believe in Jesus." This meant nothing to him, and he commanded Angel to leave with him. I hung on to her arm so he could not force her. The Lung Kong Road boy hung on to her other arm, and thus in unwieldy formation we walked out of the door and into a taxi. We were pulling away from the curb, relieved that Angel was still with us, when the boyfriend leaped at the vehicle and climbed into the front seat. He would not leave, so I directed the taxi on a long detour so that he would not find out our address. I did not want him to trace Angel.

Our front seat rider swung around to glower over the back of his seat. "My boss will be extremely angry about this. He will not let Angel go. This matter must be finished. I need your phone number."

I refused to give the number and said that I would contact him again and we could talk some more. At last he climbed out of the taxi and we went home.

It was all very unsatisfactory, and we decided that Angel should not go to the next talk-out because they might actually snatch her back. We called and made an appointment to see them again. They said we could choose the place, so I chose the Diamond Cafe, just opposite our flat in Lung Kong Road. Angel's boyfriend advised that this time it should only be Angel and myself. Nobody else should come; he would come by himself and not bring anyone else.

I did not completely trust him about this. I was also worried about the threat of violence from a different direction, for the boys in Lung Kong Road were getting quite protective about Angel and me. This was just what I did not want to happen, because if there were any trouble or any violence, despite the fact that they were Christians, their instinct would be to fight and, therefore, they ought not to be in such a situation. So we spent the morning looking up the stories of Gideon and Jehoshaphat in the Old Testament, where they were facing impossible odds but did not have to fight at all; simply by praising God or by singing they got the victory.[3] I wanted our boys to know that we did not have to fight. I was not particularly worried for myself; although I would be really frightened if somebody wanted to kill or slash me, I would not be likely to grab a knife and stab him back. More likely I would fall to my knees, pray and die. This would be rather much to expect from the boys.

A couple of hours before the meeting was scheduled, the street was beginning to fill as Angel's men were staked out at various points and up back alleys. I had the boys lined up on our roof where they could see into the cafe without being seen themselves. I said, "Your job is to pray, and if you see any violence going on you can ring the police, but you are not to rush out to defend me or anything like that." They were all ready to run into the Walled City and get Goko to send out men to fight the other gang. I had to explain forcibly, "As Christians you can't do this; you can't fight a spiritual battle this way, you're not to get involved physically." We really prayed about this, and then I went to the appointment with one boy, leaving Angel behind.

When I got to the café, I found that this time Angel's boyfriend had not come himself but had sent his gang leader, who also was a burly brutal figure. There were also five or six of his cohorts there, and I knew there were others outside. He was furious that I had not brought Angel; obviously, they had been all ready to snatch her.

"Don't think I'm going to stand on ceremony just because you're a Jesus lady or you have something to do with the church," he said. He did not know that I had anything to do with the Walled City, so I foolishly attempted to witness by mentioning some of the boys, once Goko's followers, who now were following Jesus. He leaped to the conclusion that I had something to do with the 14K.

"Right," he said. "That settles it. We're not going to stand on ceremony with you any longer." He banged on the table furiously and got up shouting until the whole cafe was terrified. "You have to produce this girl. We're not going to let you go until you do."

He ranted while I tried to tell him about Jesus; but he didn't want to hear. I was stuck. I thought, *I tried to tell him about Jesus and he doesn't want to hear that, neither is he going to listen to reason about the girl. I really am cornered.* I was frightened.

"Excuse me, can I make a telephone call?" I bleated. I telephoned my house, which they still did not know was opposite, and spoke to Willie, an old Etonian, who was helping us for a year.

"Don't look now, but outside the cafe there are two cars with men with knives in them," he said, and it sounded as if he were speaking out of the side of his mouth. "They're waiting there."

I was terrified out of my mind, so I whispered to Willie, "Call the police." I went back to my seat and told them that Angel was not coming, so they would have to do the talk-out with me, and that Angel wanted to follow Jesus. They could not understand what I was talking about; I was certainly no substitute for her.

As the police cars arrived, the weapon cars slid away, and when the policemen came into the café, all was tranquility. Here were all these young men having a cup of coffee with a European girl. The young men, of course, did not have knives on them, and I could hardly say to the policemen, "Look, these men are threatening me," because they were not. I went out to the lavatory at the back, and there was one of the policemen there too, so I said, "Excuse me, but there are men with knives outside in cars."

"There's no one there. Do you want me to search the cafe?" he asked helpfully.

"It's no good searching the cafe," I said. "You won't find anything."

So the police all went away again, and as they went the cars came back. I was still stuck there, not knowing what to do. The one thing that I could do in this situation was pray, but I could not pray in English, for I was in a complete blue funk. I decided to pray in tongues very quietly so that they could not hear.

My knees were shaking under the table, and I went on praying. I had no idea what I was going to do next, for this gang was

getting more and more furious and I could not see how it was
going to end. Finally I got up, saying, "I have to go and buy
some vegetables."

Trembling violently I walked out of the café, and as I walked
out I could see men getting out of the cars, which were parked
close together. They were walking toward me. I did not know
what would happen and was still more frightened that the
Walled City boys would leap in and fight on my behalf.
Mercifully, a minibus was passing, and although I did not know
where it was going, I jumped on and got away. I went straight
to the police station.

"I want to report something. I'm afraid there might be a
murder." I tried to tell the police about the emergency phone
call and about the men with knives looking for Angel. "I'm sure
they are going to go to her family's home. They don't know
where I live yet and have no way of finding out my address. But
they're going to go to her home, and I know they're going to
give her family members trouble." I gasped incoherently.

They all looked very bored and asked, "Where does she live?"

"In Shek Kip Mei," I told them.

"Well, that's not our district." They sounded irritated.
"Would you mind going to the Shek Kip Mei police station?"

"But can't you call from here?" I asked them. "I'm afraid
there might be a murder."

A police inspector sitting there looked around at me and
smirked. "Madam," he intoned, "people get killed every day."

"Yes, I know they do," I said impatiently. "But I just want to
tell you before it happens, because I'd like to stop this one." I
made such a fuss that eventually they said they would take me to
Shek Kip Mei police station in one of their vehicles. I found the
second police station equally unhelpful. "This should be
Kowloon City business, as the 999 call was made from there," they
complained. "Anyway, what do you expect us to do about it?"

"Look, here is her address," I said. "Here is where her family lives. I'm pretty sure that this gang is going to go to her family and give them problems."

"We can't send someone to watch there all the time. We've got a lot of jobs to do."

"I know you can't, but could you tell the policemen on the beat to watch out for this address and to keep their eyes open?"

This all took about six hours and eventually a very helpful inspector took an unofficial report, as there was no way that he could make it official since nothing had actually happened. Twelve hours later, I got a desperate phone call from one member of Angel's family. I deliberately had not given them my address, as the gang would have got it out of them. "I'm out shopping and I can see up onto the balcony of the resettlement block," she said in a shaking voice. "There are five men sitting in my family's house, and they won't leave. And there are other men sitting on the stairs with weapons, with iron bars."

I straightaway rang the police. The long six-hour wrangle with them the night before proved its value, because they were already informed and got their policemen there very quickly. Most of the men managed to escape, but they captured two or three of them. The police managed to put fear in them by implying that if they felt like it, they could get this gang into a lot of trouble. Angel was never bothered again.

The strangest part of the whole story was yet to come. Angel's family told me later that they had been terrified when the gang came and sat in their house. They were questioned as to where I lived and where our church was. Mercifully, they did not know and so could not tell.

"Anyway, who is this Jesus lady and who are these Christians?" asked one of the gang. "Our Angel used to be so obedient; she'd do anything we wanted before, and now she dares to resist us. Did you see that Jesus woman's eyes? When we were sitting in that café, we were frightened; we dared not look in her eyes because she has some kind of power." The word they used implied a supernatural power or strength. When I heard that, I really rejoiced, because it had been one of the most frightening moments of my life and I was completely out of my depth, yet they were more frightened than I was and had not dared touch me because they recognized a spiritual power.

Now that her freedom was secured, we could not keep Angel in Lung Kong Road in the middle of boys who were trying to start a new life. Since Jean and Rick had moved to the Hong Kong side to accommodate more people at the Saturday meeting, their Mei Foo house was available for the few months the lease still had to run. We decided to put Angel there together with two girls who had been referred by the courts and the girlfriend of one of the addicts who was going through withdrawal in our houses. Sarah stayed to be the housemother, and so the girls' house began.

Another of the difficulties in rehabilitating girls was that no one ever forgot their past. Somehow there was a kind of glory attached to a man's crimes; he could be forgiven, and if they were not forgotten at least no one blamed him for them. For a girl, however, it was different: Even if she became a Christian, no one forgot what she had once been.

Although the lease soon expired and we were unable to continue the girls' house, we had learned much through this experiment. Angel, who had never been to school in her life, had begun to read a little. She was never molested again and later married a very nice young Christian man with a proper legal job.

It was a year later when another member of the judiciary—this time a district court judge—telephoned Jean and asked if she would consider taking a middle-aged woman into our houses. She had been caught at Kai Tak Airport with four and a half pounds of raw opium in her underclothes. The judge felt that this was an isolated incident in her life, and although the crime actually merited several years in prison, he was unwilling to pass this sentence as it seemed of no benefit to her. The probation report on her home was so discouraging that unless an alternative could be found, probation would be ruled out.

Jean hurriedly told the judge that we no longer had a girls' house and could not consider mixing a female drug peddler with our boys. However, she agreed to visit the court the next day and talk to the woman.

I went with Jean to translate, and when we arrived the judge, who remembered us from Ah Kit's case, cleared the court so that we could talk for as long as we liked without being disturbed. We saw a Chinese woman in her late 40s sitting in the dock like a rabbit frozen with fear.

We did not want Ah Ying to think that her future depended in any way on her response to our message, as that would have provoked a weighted decision from her. Without saying where we were from or who we were, we told her about Christ and how He could take away the heaviness of sin and give her a new life with power.

She told us that she had been trying to pray in prison while on remand and that we were an answer to her prayers. She smiled as she realized that Jesus had forgiven her and prayed eagerly with us to receive the power of His Spirit.

Jean looked at me. I looked at her. We both shrugged and smiled as we said in unison, "Well, we had better go in to the judge and tell him we'll take her."

Ah Ying went to live in Third House, staying in one of the helpers' rooms. She was very churchy at first and liked long, flowery, repetitive prayers. She was also very contentious and difficult to live with. But gradually, she grew into a completely different person. It may have had something to do with the fact that she always prayed in the Spirit while she did the establishment's ironing—and some days she ironed for hours . . .


*God, I can't tell them about Jesus. Wouldn't it be awful if they believed?* I used to hurry past some of the old prostitutes, avoiding them for that reason. I was at the stage where I knew that Christ could overcome the power of drug addiction, but I also knew that the new believers needed a safe, strong house to grow up in. We no longer had a place for girls; we had quite enough problems with the boys as it was. So what would I do with a repentant madam? Leave her on the streets?

I could not resist speaking one night as I passed one old crone who had her pitch just near Lung Kong Road. She sat on an orange box and had no home, nowhere to sleep, nowhere for her belongings. The only way she got a bed for the night was if a man hired her, and then she could sleep the whole night in the apartment house room that he rented. She had no cupboard for her clothes but kept them all in a laundry, taking out clean ones when needed and changing them for her dirty ones.

Ah King was nearly 50 and endured her prostitute's life by taking heroin. Perhaps she had been led into prostitution to make money for her heroin habit. In any case, the two were now inextricably combined, and she was on a hopeless course. She knew who I was, as I had walked by her for years.

I began to tell her about the woman who washed Jesus' feet with her tears and wiped them with her hair. How she was a prostitute but He, who was God's Son, liked her and spoke kindly to her. I spoke of the religious people whom He was not so keen on, and how upset they were at Jesus' manners in public, letting a soiled woman touch Him; how He had said to her, "Your sins are forgiven . . . go in peace."[4]

Ah King listened and believed. "That's the Lord I want," she cried.

I told her how she could receive this Lord, and she prayed out loud in Chinese, completely naturally. The old man who was the street pimp was close to us; he was not a very high-class pimp but one who took a few dollars from each of the elderly street women. This coolie watched us sitting with our eyes closed praying and nearly split his sides with laughter. His howls of mirth did not put Ah King off. She sat there talking to the Lord who loved prostitutes.

"This Lord will also give you power to help you pray, and this power will stay with you to teach you everything," I told her. She began to pray in a beautiful new language quietly and clearly as the Holy Spirit taught her.

When Ah King had prayed for 10 minutes, she looked up with happiness flooding her face. Now came the awful moment.

I had nothing to give her. I had no house for prostitutes; my floor was already covered with boys. My purse was empty. I had not even a bus fare. She continued sitting on her box.

"You know, Ah King, you don't have to look to men anymore for your daily rice," I said. "Look to God."

She roared with good-humored laughter. "Do you mean to say it will fall down from heaven?"

"Maybe," I replied seriously. "If God really is God, He could quite easily send you rice from heaven. You cannot live this kind of life anymore."

She seemed to catch the idea. "I tell you what," she said. "Next time I see you, I'll tell you how it came."

I walked away, leaving her on her box. I did not like doing that—it was hardly an auspicious beginning to a new life—but I decided to put her completely into God's hands.

A week later, I saw her again.

"I've learned some things," she told me. "I think it is reasonable enough for God to provide my rice money but not my heroin money." That was the last time I ever saw her. When I asked the other prostitutes where she was they replied, "Oh, she does not do this anymore. She has gone away. She has gone somewhere to get off drugs."

I always like to think of Ah King sitting somewhere in the best house God can provide while He rains rice down upon her.

# WITNESSES

It was dark in the Walled City that night; only the lights of our little room blazed out bravely in the sultry gloom. Four or five boys lounged around watching a table tennis game. Into the light slipped a pathetic figure, very young and very thin and clearly addicted to heroin. I recognized Bibi, Winson's youngest brother, who was called "Bibi" because he was the baby of the family. He was on the run from the police; they had let him out for one day's holiday from prison and he had not gone back.

I called him, sat him on a wooden bench away from the tennis table, and told him about Jesus. He seemed to begin to understand, but he did not stay more than half an hour; boys on the run can never stay long in any place. He promised me to come back again, and some days later—or it may have been weeks—he did come back. I told him more so that he knew enough to make the decision to follow Jesus if he so chose; I warned him that he now had to make up his mind for himself. "I can't go on seeing you, because I'll be breaking the law if I encourage you to visit me here," I said. "If I do not know where you live that is one thing, but if I am regularly seeing you here, I will be obliged to turn you in. I will pray for you, and as soon as you are ready to follow Jesus, tell me and I will go with you to the police station and help you give yourself up. I will go through the whole thing with you, because if you really start to pray, I know you can be helped."

Bibi did not turn himself in. Later, he was arrested and sent back to prison. I went to see him there and we talked, but on his release he went back on drugs. For the next few months he dropped into the Youth Club occasionally, and then I heard he had been arrested for two very serious crimes. One charge was for wounding a newspaper seller and stealing his watch; the second charge was for robbery with assault. The police claimed that they had found identity cards and property from the victims on Bibi when they arrested him. As soon as I heard the details, I knew that Bibi could not be guilty of at least one of the charges: He was in the Youth Club talking to me at the time that he was supposed to have been robbing the newspaper seller. I hurried to see him in prison and discovered to my horror that he wanted to plead guilty because, although he was innocent of these particular charges, he had done about 20 other robberies in a completely different area of Kowloon. He said in a resigned tone, "Let's just get it over with and plead guilty."

"You can't," I insisted. "You really can't. It isn't the truth. Tell the judge you have done the other things, but tell the truth."

When the case came up, Bibi pleaded innocent but was found guilty in spite of my evidence, which was the only time that I have ever been a witness. In his summary, the judge said that he believed I had spoken the truth, but he thought that another witness was confused about the time of the incident. And the case was closed.

I had spent days in court praying throughout the proceedings, so inevitably the policemen and the prison officers got to know me. At the end of the trial I was walking out of the courtroom when the police inspector stopped me.

"How come you are involved in all this?" he asked.

"Well, I'm a Christian."

"Why are you giving evidence for the criminal then?" pressed the officer.

"I know he is a criminal; I know he is a drug addict; I know he has done many robberies, but he did not do this one. I know he didn't because I'm his alibi."

"Oh," said the policeman. "Well, I'm a Christian too. Look at it my way. When these people commit crimes, we know who did it but we can't always get them for it. So we charge them with what we can make stick. It's rough but fair, and society benefits."

"You may think it's fair enough to arrest someone on the wrong charge, and he may even think it's fair enough because of what he has got away with, but in the long term the effect on society is bad. There is no respect for the law or the police or truth. The criminal learns to think the way all criminals think—that getting caught is not connected with guilt or innocence; it is merely bad luck. They certainly never learn to tell the difference between right and wrong." I felt very strongly about this, and I launched into the attack.

"Well, at least they receive some kind of punishment for their crimes," reasoned the inspector.

"But they don't feel they are paying for the wrong that they have done," I countered. "I know men in prison for crimes they claim they have not committed: They are viciously bitter at being locked up on a false charge. The first thing they want to do when they get out is to do the crime to fit the punishment. Never mind the other ones they did before. They feel that having already served time, they are owed the crime."

Surprised at my tirade, the officer ended the conversation lamely: "I have never thought of it like that." He hurried away.

I met Bibi when he came out of prison again. He looked like a rat that never saw the sunlight. His face was a mauve-gray, and he had dark shadows under his eyes. He went straight back to his drug. He had promised to change, but like most addicts he was powerless; he had a celebration meal of heroin on the day of his release, although he did not plan it that way. Addicts have a favorite saying that describes their feeling on arriving in a drug den: "My heart had not decided where to go, but my feet walked themselves."

To pay for his habit, Bibi found a job as a refuse collector in the Walled City. He had to drag large rattan baskets slopping excrement through the alleys. It was the lowest form of work, but it gave him a little money to begin buying his heroin; to supplement his earnings, he went back to robbing people as well. Whenever he saw me, he would run away. But I kept in touch by getting things on the grapevine and by walking around the streets, and I usually knew where he was living. When a television film unit came to make a film of our work, we contacted Bibi and filmed him at home. The drug had eaten into his flesh and sharp-etched his bones; he shivered continuously. His family turned it into a soap opera. His mother sobbed. "Make my son good, Poon Siu Jeh, make him good. Take him into your house and make him good." His elder brother whined in chorus, "Make him good, Miss Poon, make him good."

It could not work like that, of course. Bibi knew the truth—that he alone had to make the decision to change and that no one else could make it for him. I learned that there is a time for meeting and talking and then ultimately a time for not meeting anymore. For Bibi that time had come, so I told him that we had reached the end.

"This is the last time I am coming to see you. From now on I am not going to visit you anymore, because you know the way to Jesus. It is up to you now. You can choose if you want to follow Him or not. You know about Him and you know I care about you. It's because I care about you that I don't want to see you again. I don't want to see you in this state anymore. When you are ready to change, this time you must look for me."

A week later, Bibi came.

"I'm ready now," he said. "I've had enough. There's no way I can get off drugs myself. My family despises me. I can't stay at home because I've got to sell drugs to buy my own; I also have to be involved in the gambling dens because I need the money. Please, please help me."

We prayed together for a long time. Bibi was filled with the Spirit and began to speak in a new language. Then he looked at me and stated, "Now you've got to take me into your house." He meant that he wanted to be admitted to Third House. I took a deep breath and said, "I'm very sorry, but there's no room."

Bibi was frantic and very angry; for him the chance to get into one of the houses of Stephen was his only escape left.

He shouted, "But you have to let me go there! Now I'm going to follow Jesus, you can't expect me to live on the streets. I'll go on taking heroin there, and you can't be a Christian and go on taking heroin."

He was right, of course; so I pleaded for him with the Willanses and the workers in Third House, but they turned me down. "We can't take him into the house because the house is not in good order," said Sarah.

"You just have to," I argued. "That's the whole reason why we have houses: They are there so that we can take care of the boys who come to Christ so that they can grow up into a new life. Now you won't let me bring in boys because you want a nice tidy house."

Sarah replied firmly, "It's not helpful to anyone at all to bring a boy into a house like this if the relationships are not solid enough to support him. He must wait until the boys we already have settle down. The houses are like a family; it's important to have the relationships right inside before we take in more people." She was right, too; while I was desperate to bring people into the houses as soon as they became Christians, her duty was to protect the family members. If I recklessly poured people in, the whole situation would become as chaotic as it had been before we had the Houses of Stephen.

When they refused to take Bibi, I had to go back and tell him that there was no room. We met at Ah Wong's noodle stall in the Lung Kong Road—you could get marvelous little *wunton* dumplings and noodles there. Bibi raged at me in desperation when he heard the news, and I had to answer, "Just for a moment, Bibi, take your eyes off yourself. Forget that our house is going to save you. Just look up at the sky. It's not a very beautiful sky down in Kowloon City, but just look up and imagine the One who made all of that sky, the heavens and the earth and the sea and the birds. He's the One who makes even the things like drops in buckets. And He stretches out the heavens like a tent, and makes the mountains and the animals and the flowers.[1] That One actually chooses that His Spirit should live in us.

He chooses that His Spirit should live in us, rotten as we are. Why? Because Jesus left all that glory and walked through the miserable Walled City and got beaten up and killed and died and rose again so that we could have His Spirit. Isn't it amazing that the Spirit of the God who created the whole world should actually come to live in us?[2] Just take your eyes off our house saving you; instead imagine the wonder of our God."

I left Bibi there at the noodle stall, praying, so that I could talk with another addict who was pressuring me to be admitted. Half an hour later when I came back to Bibi, I found him, eyes shut, with a soft smile on his face. I called to him, but he did not reply. I called more loudly, but still there was no answer. At my third shout Bibi very reluctantly opened his eyes.

"What did you see?" I asked him.

He told me that he had seen Jesus—at least he thought it was Jesus—wearing a long white robe. He had been on a mountain and Jesus had come toward him with his hand held out; He said to Bibi, "Bibi, will you follow Me?"

Bibi replied, "Well, yes, Lord, who else?" Jesus had taken him by the hand and led him along the most beautiful path. "I can hardly describe it." Bibi searched for words in his meager experience. "It was so beautiful. There were lovely flowers and birds and it was very sweet smelling. It was the most lovely place. We walked along this path and I heard you calling but I didn't want to come back. I heard you calling again and I still didn't want to come back."

From that time onward, instead of believing that our house was going to save him now that he was a Christian, he looked up again at his Creator to do so. His peaked face was illuminated by a glow. There was room for him in our Third House just one day later, and he stayed for two years. He became one of the best boys we had, never difficult even when he was coming off drugs, which he did without so much as a headache. He simply got up and lived normally all through the withdrawal process.

Bibi's family called Jean and Rick saying that Bibi's father was ready to die, so Bibi went to see him in the hospital. When he arrived, his father, who had come off opium himself and become a believer, said simply, "Now that Jesus has made my sons good, I'm ready to go to heaven." He kissed both his sons a tender farewell; but instead of dying, he was healed as his sons prayed for him, and a week later he was discharged.

Now that I was free of the need to be a homemaker because there were several of us working together at Stephen, I could go back into the streets. So many of the addicts passed on the word that people came from areas all over the colony asking for help. A converted policeman gave me a two-way radio so that I could be reached any time or at any place, and I found myself more and more involved in the courts and prisons where so many of the boys were shocked into facing their problems. One day I attended a trial in Causeway Bay. As I was walking out after the case, I heard a cry behind me.

"Poon Siu Jeh! I've been framed! Help me, help me!"

I looked around to see the next defendant being led into the dock. He was a stranger to me. I could see the desperation of his dirt-streaked face. It was a very cool air-conditioned courtroom, and he was standing in the cotton shorts and singlet in which he had been arrested. The boy was still gesticulating wildly to me as the magistrate came into the courtroom to start the case. I had no means of knowing whether he spoke the truth or not, and no right to speak in court even if I had known. However, this unimpressive boy was about to go into battle alone, as there was no legal aid offered in Magistrates' Courts at that time. I stood up with an inspiration. "Your Honor," I said, "I am not familiar with the defendant, but I think it possible that he has not had reasonable access to legal representation. Could you remand this case so that enquiries can be made on his behalf?"

The magistrate raised his eyebrows. This was an unusual request coming from a layperson. He turned to the defendant shivering in the dock. "Do you wish to be represented?" he asked him.

"Yes," replied the boy, "But I have not been allowed to make a telephone call since my arrest, and so none of my family knows that I'm here."

The magistrate remanded the case for one day, and I went down to the police cells below the court to talk to the boy. In the two minutes allowed me, I learned that his nickname was Sorchuen, or "Crazy-boy Chuen," and that he knew of me through his Chaiwan brothers.

He was shaking violently, and his stale sweat was sour; his eyes were red and running, and he sniffed constantly. I had one minute left.

"Listen to me," I said. "I have no time to tell you about Jesus, but if you call on His name He will hear you and save you. He is God." Under the astonished gaze of the prison guard, his withdrawal symptoms immediately vanished and his face relaxed. When I saw him the next day, he was still dressed in the dirty shorts and singlet, but his face was clear and happy.

"I really did call upon Jesus and now feel quite different," he said.

Sorchuen was found guilty of the charges laid against him and went to prison briefly. Shortly after coming out he was arrested again, and this time he telephoned me from the police station. I went down to see him with an excellent young solicitor who sometimes helped us. Sorchuen had been arrested on a charge of attempting to break into several cars in the Shaukiwan district. According to him, this story was quite untrue. He claimed that he had actually been watching a pornographic film called *Legends of Lust* several miles away in Wanchai. After the movie finished, he had boarded a 14-man bus for Chaiwan but was stopped on the way by two detectives who asked him to alight from the van and "talk." They asked him to help them find another Triad nicknamed Morgwai, or Devil, and drove him in a private car to a cinema looking for the Triad. Sorchuen saw a friend there but Devil could not be located, so he was taken to the police station and booked on the attempted robbery charge after signing some kind of incriminatory statement in the policeman's notebook.

Nearly every time that Sorchuen was arrested, he yelled "Frame!" He, like many other boys, claimed to have been beaten up to make a confession. I discovered that a good number of them were not beaten, but they were so sure of the inevitability of the beating that they convinced themselves that it had as good as taken place and signed statements incriminating themselves. A high proportion of defended cases contained a *voir dire*, a trial within a trial, to determine whether a confession was admissible as evidence. Many a defendant was convicted solely on the strength of his "confession" in a police notebook without witnesses, exhibits or corroborative evidence.

David, the solicitor, and I decided to do some investigative work. David was willing to defend Sorchuen without fee, provided he was convinced of his innocence; so he wrote to the police for the registration numbers of the cars that Sorchuen allegedly tried to enter. I went looking for Devil but found that he had just been arrested, too. However, I found the friend in Chaiwan who had been outside the cinema when Sorchuen arrived with the detectives looking for Devil. He remembered the time and the date; it was three hours before the official time when Sorchuen was arrested in Shaukiwan. While I made these enquiries, Sorchuen was still in prison on remand and had no opportunity to contact his friend; I was convinced that he was telling the truth, as their testimonies were identical.

When we got the vehicle registration numbers, we took a taxi to Sheko, where there lived a boy who owned one of the cars involved in the alleged crime. He worked in a button factory in Wanchai, so we chased back, located the button-holer, and asked him where he usually parked his car. "Usually in the Shaukiwan parking lot," he said. But on the date of the crime it had not been there. Now we had a case; now we had witnesses.

All this fuss over such a minor case was unusual, and the Attorney General's department was alerted. They sent counsel to conduct the prosecution. Usually in Magistrates' Courts a police inspector fulfilled this function.

During a break in the case, the prosecuting counsel asked to speak with me. I had noticed him becoming more and more tetchy as the morning proceedings crawled along. He was extremely annoyed at the detailed cross-examination by the defense and kept looking at his watch.

"Why are you two going to so much trouble for such a minor case?" he asked. "We should have disposed of it by now. As it is, we will have to continue into the afternoon; it is such a small matter anyway."

I knew that I should not discuss this case, but I said, "Shouldn't one present the best case possible in the interests of the defendant?"

"Yes, but why waste time on such a case at all?" he objected, very upset at spending his valuable time on a trivial affair.

"Because I believe the defendant is innocent," I said.

He looked at me astounded. "That man has a record of a dozen or so convictions! Didn't you know?"

"Yes, I know. But we are talking about today's charges. I am sure he did not commit that crime."

"Well, my dear," said the barrister, patronizing me, "I've been in Hong Kong for six months now . . ."

This was one of the few cases I was involved with in which the defendant was found not guilty. But as a rider, the magistrate also handed a bouquet to the police, saying that they had done an excellent job and that the fact the accused had been acquitted reflected in no way adversely on their testimony.

So I was landed with Sorchuen. Praying in the cells after our first meeting had taught him that Jesus was alive, but he had yet to learn that the way to be His disciple was not by going to see *Legends of Lust*.

Following this case, David helped with several more and helped to pull off a legal first in Hong Kong. It was on the occasion when two Chaiwan boys along with some others were arrested for claiming to be members of a Triad society. The legal point was interesting: While you cannot be arrested for being a silent Triad member, you can be arrested for claiming to be one. For this reason, the police needed signed confessions for the charges to hold up. The two boys had signed alleged confessions in the police station but later said that they did so under duress and that they were taught what to write. The others pleaded guilty.

MOTS (Member Of Triad Society) cases, as they were known, were usually rapidly dealt with, but this one became extremely complicated. Both the boys charged had become Christians a year previously; a number of us were praying that this trial would somehow glorify God. One of the issues in the case was indeed a spiritual one: To join and remain an active member of a Triad society was a self-commitment that could not be consistent with Christianity. To take part in a Triad initiation ceremony, there was bloodletting and an invoking of spirits, which the law recognized as evil by defining it as an indictable offence.

The police produced their expert witness, a 426 Redpole fighter. He got up in court and gave his evidence.

"I am a 14K office bearer. I say that according to Triad rules, you are always a Triad member—forever. You cannot leave the Triads. Even though I now spend my life giving evidence at police trials, I still remain an office bearer in the 14K."

The case for the defense rested on exactly opposite assumptions. We claimed that our boys were no longer Triad members because they had renounced their Triad membership by being baptized as Christians. The boys stated in court, "Yes, we were Triad members, but we are no longer." Our solicitor produced another expert witness, a Chinese language scholar, who pointed out that when the boys' confessions had been translated as saying, "I am a Triad member," the translation was open to question because there is no present or past tense in Chinese. We contended that what their statement meant was, "Yes, I was a Triad member; yes, I did join a Triad society, but now I am not actively involved."

Then we produced yet another expert witness, Ah Kei, who held the same rank as the police witness in the 14K Triad society. He rose to his feet in court and said, "I too am a 426 Redpole of the 14K, but I've become a Christian. I have renounced my entire gang; these two boys here on trial were my younger brothers. Since I have given up the gang, I have told the members that I no longer hold responsibility for them; if they want to follow Christ they can, or else they can go their own way."

This clinched matters for the judge. He had been forced to spend hour after hour listening to talk of baptisms and conversions, whereas usually in Triad cases the accused were speedily found guilty or not guilty. He announced to the court, "I see no reason why a man should be branded for life; if he wants to change and become a Christian, then good."

Then the judge turned and said, "And now, Miss Pullinger, it is your responsibility to see that they continue to follow what they are supposed to have confessed. Case dismissed."

One of the reasons why there were not more acquittals was that people in Hong Kong were very unwilling to give evidence in court. There was a deep distrust of legal proceedings and a feeling that every case was rigged. Being a fervent believer in the fairness of the British judicial system, I tried to persuade them that if only they spoke for themselves or their friends with complete honesty, they were bound to be justified. The fact that so many cases went against them was largely due to their own apathy; they contributed to the inequities of the system they so berated.

Through attending so many court sessions, I began to notice some characters who seemed to appear with remarkable regularity. There was a little granny with a long plait down her back, a total of two teeth and a beautiful deeply lined and weathered face. She held what appeared to be a shopping list and sat in court each morning pleading guilty to at least 20 different hawking offences, all under different names. As each one was called out, she would raise her hand and squeak "Yauh," meaning "I'm here," and then mark off on her sheet of paper the amount to be paid. I discovered that this was her career; she no longer stood laboriously in the streets hawking her goods. Instead, for a small fee, she stood in for all her market friends at court so that they could continue their little businesses.

She had a male counterpart, a delightful 70-year-old man who squatted outside the courtroom playing cards with his mates. He knew exactly when to go in for his hearing, and every week he was there. The charges were read out: "Smoking opium and being in possession of instruments for doing so." He nodded happily. "Fifty-eight previous convictions for similar offences." He went on nodding and beaming. "One hundred dollars, or 50 dollars and one day in prison." He looked as if he would explode with joy and walked out smiling broadly. I mentioned to Ah Keung, who was sitting with me, what bad luck it was that he always got caught.

"Oh no, it wasn't an accident," laughed Ah Keung. "He is an 'actor.' He is paid to be arrested by the drug den owners." I learned that when the den operators were informed of a police raid, they closed the premises and left behind one old addict, who was then arrested and charged. Because of his age and number of convictions, he was given a minimum sentence. The den paid him 150 dollars for this and provided free opium, so he was able to indulge his habit and, after paying the fine, still make a small profit. The police were pleased, the operators were pleased, the actor was delighted, and Hong Kong's arrest tally was impressive.

Ah Keung's father was one of those who would have nothing to do with the courts. He asked me on one occasion to help his fifth son, Ah Pooi, who had been arrested for stealing a radio from an elderly man outside the Walled City. At the exact time, Ah Pooi had actually been inside the Walled City, talking to an old woman. The woman refused to be a witness, as her job was to sweep a gambling den. His father also saw two detectives take him away from there, but he refused to give testimony on behalf of his own son.

"*Pa mah fan*, don't want to get involved, too much trouble." Because he was involved in illegal gambling himself, and because the den had some arrangement with some policemen, he felt that keeping good relationships was more important than vindicating Ah Pooi. Nevertheless, he hoped that I would help his innocent son. I explained that because he was withholding the vital evidence, there was nothing I could do. He, however, had an unshakable conviction that I knew the judge and merely had to wink at him in court to free the boy. Had he known the judge, he would have winked . . .

It was a hard line to take. I had to be careful not to be eaten up with anger over the injustice when truth was rejected. I also had to avoid being used as a source of free legal aid by rascals who had no desire to change. In one case, a young man returned from seeing a solicitor I had recommended, complaining, "He is no good. He did not even teach me a story to tell in court. What a waste of money."

Yet it was not a waste of time. Many people's lives were touched through the legal cases, and if there seemed to be a lack of justification in earthly courts, there was a growing number of people who understood being justified in heavenly ones. A reformed criminal named Suenjai was a glowing example of this. He had led a straight life for 10 years, working very hard to support his wife and four young children. When he was arrested and convicted for a pick-pocketing charge, I was certain he could not have committed it. It was a particularly cruel blow for him to be imprisoned for a crime he had not done.

Suenjai's wife contacted me, and I visited him in remand prison. He was an angry and bitter man. He wanted to talk about his retrial; I wanted to talk about Jesus. He did not want to be preached at and was still abrasive, so I prayed. Then he stopped raging and became calm. I had no Bibles with me, only a little booklet containing extracts from the Sermon on the Mount. I did not feel this was very suitable, as it did not contain much about God's love and forgiveness or the means of salvation; it was mainly "good work" teaching. However, I had nothing else, so I left it for him to read.

When I next went to visit a small group in the remand center, Suenjai was sitting among them. I asked them, "Why did Jesus have to die?"

Suenjai answered straight off with a most academic reply: "Because it says, 'Do not think that I have come to abolish the

Law or the Prophets; I have not come to abolish them but to fulfill them. I tell you the truth, until heaven and earth disappear, not the smallest letter, not the least stroke of a pen, will by any means disappear from the Law until everything is accomplished.'"[3]

Suenjai had never been to a Christian meeting in his life and had only studied four years of primary school, but he had an amazing understanding of Scripture. Jesus' Sermon on the Mount led him to belief. He asked Jesus into his life and received the Holy Spirit.

Shortly before his retrial, I asked Suenjai how he would present his defense. He said that previously he had been very angry and had lots of abusive things to say; he now decided not to present a defense apart from saying, "not guilty." I began to advise him differently, but he stopped me short.

"It says in the Bible, 'Simply let your "Yes" be "Yes," and your "No," "No"; anything beyond this comes from the evil one.'"[4] I said no more.

Suenjai was found guilty. Although I was convinced he had been framed and was serving 15 months for a crime he had not done, he remained cheerful and never stopped praising God. In fact, his neighbors who heard about his demeanor at the trial were so impressed that they organized a meeting in a resettlement block and asked me and some of the boys to go and tell them about this Jesus who could change a hard man's heart.

One day Suenjai told me that he'd led 12 prisoners to Christ. I was a bit doubtful, as I knew that his theology was only based on three chapters of Matthew, a few visits from me and his own experience: He had never read *Personal Evangelism*, *Four Steps into Christ* or undergone a counseling course. So I questioned him about the circumstances.

"Well," he said, "one night one of my cellmates woke up screaming. It was as if he had been grabbed by the neck, and he began to writhe on his bunk and suffocate. I could see that he was in the grip of a spirit and couldn't breathe. So I got up and said, 'Satan, in the name of Jesus, get out!'—nothing happened.

So I said, 'Get out, I tell you!' I made as if to kick the spirit and it left him, so he lay quite relaxed and peaceful. At that, the 11 other cellmates got up and asked me, 'What was that? How did you do that?' 'That was Jesus,' I replied, and they said they wanted to believe, too, so I told them how."

Three days after his release, Suenjai's wife ran away with another man and prostituted herself. Suenjai was then supporting and looking after eight children, as his widower brother was a drug addict with four children. He remained faithful in prayer, and in future meetings with his wife so impressed her with his compassion and forgiveness that she eventually came back to him. His family and friends despised him for the weakness of his approach to her. His behavior was particularly remarkable in view of the Chinese culture that demanded divorce or a savage beating for errant wives.

For some time he continued the prayer meetings in his 10-by-12-foot resettlement room, inviting all the neighbors. One ex-prisoner who attended explained, "I received Christ because I saw what happened to my friend after he believed in Jesus, and I couldn't not believe."

Not only did God work miracles in the hearts of criminals but also, on several occasions, He deeply affected others involved in the trial. When Ah Kit's case had come up in court, Jean, myself and several members of our group went to listen. We prayed for a long time in the Spirit before arriving and also silently in the courtroom.

After the verdict releasing him into our care was announced, the arresting police inspector came to chat with us and was extremely friendly and interested in our work. He suggested that we lunch together so that we could continue the talk. He liked talking, and it was several hours later that he at last managed to say what was important to him.

"You know, I feel terribly embarrassed saying this," he confessed in his charming Scots brogue, "but when you came into court this morning, I looked at you and—well—it was like those Christmas cards . . . I know you'll laugh, and I feel awfully

silly saying this, but—well—there was a halo over your head."
Ted was a big man, a Hong Kong judo champion, second row
forward in the police rugby team, and obviously serious. I did
not feel a bit like laughing, but I swallowed several times.

We invited Ted to our usual Saturday evening prayer meeting, and he came gladly. I don't think I have ever seen anyone
more knocked sideways by a prayer meeting. At the end of the
meeting, he was sitting there gasping. Jean chatted to him and
gave him a drink and some canapés. He continued sitting there
in silence for a while, then he said, "You'll never believe me, but
that is the strangest Saturday I have ever spent in my life.
Normally I'm out with the boys every Saturday night drinking.
Tonight I have watched you people really inspired by something I don't quite understand."

I was relieved to hear him so positive, because during the
meeting a girl had come up and asked him bluntly whether he
was saved—I was worried lest he had been put off by such a
direct approach. Clearly he had not been; so we sent him home
with a copy of Jean's book.

All Sunday, Ted read the book. He was most upset because
he could not dismiss the evidence in it. Finally, he got down on
his knees and prayed. Then he rang us up and asked if he could
come around, because he wanted to receive the baptism of the
Spirit for himself. He said, "I just couldn't sleep. I kept thinking about last night. I came to the conclusion that either you
are all completely crazy or what you said is true. I've heard for
myself people speaking in tongues; I've seen for myself the way
these boys' lives have changed. So I came to the conclusion that
Jesus has to be true. And if He was true, that affected me, and
I asked Him into my life this morning."

The following Sunday, Ted was baptized in the sea together with a former gang member and his wife. The officer's conversion became widely known. His friends could see that his life
was completely changed in big ways, like his general attitude to
work, and in small ways, like no longer swearing in the rugby
scrum. One of his superintendents joked with him at a match,

"No praying in tongues in the scrum, Ted; it gives you an unfair advantage." Though the superintendent was joking, there was no doubt that Ted's conversion made a big impact on the Hong Kong police.

Not long afterward, one of Ted's colleagues who was opposed to his conversion said, "At least I hope you are not trying to change me."

"No," replied Ted, "I'm not trying to change you. I know you'll be all right when you repent, so there is plenty of time."

"But what if I snuff it first?" said the scoffer.

"Well, yes, there is that," said Ted.

# SET THE PRISONERS FREE

One day, I received a beautifully written letter from a Taiwanese man in the remand center. When I saw him there, I found a man full of spite and venom with a white stripe around his uniform, indicating that he was dangerous. He had faked illness and tried to escape from the hospital, attacking the guards in the process. He was sharing a cell with one of the Walled City boys who had told him about me.

I told Ah Lung about Jesus. It was a great disappointment to him, as he had hoped to receive advice on how to get out of prison. However, after listening, he said he would like to believe; I told him he should be willing to forgive his prison guards and lay aside his bitterness.

"Huh! They treat us worse than animals!" he snorted. "Don't ask me to do that. I could never love them. You asked the worst thing you could ask me."

"I'm sorry, Ah Lung," I apologized. "Of course you can't forgive them until you understand that you have been forgiven yourself." I told him that whatever he had done Jesus still loved him and would forgive his sins. I then prayed and felt impressed to speak in the language of the Spirit.

Ah Lung looked up at me. He interpreted very softly, "God has spoken to me and told me that He cannot forgive me if I do not forgive others.[1] I freely forgive my prison guards." He meant it.

Ah Lung became a model prisoner, as I learned from other inmates and prison officers. He changed his plea to "guilty" in court and sat there praying, which amused the interpreter and infuriated the barrister who had prepared his defense. "But," he said wryly, "I had to admit I had done a lot of rotten things. I was a very mean man. When I heard Jesus speaking to me, it was the first time in my life I've ever admitted I was wrong."

Ah Lung spoke to a 19-year-old youth awaiting trial for rape who joined us when I went to the remand center one day for a Bible study. "I've seen my friends here in prison and I've seen a very hard and a very bitter man and I saw what happened to Ah Lung when he believed in Christ. What is it that has made this hard man change into a softhearted man? I want to know this Jesus." I told him that Jesus was the One who came into the world and did all those miracles; He was the Son of Almighty God and yet died for sinners.

"Do you believe He's the Son of God?" I asked.

"Oh," he said, "I don't quite understand about that." His eyes were fixed on the prison table.

"Well never mind—are you willing to believe it?"

"All right." He kept his eyes downcast.

"Do you believe that He died for your sins?"

"I don't understand that either." He was almost cowering; he was so nervous.

"It does not matter if you don't understand completely— are you willing to believe it?"

"Okay." He was willing but still did not raise his head.

"Do you believe that He rose again from the dead?"

"Oh, yes," he said immediately, and looked up at last.

"How are you so sure that Jesus rose from the dead and you're not sure about the other bit?" I asked curiously.

"If Jesus didn't rise from the dead, you wouldn't be here talking to me in prison."

"Well, do you want to follow Him?" I asked.

He replied in the way that many of the gangsters replied, as if to a rather irrelevant question. "If He is the true God—of course, who else am I going to follow?"[2]

"All right. This Jesus will give you power, because He doesn't expect you to live a Christian life by following a set of rules—it's impossible. He will give you His Spirit to help you," I explained. He began to pray as God gave him his new language there in the prison.

Two weeks later, I picked up a newspaper and read that there had been a dramatic change at this young man's trial. He had gone up to the judge and said, "My solicitor has instructed me to plead not guilty, but I have to tell you that I am guilty. I have come to believe in Jesus, and I am guilty of this crime." He was sentenced to nine years in prison.

When I visited him there in prison, he smiled at me. "I have such joy to know that my sins are forgiven, Miss Poon," he said.

Although his wife and his child were killed in a fire one month later, he never stopped believing and sharing Jesus with others. "It's such joy to know that I am forgiven," he said. "Jesus took upon Himself even such a terrible sin as rape." He discussed with me a chapter on redemption in the Bible until it was time for me to depart. It is hard for me to say who was the more edified by the visit.

This was in direct contrast with an incident that occurred two years previously in the same prison. When I visited Daih So, Ah Keung's eldest brother, I was not allowed to use a special room, so I saw him in the general visit room. It was bleak, cold and damp. The prisoners were separated from the public by a cage of wire with so fine a mesh that it was difficult to see their faces. I had to peer very closely, because there was also a highly reflective pane of glass that made Bible study impossible.

Daih So was only 30, but as he had been taking heroin since he was 13, he already looked an old man. Even during his father's funeral, he dribbled continuously into a spittoon and had to go out several times for drugs. He was always drooping, but I liked him very much, for there was a pathetic innocence that hung around him. He once gave me the clearest definition of sin I have ever heard, startling in its profound simplicity.

When I asked him, "What is sin?" I thought he would say, "Stealing, hitting old people or pushing dope." Instead he replied, "That's simple. Sin is walking your own road."

"It's no good talking to me, Miss Poon," he said that day in prison. "I'm not going to change in here. And don't tell me to get off drugs while I'm here either, because that's impossible."

When I looked at his arms, they had several lines of fresh track marks running down them. He had gone into prison chasing the dragon but inside had learned to inject, as it was more economical and easier to take.

"Don't ask me to pray! Don't!" Daih So insisted. "And if you leave a Bible here for me, I shan't read it." He turned his back on me to make further conversation impossible and called a guard to take him away. I left feeling desolated. I went away and prayed for him. This poor man was saying he could not stop taking drugs in prison—to follow Christ would cost too much.

About six months later I was in the Walled City, and a plumpish stranger ran up to me and said, "Poon Siu Jeh! It's me, Daih So."

"Daih So! You're out of prison. When did you get out? And how come you look so fit?"

"Oh, I just got out of prison a few days ago, and I wanted to come and tell you that on that day when you came to visit me and told me about Jesus, I didn't want to hear. I called the warder to take me out, and when I got to the door I looked back and I saw you sitting there looking sad. I felt really convicted in my heart suddenly, and so I asked the jailer if he would bring me back because I could see you sitting there, but when I came back there was someone else there, so I did what you told me to. I went back to my cell and I prayed in Jesus' name, and I got off drugs."

We sometimes sent people toward jail rather than helping them avoid it. Many of the boys who came to our House of Stephen to withdraw from drugs had committed crimes for which they had never been arrested. We did not always insist that they resolve every incident, as they had put the past behind them. However, sometimes something continued to trouble them and they needed to make settlement on a human level.

Ah Wah wanted to go to the police station and give himself up for jumping bail. It turned out that he had been arrested a month earlier for possession of dangerous drugs and released on bail on the understanding that he appear in court two weeks later. Of course, being a heroin addict, he had no intention of turning up. We did not know that he had jumped bail, and when he said that he really wanted to change his life to become a new person in Jesus, he was admitted to the Houses of Stephen.

As the months went on and he continued praying in the Spirit and reading Scripture, his conscience began to bother him. Then came his confession of his outstanding court case. Jean thought that as I had been on the unhappy side of so many cases, it should be left for me to tackle as a welcome change. As I talked to Ah Wah, however, I thought his chances of release rather slim: It became clear that not only was he liable to be sentenced for the drug case and jumping bail but also that when he committed his last crime he was already on a suspended jail sentence. So under the law, he was bound to go back to prison. Although I was really pleased that he wanted to give himself up, it seemed unlikely that we could avoid his being taken into custody. I told him to pray, and all the boys in the houses also had a huge pray-in.

Although we prayed continuously in tongues all of that Monday morning, we had quite a lot of difficulty getting Ah Wah arrested. We could not start the Willanses' car, so we waited for a taxi. One hour later, there was still no taxi. Finally, we arrived at the police station, where we were kindly asked to have a cup of tea and wait. We kept saying that Ah Wah wanted to be arrested, but they were not keen and could not find the papers, so they sent us out to have lunch. When we came back, they fingerprinted Ah Wah to see if he really was the one on their files with nine previous convictions. He looked so good that the men taking his prints thought he had come to the police station to apply for a job. When he said no, they thought it must be that he was applying for a gun license. He eventually persuaded them that he was giving himself up for a drug offence and told them how Jesus had changed him. Then they asked him to teach *them* how to take fingerprints, as they had less experience than he.

Eventually we were all invited into a car and driven to court, praying all the while. The magistrate asked Ah Wah why he had skipped bail, and he told him, "Yes, it's true that I ran away last July. I was a drug addict, and I'm sorry for offending the court. But now I have believed in Jesus, I know I was wrong and I have come to give myself up."

"Congratulations," said the magistrate. "You have made a very sensible decision—and I wish you every blessing in your new life. You may go."

Ah Wah had only to sign a good behavior bond, and never at any time did anyone lay a hand on him. His relief was enormous, and there was great rejoicing in our houses when he returned. We had no calf to kill, but we bought ice cream to celebrate.

In many ways, it was easier for the boys to be Christians inside prison than outside. They suffered mockery, but they also gained respect. Through meeting so many prisoners, I learned to distinguish between *hauh-fui* (regret) and *fui-goih* (repent). Most criminals regretted being arrested, but very few really repented what they had done. Until this happened, there was no hope at all that they would be able to live anything but a life of crime outside.

One such habitual offender was Ah Bill, who stayed in my Lung Kong Road house for only 10 days before deciding he could manage his own life. But he could not cope with freedom and its choices. He wrote me a letter from prison:

HM Prison Stanley

Dearest Pullinger,

I have left the people in the house [of Stephen] for a long time. Please, ask after every brothers for me. I also ask after you. Hope that Jesus will help you on everything.

I have to stay here for ten more months. Then I can have my new life over again. I hope that in this time I can make my last repentance and will be accepted by the Lord, so that my dirt can be cleansed. Can you pray for me?

Last time when you came to visit me, I was transferred to Cat A because I have done something wrong in the prison. But now everything is just O.K. After this punishment, I have learnt how to be obedient. Every time you visited us and have meeting with us, and explained the Bible and really considered our condition. But I still did not give hear and broke the regulations. I was ashamed of myself.

When I first entered the prison, I came to the chapel every Sunday and I prayed in tongues every night. Some people just said some bad things against me. For example: Ha, you believe in Christ, but you still have to stay in prison. You don't need any food if you believe in Christ, do you? There are many other bad words. But I did not want to write it down. I think you can guess some. At this moment, I was very angry. But when God's miracle came in my mind, I just neglected all their words.

I have written quite long already. I am now following Jesus. Lastly, I want to talk with those new brothers. It is time that God has given us many opportunities. But have we taken these seriously? Have tried to get Him? Although I have come across many difficulties, I could get a little bit of His grace. In the past, I have wasted my time and life in a wrong way.

I would be very happy, if I can receive your letter on next month. And I would write back to you in order to ask some question concerning about the Bible.

Hope you have good health.

Ah Bill

Ah Bill was one of those who found it easier to be a Christian inside prison. Like other recidivists, he actually looked relieved when he was inside. This was not because he liked prison; in fact, he hated it. But at least inside he was spared the necessity of making all the daily decisions, like whether he should get up and whether he should go to work. Each time he was released, he found himself less and less able to cope with the world outside.

When Ah Kit was released into our care, he told me of his friend Kwok, whom he had met in prison. He was in very serious trouble, for although he was a 20-year-old policeman he was also a Triad and had taken part in a gang battle. One of the rival gang members had been killed in the fight. No one was quite sure who had actually put in the knife, but five boys were on trial.

Kwok was a quiet country lad, the son of a chicken farmer from the New Territories. He was courteous and clean looking, but drawn and thin from the worry of the remand period. Like all Chinese his eyes were dark, but his were still blacker with a bleak despair. When I told him about Jesus dying for him, he could just about understand and could accept that He was God's son, too. But he repeated sadly, "What hope is there for me—I mean what future?" I prayed quickly, hoping to give the right answer.

"Did you know that the two men in the Bible that God used more than any other men in history were murderers?" He looked stunned while I continued, "One was called David and the other Paul. Paul was chosen to spread the news of God's forgiveness to more men than any other man in history. He had murdered Christians, but God showed the whole meaning of the gospel when He used such a man."[3]

When Kwok heard this, his face lit up and his black eyes shone a little. "Do you mean," he exclaimed, "that as well as being forgiven I can have work to do for God?" This idea that he could be useful so encouraged Kwok that he prayed as if his heart would burst with joy.

Two days later, I saw him again. He was positively glowing as he told me, "Miss Poon, I have such peace in my heart. It is what I have been looking for all my life. I know my past is forgiven and

I have hope for my future. I do not fear the results of my case any-more. If I am found guilty or not guilty, I do not mind. I have hope." He talked as if we might never have the chance of meeting again, packing as many words as he could into the time.

He was sentenced to death the next day. I remember watching him as the verdict was announced. He was calm. But the other youth sentenced with him looked terrified. This youth immediately made a show of bravado, and as he passed me in the Supreme Court lifted his handcuffed hands to his neck in a dreadful gesture meant to convey hanging. He laughed.

I was not allowed to see Kwok for two years, while they were deciding whether to execute him or not. Eventually, his death sentence was commuted to life imprisonment . . .

When at last I went back to see him, I was nervous because I had only seen him twice and had told him very little. He knew that Jesus was God's Son and loved him and died for him, and he had prayed and received the power of the Holy Spirit, but that was all. I thought, *Poor boy, he does not know very much. He has not had a Bible all this time; no minister has visited him, and maybe he does not really remember all that much about Jesus. He has probably forgotten all that I told him.*

When I went into the special little room provided, I was not quite sure what I was going to meet. But when Kwok came run-ning into the visit room, he was still absolutely radiant. I had never before seen such pure joy on a man's face. "Oh, Poon Siu Jeh, it is absolutely wonderful," he gasped. He was so excited that he hardly paused for breath.

"I have got such peace in my heart, such joy to know my sins are forgiven. I sit in my cell every morning and every night and I pray. I do not know what I am saying because I am speak-ing in that language that God has given me, but I know He understands what is in my heart, and I have been telling all the other prisoners about Jesus and six of them have believed, too, and here are their names, and here are their numbers."

He thrust a list at me, and later I visited the men on it. All of them were either long-term prisoners or convicted killers, and one of them was the youth who had made the hanging gesture in court. They did indeed believe. Their teacher had known little with his head but much in his heart, and I never met a group of men who understood better the meaning of Jesus giving up His life for them.

I gave Kwok a Bible, and he had finished the New Testament within two months. He wrote his questions on a minute two-inch square scrap of paper, and there was never enough time to talk. He had read through the New Testament twice before he had time to ask, "Excuse me, Miss Poon, but what is a Gentile?" His converts grew well too, and since all were baptized in the Holy Spirit they used these gifts quite freely. They had their own songs, which the Spirit gave them as they prayed and prayed for one another when they were sick.

One day, I visited Kwok when I was a little tired and worried that I would not be allowed to see him and his friends again. "Don't worry about us, Poon Siu Jeh," he told me and smiled encouragingly. "We're all right here. We're praying for you." They are the freest men I know.

I received several letters from them, and some of the young people in our group helped me to write return letters or wrote the letters themselves, as my written Chinese was still very poor. The English was delightful, as they lifted whole phrases out of dictionaries or the Bible or translated the Chinese themselves, word by word. William was one of the students, and Kwok wrote the following letter to him:

Dear William:

It is with much pleasure to hear from you and thanks be to the Lord Jesus Christ, for by His Wonderful name we know each other, Praise God!

In reading your letter, I was so delight to communicate with you and I want to thank you for writing me giving me so great encouragement and message in understanding the love of God—thank you! You know, Jackie uses to come and visit us in the prison every month even it is in hottest day; preaching and explaining us the Gospel. And there, we find not a word could be good enough to tell you how great is her kindness to us! We really feel deeply impressed by this—the wonderful love of God. Every time she comes to see us, we would be very happy and there we would ask her many questions in the Bible and she would be very willingly to give us every details and explanations and that is why we never find time enough for us to be with her. Now and then I greatly believe in what the Bible says that Jesus Christ is truly died for us and I sincerely hope to do my best for Him.

It is through the power of the Holy Spirit, God gives me very many opportunately to witness to others here and many of them wish to see Jackie but I did not dare to give any answer or even tell Jackie about this, for I sense that they are asking this on purpose. I know there is nothing I can do about this and I just pray that the Holy Spirit will touch them and that they would be changed perfectly.

Now I have to close my words because it is very late at night. Please pray for us here and greets to you in His name. KWOK.

On the first occasion I had visited Ah Lung, there was another white-striped Taiwanese prisoner who was on trial for bringing into Hong Kong the largest amount of heroin ever discovered on a ship. He was the second officer, and he started to discuss his case with me as soon as we met.

"I'm sorry I cannot discuss court cases with you," I said. "The only reason I am allowed in here is to talk about Jesus."

"But I cannot be a Christian," said Go Hing. "Let me tell you a story." He told it in Mandarin Chinese with the odd word in English.

Over 20 years ago there was a family who fled from mainland China and ended up as refugees in Taiwan.

In this family there was a young boy, about four. He ran away from home one day with a young friend and went to play at the schoolhouse. There was a large water pool there, and as he was playing with his friend, he fell in. The little boy's friend was so frightened because he knew they should not have been playing there that he ran away and did not tell anyone.

Several hours later, the Headmaster got back to the school and saw to his horror and distress the body of a child floating in the water. He fished him out but was unable to revive him. Recognizing the child, he sent for his parents, and the mother arrived beside herself with grief that this beloved son of hers had died. She insisted that they take him to hospital. Of course, it was too late to save him and the doctors certified him dead; but she would not believe it, so she took him to another hospital where he was again certified dead. Sadly she took the body home, as is the Chinese custom, and dressed him in his burial clothes. She was going to sit by the body all night keeping vigil.

In the middle of the night the boy sat up, looked at his mother and said, "Why am I dressed in these clothes?" She could not believe what she was seeing. She thought it was a vision. She said, "Do you remember falling into the pool?" and the little boy said, "Yes, I remember, and I remember I was going down in the water and I opened my mouth to shout for help, and the water went in, and then I saw a man come."

The mother interrupted him to ask, "A man—who was he?"

"Well, he came and he held out his hand to me, and he pulled me out of the water," he said.

The mother supposed that the boy had seen the headmaster, so she asked, "Do you know his name?"

"Don't you know?" replied the boy, "It's Jesus." The family had never heard Jesus' name before. They had no contact with Christians, but from that time onward the mother and the whole family became disciples of Jesus.

Go Hing told me this story very dramatically and very emotionally. Then he looked at me and asked, "Do you know how I know that story is true? I was the boy. I was brought back from death, and since that time my family have been Christians. That is why I cannot be a Christian, because I knew the truth and I have not followed Jesus."

"I've got very good news for you," I told Go Hing. "Jesus doesn't expect us to follow Him in our own strength, so if you are prepared to tell Him that you are sorry and ask forgiveness, then He will forgive you. You can start again, and He will give you the power to help you follow Him. The power is His Holy Spirit. He will give you a new language to help you talk to Him, because there will be so many things in your heart that you will want to tell Him after all this time."

I could not lay hands on him under the gaze of the curious prison guard, but as we prayed together he began to pray in tongues, and he then began to cry.

He looked up afterward and said, "That's the first time that I've cried since I was a boy. I feel so happy. I know Jesus is with me now."

I went back to see him some days later and told him, "You know you have to tell the truth in court. You have to tell the truth."

"I'm too frightened to tell the truth. I can't."

"You have to tell the truth. You are a Christian now."

"I can't, because if I plead guilty to this case I'll be killed. According to Taiwanese law, whatever country you commit a crime in you are liable to be sentenced again in Taiwan, even if you have already served a sentence. In Taiwan they still execute a man for drug peddling, armed robbery and for murder. So I can't plead guilty."

"I'm not your solicitor. I'm not giving you legal advice," I told him. "I'm just telling you that you have to speak the truth.

You know Jesus saved your life, and you can't go only halfway with Him."

Go Hing was found guilty and was given 12 years in prison. I wasn't able to see him for some time, but just before I went back to England, I was allowed to visit him in Stanley prison. As I looked at him through the panel he began to cry, but he was smiling.

"Because you are going, I just have to tell you this," he said. "I am known as a very hard man. I've been a seaman for many years; I'm not afraid of the great wind and I'm not afraid of the big waves. When my father died, I didn't cry; when I was arrested and I knew I would not see my wife and children again for many years, I didn't cry. There are only two occasions in my life when I've cried. One occasion was when you came to the prison before my trial and I received Jesus and His Holy Spirit, and the other occasion is today. But today I'm crying with joy, because I know my sins are forgiven.

"There is one thing more I must tell you before you go. When you kept telling me I must tell the truth, I had no intention of doing so, but I was praying and I made a bargain with God. I said, 'Okay, if she comes to see me today, I'll tell the truth this afternoon.' You came, so I went and I disclosed to the police that there was as much heroin on the ship that had not yet been found as had been found. Nobody was pleased with that. Of course, my own people were furious because they had a fortune hidden away, and the police were not pleased because they were made to look foolish. The judge was very angry because the amount of drugs was so enormous and gave me a very heavy sentence."

Go Hing smiled at me as he finished. "I have a heavy sentence here on Earth, but my sins are forgiven and I go to heaven—better that than to have a light sentence here on Earth and go to hell."

# WALK IN THE SPIRIT

Adelightful American sailor once took me to task about my praying in tongues. He thought I went on about it far too much. He had this gift himself, but he felt it should only be used sparingly for spiritual highs and for special occasions. I explained to him that one reason why God was able to use me was because I kept in touch through using this gift all the time. I prayed in the Spirit as I went around the colony— in buses, on the boats and walking along the streets, very quietly under my breath. That way, it is possible to pray all the time. I offered, if he had time, to take him on a day-long tour of Hong Kong while we prayed continuously.

The next day, we met up and walked down through Western District to the waterfront. The route reminded me of my first few days in Hong Kong when I began to see beneath the tourists' glamorous façade to the dirt, poverty, struggle, ceaseless work and more work.

In one steep-stepped ladder street, I passed an old man living in a cupboard five feet high, six feet long and three feet deep. He sold vegetables from his cupboard by day and climbed on top of them to sleep at night, as there was nowhere else for him to live. With four and a half million people crammed into every available square foot, whole families in Hong Kong had to live in one room. This man had no family.

Further down the street, I found an old lady holding out a plastic rice bowl. No one in Hong Kong had money or rooms to spare and there were no pensions either, so she stayed alive by begging. There were so few old people's homes that she had not a hope of getting into one.

Walking on, I saw a little girl about five years old with a child strapped on her back, because both of her parents had to work long hours to support their children. Nobody looked after the dirty little five-year-old—she was looking after the baby.

Then I passed a teenage boy who paid rent for the privilege of sleeping on a four-foot shop counter. He had stopped school at the end of his primary years when he was about 13. He was bright and wanted to continue school, but his parents took him away to work. When he got his job, he gave all his money to them so that they could send all his younger brothers and sisters to school. Every time I walked past him, he asked me to practice English with him to help him to get a better job.

I reached the end of the street feeling that if I spent my entire life down there I could just about get to love this street—I could just about get to love all the people and know them and their needs. But when we turned into the next street, it was a duplicate of the first, and beyond that was yet another . . . more people. I told the American sailor how I had prayed during the early days, asking God to show me which bit of His work was mine; He had answered by sending me to the Walled City and the miraculous events of the next dozen years. I could never have dreamed of anything so extraordinary and wonderful.

My sailor was as overwhelmed by this sight of Hong Kong as I had been. But the purpose of our day was to encourage him to walk in the Spirit, so I began to pray as we went.[1] We crossed the harbor and arrived at Jordan Road, an area I knew well, as I had lived there for a while. I took him inside a building that boasted both brothels and ballrooms. It was a place where heroin addicts hung out, looking deathly sick and half-starved. We walked up the back staircase; there were various people sleeping on the stairs, and we picked our way over the bodies, looking for a large tramp. I had come to find Mau Wong, the "King of the Cats"; he was much fatter than the others there because he

was a "protector" for various prostitutes, and so earned quite a
lot of money.

We found Mau Wong in an extremely unhappy state: He
had a terrible stomachache and was sweating profusely and
retching. He could not listen to me telling him about Jesus, so
the young American and I laid hands upon him and prayed quietly in the Spirit for his healing. Very quickly his pain vanished
and a look of great surprise crossed his features. He could hardly believe what had happened to him, but he was now ready to
sit down and listen. He accepted Jesus and was baptized in the
Spirit then and there.

We had hardly finished praying when he got up, ran away
and reappeared, bringing with him a pathetic specimen of a
man with sunken cheeks. Mau Wong explained that this friend
had toothache; would we pray for him too? So we took him up
onto the roof of the building, which was flat and empty, and
prayed with him also. He was healed at once; then we told him
who Jesus was and what Jesus had done for him. He was ready
to receive Christ and His Spirit and did so straight away. Then I
had a message in tongues, and Mau Wong was able to give the
interpretation about repentance, which thrilled him very much.

I was to visit Mau Wong on the back staircase several
times to tell him more about Jesus; the second time I met
him, he gave me a knife and various equipment for smoking
heroin, which he asked me to dispose of. He explained that
now he was a Christian, he had to earn his living in an hon-
est way, so he had bought some shoe brushes and was going
to become a bootblack.

The young American and I left Mau Wong to continue our
tour of Hong Kong; we crossed back over the harbor and took
a minibus to Chaiwan. All the time I was praying aloud but
quietly so that no one could hear. My sailor had thought that
praying on buses was a bit much, but after seeing what had
happened at Jordan Road, he began to join in too. The whole
day we prayed without ceasing except to eat and to talk to
those we met along the way.

At Chaiwan we headed for a drug den, which was quite a dangerous place for the young American to go. But they welcomed us both as if they had been waiting to hear about Jesus and we had been anxiously expected. "Poon Siu Jeh, can I have a Bible?" asked an addict.

"How can I start a new life?" asked another.

"Am I too old to be saved?" enquired an old man. "Where can I hear about Jesus and learn doctrine?"

"There is no need to wait until you go to a meeting to hear about Christ. I'll tell you now," I said to him. I sat down and talked while a small crowd gathered and listened. The old man listened wonderingly to Bible stories and accepted Jesus like a little child. He renounced his petty fencing business and became a regular attendee of the Saturday meetings.

As we left the den, we were followed by Ah Wing, a mean man who sold heroin, killing others' bodies as well as his own. He came to eat noodles with us through no good motives at all—he just wanted a free meal. I was telling him about Jesus, and he was hurrying this bit through to get to the noodles.

"Are you willing to believe that Jesus is the Son of God?" I asked him.

"I'm not sure," he replied. "Maybe."

I didn't think he was all that convinced, but I went on to the next question. "And do you believe that He died for you?"

"Don't understand that."

"Well never mind, are you willing?"

"All right," he mumbled.

"Are you willing to believe that He rose again from the dead?"

"Well, I suppose He must have," he acquiesced, "because I've heard of the things He is doing."

"Are you willing to follow Him?"

He answered scathingly. "Oh yes. I mean, if He is the true God, of course."

"Ah Wing, why don't you ask God if Jesus is His Son or not?" I suggested. "I am sure He will let you know."[2] I began to pray quietly, motioning the American to join us. As we prayed there at the noodle stall, Ah Wing joined in with us gently and confidently in tongues.

After a few minutes I lifted my head, thinking we had done enough praying at that stall even for me. When I looked at the drug peddler, I saw that he was still praying on and on and on. My sailor had moved one seat farther away, trying to pretend that he did not belong to us, although it was difficult for him to disown me in an area where there were no other Westerners. His attitude changed when he looked up to see the extraordinary expression on Ah Wing's face as he prayed. He had a look that was seraphic. When eventually he looked up after about 20 minutes, I asked him, "What did you see?"

"Well," he said, "when I was praying I saw what was like a picture, and I think it was Jesus. He was sitting at a table, a long table. There were several other men around; I think there must have been about a dozen or so. They were passing around some bread, and then a wine cup, and drinking from it."

I explained to him the meaning, that Jesus was giving His body and His blood for us and rejoiced that God should have revealed Himself to Ah Wing through the breaking of bread.

Two more people were converted later on our walk, and my American friend needed no more convincing about praying in the Spirit.

When I got back home and told Rick and Jean about Ah Wing and the others, they groaned and said, "Oh no! Anyone else and we'd be pleased—but yours are all addicts, and where are we going to put them?"

We often had no room to house those we had brought to faith in Christ. Ever since Winson and Ah Ming, I felt that I was responsible for the welfare of each believer until his life was straightened out, but each one needed so much care: Most had no home, no clothes and suffered from severe personality problems as well as drug addiction and disease.

I felt that I must go back to Chaiwan to look for Ah Wing so that I could do some follow-up. I did not see him, but found an old acquaintance, Ah Kwan, talking in a drug den with some wholesale drug peddlers. They were all being very nice to me, but I felt compelled to say that although Jesus loved them, and I did too, I thought their business stank. Ah Kwan, who had joined the peddlers, said he would "repent" the week after because he needed three days' money first. (He lived in a wooden hut with a plastic tarpaulin for the roof, five buckets to catch the water, a tired wife only 25 years old and four children under six. They had no income.) I told him that no one chooses when to repent and that if he did not follow Jesus immediately and come with me, he would be in jail within days. He was caught four hours later and sentenced to 30 months. So the word was out in Chaiwan that I was a prophet, and they began to be more careful about talking to me!

I never saw Ah Wing the drug peddler again and could not tell what happened to him afterward. But I trusted fully that since God loved him better than I, He would definitely take care of him better than I. I had come full circle: I first believed that God would heal all addicts instantly, then I believed that they could only survive if I provided a safe environment, and then I trusted again that I could leave them completely safe in His care.

The sailor wrote to the Willanses, asking if he could come and help our work when he came out of the navy two years later. They replied by saying that by that time we might have 5 houses, 50 houses or none at all. Since none of us was called to do drug addict work but to preach Jesus, we did not feel we should necessarily perpetuate the program, lest it become a burden. We would therefore be open to whichever way God moved, whether it would be into China or a dozen more flats for boys . . .

Goko's second real brother came back from Canada. He was tall and suave, dressed in an immaculate suit. We met when Johnny married a Christian nurse from the hospital where he worked. Johnny had invited the members of his old gang so that his wedding could be a witness to them.

"I have to shake you by the hand, Miss Pullinger," Goko's brother said in perfect English. "I grew up with the boys in the Walled City and I determined to study law so that I could come back and help them. But now I am back, I see that there is nothing left for me to do. You have done it all. I must shake you by the hand." Quickly I disclaimed the praise, telling the brother Who had done all the work.

We walked together down the Walled City streets toward the clubroom. They were empty now, as many illicit businesses had ceased. This was due partly to the success of the anti-corruption commission but also partly to the fact that so many of the 14K boys had become Christians. There was a local story that Sai Di, the number two in influence, had telephoned a 14K cousin across the harbor and asked to borrow some brothers for a gang fight.

"Sure," replied the other leader, who knew of both Goko and Sai Di's reputation, "but what about your own gang?"

"Well," replied Sai Di, "half of them are drug addicts, the other half are Christians, and they are all lousy fighters."

Goko's Canadian brother walked into the clubroom and approved of it. Night after night he appeared for the singing and then talked to me.

One day he asked, "What do you do for money?"

I was a bit offhand and answered tritely, "Oh God looks after us. We pray for it."

"Okay, okay—but *practically* speaking from where? It does not just fall down from heaven, does it?"

"Well, it may," I said, and at that moment there was a knock on the door and in came an old man. He lived in a little cubicle in the Walled City, into which he could just squeeze to sleep. He handed me a grubby envelope.

"Poon Siu Jeh," he said, "I was walking along the street and somebody gave me this letter." I looked at it; it was addressed in English, "Jackie Pullinger—Walled City," and that was all. There were few post boxes in the Walled City, and it was a dangerous place to send letters anyway. No one there knows English, so how he got my letter was a mystery. I opened it up, and there were 100 American dollars from a man I had neither met nor heard of before. I showed it to Goko's younger brother, and he held up his hand as if calling a truce and said, "Enough said, point taken."

He went off home and left me to walk down the streets alone. Past the prostitutes, past the blue films, the gambling dens and drugs. Past Ah Keung's house, where I had sat with him on the night his father died, watching the body and listening to the howls of the dogs as they were beaten to tender flesh for the cook pots. Past the spot where one year previously I had witnessed the beginning of a vicious fight between two knife-wielding strangers.

"Stop. Don't fight," I had said, feeling sick. Two minutes later an emissary was sent along the street to calm me down.

"We are sorry, Miss Poon," he soothed. "It won't happen again. We did not know you were here."

I walked out of the city and looked at the rubble where the Lung Kong Road house had stood and thought of Goko, who now lived in the opposite building. His wife had gone missing a few months earlier after gambling away a large amount of his money in one of his dens: She was too frightened to return, knowing that he would beat her. She stole the four-year-old son of his former mistress and hid out in an apartment house. When she phoned him, she said that she would return his son if he promised pardon. Goko was uncompromising. He promised no such thing and set his Triads to work tracing apartment houses, which would not take long through the Triad affiliations. His wife did not wait to be found, however; terrified of her husband, she drank poison and then forced the little boy to drink too, killing them both.

I made a point of seeing Goko about once a year, and when we next met for tea, I offered him my sympathy. He had lost weight. He sneered at the mention of his wife, but I guessed the hurt at the loss of his son. I saw the fear of being alone too, and because I wanted so much to reach him I told him I knew of his fear. He was surprised but he also longed to confide in someone.

"How do you know? I've never before told anyone I am afraid," he admitted. "I feel so lonely."

A double funeral and a luxury burial had been held, as part of keeping face before his Triad brothers. Goko told me he never confessed his emotions to another soul.

Goko and Sai Di voiced similar attitudes about Christ, although their Canadian brother believed openly. "I'm not saying I don't believe in Jesus—I've watched those who do. But I've also watched you Christians and noticed that most of you have jobs with poor pay. I cheat, lie and steal in order to provide for all my dependants, and I know Christians don't do these things. So I'm not going to be one because I'd want to be a real one. I understand that Jesus can provide for me but I need to be sure He can support my followers."

I have always respected the brothers' position and have prayed for them to see God as big enough to care for all their needs. Certainly neither would ever make a commitment lightly. More than once in conversation with Goko, I have heard him say, "Okay, if that brother wants to be a Christian, okay. But let him follow Jesus good. I don't want him gone tomorrow and back the next day. If he is to be a Christian, let him be a good one."

I left Goko's house behind me and headed back toward the Houses of Stephen, where those of the boys who continued to walk in the Spirit became fine and trustworthy men. Those who had known Christ but who left prematurely to follow their own desires got into trouble. One Chaiwan addict summed it all up when he applied to enter one of our houses: "I have heard that Jesus does the same miracle for each boy who comes to your place. But whether or not you choose to continue is up to you."

# OLD MEN'S DREAMS¹

It is the year 2000, and down in South Wall Road sit two old men—I never knew their names, but they call loudly, "Poon Siu Jeh, Poon Siu Jeh," so I stop and they lead me into nostalgia.

Quite clearly they have been inhaling beer for some time, for as I draw close to the noodle shop they huff fumes all over me and my friend. Now I recognize them, although it has been a dozen years since we often nodded to each other in the Walled City. The one with red rheumy eyes is very excited.

"Beer? Noodles? Anything. I invite you."

I must accept something or there will be a street riot. He is waving his arms around and shouting. The traffic has stopped, and even though I do not feel like a foreigner after more than three decades in Hong Kong, the sight of one talking to a crazed local in a stained singlet draws the inevitable crowd.

"Thank you so much—I've just eaten. Just a drink," and I sit down in the street with them although my host is still wildly gesticulating.

"We all want to thank you, Poon Siu Jeh. Do you know, do you know," he turns to my companion, Margaret, "what happened in Walled City?"

Before he can continue I fill her in a bit. This old man was a guard, a "tin man *toi*" in the days when the city was in its heyday, when illegal gambling, prostitution, drug dens and blue films made it a haven and a magnet for criminals and gangs. Now the Walled City's walls have come down, and the city itself, too. Now he has to sit outside and look at the beautiful new park with memories of wonderful old squalor. Now he is unemployable. Today drug pushers use mobile telephones and hide in proper apartments. His day is gone; he has neither. But he remembers. And with maudlin passion, he enthuses some of our story to Margaret.

"She cared about us, and miracles happened. People who could not change were changed. It was that Jesus."

I am surprised by him. I cannot recall ever talking to him about Jesus. He used to sit in the *congee* shop, where the poor old men ate the cheapest food. It was where the unsuccessful law-breakers hung out and for a dollar or so could spin out hours in the familiarity of the Dark City.

"All these people, Goko, Johnny, Geui Jai, Winson, many, many, all changed by Jesus. You know maybe one day I will believe, too. That has to be the true God. Can I find you?"

As he speaks he wipes his eyes, which are leaking yellow, and the other old man gulps and joins in too. Then our potential evangelist includes the noodle seller in his oratory, and suddenly the whole street is challenged to believe in a God that he has seen change a city, a gang boss and many hearts.

"Excuse me," I am leaking tears, too. "But could I introduce Him to you now?"

It is a struggle between the alcohol and the Spirit.

"Could I reserve that hope?" he finally compromises.

It was unfair, most moving and totally embarrassing. I had never done anything for this ex-guard. I had never spoken to him, helped him personally or been involved with his life. His toenails were still black, yet there was a fuzzy hope in his heart that he somehow attributed to me and Jesus. That was the awful wonder. Long after the walls crumbled, the desire for glory still smoldered in his heart.[2] I tried to tell Margaret that it was over the top, an intoxicated exaggeration of my importance in his life, but it was still there.

So we were present at one of those times in history when the past blares, intruding the present, and I am in them both. I often tell visiting mission teams of this unjust phenomenon. It is fashionable nowadays to visit Asia, China and the poor for a few days, weeks or months and call it outreach.

Over the years we have had hundreds of short-termers who want to get the picture immediately—if possible, on video—so they can show it to their home church and have an inspired evening. I have begged them to love the people and stay, just like Sai Di did of me 30 years ago. The disadvantage of short-term missions is a wrong perspective based on this generation's need for instant results.

Many have stayed with us and lived in our new houses, now called St. Stephen's, which currently house over 300 men, women, teenagers and children all over Hong Kong. Sometimes everything goes well and there are real conversions, healings and glorious glimpses of changed lives. The visitors leave and wonder why it does not work at home. They wonder why everything seems so easy in Hong Kong. At other times nothing goes right, even here. The man who prophesied last night beats up a helper the next morning, or the whole house runs away. Then the visitors leave disillusioned.

"It is nothing like she wrote in her book. We had a hard time."

The remarkable fact that after so long we still see most addicts who come to us believe in Jesus, pray in tongues and detoxify from drugs painlessly does not obscure the fact that they need a changed mind. So the voyeurs leave. They have their video clips, but they never saw. It was either all too good or all too bad, and neither was accurate. We love our people whether they turn out well or not, and the successes do not vindicate our ministry nor do the disappointments nullify it. What is important is whether we have loved in a real way—not preached in an impassioned way from a pulpit.[3]

And then there is time. If God meant a child to grow slowly and safely in a loving family for up to 18 years, why should we be angry at those who do not change at our pace for the sake of our statistics, furlough or, sadly for some, funding? All the unreasonable benefits came for me after nearly 20 years. People

I had spent time with so long before never forgot, even though we lost each other for a while. Suddenly, someone from the past would appear again, and it would turn out that he had not killed the memory of a love that was so extraordinary that the giver spent Himself in giving until He died. So we have been the delighted, sobbing representatives of the Father whose prodigal son crawled or rushed home after all.

Our summer missionaries did not stay to see this, although we hoped they might yearn for it somehow. Stay for the party. The fleeting volunteer sometimes catches a course—sweet and sour—but no one savors the whole menu like me.

"Everyone brings out the choice wine first and then the cheaper wine after the guests have had too much to drink," said the master of the banquet when He called the bridegroom aside, "but you have saved the best till now."[4]


Grandpa Chau Bat used to live in the same South Wall Road. He had a cubicle, a "cage," which was one tier of a three-level bunk bed enclosed by wire netting so that he could keep himself and all his belongings in and intruders out. The wooden shelf was heaped with his life, such as it was, and there was just enough room for him to lie down. He was the "actor" I had noticed in court years earlier. And he had a bad cough. He had fallen on bad times since the opium dens became too smelly to deter detection dogs and detection men. Even the Walled City had been affected by the ICAC (Independent Commission Against Corruption) in the 1970s, and Chau Bat's role as the actor who was tokenly arrested in the many reported raids became obsolete. He had to switch to heroin, less detectable but more expensive, and he constantly hawked phlegm. I often passed his street and, seeing him wheezing, offered to pray for him.

"No need. I am an idol worshiper," he politely responded, but I persisted and blessed him anyway.

Some time later, I was walking down a neighboring street on the outskirts of the Walled City and they told me he was looking for me. I hurried to his patch, where he looked annoyed. "I was waiting for you. I have been waiting for days."

Then he pointed to his leg, obviously poisoned with escaping pus.

"Why didn't you see a doctor? This is serious," I asked.

"I was waiting for you."

He admonished me as if I should have known. So I hurried him to a doctor I knew for advice. We learned that the infection needed hospitalization and prepared for the journey. Again, it was an old Walled City brother I invited to ride with us in a taxi to the Haven of Hope hospital. As we traveled, I preached as usual.

"When you feel withdrawal pains from the heroin, just call on Jesus. He will help."

"*Yau moe gau chor*. You must be joking."

He became churlish and tetchy. He was in pain.

"No, it is true," said my brother. "Lots of people like me have tried, and we got off drugs without pain."

It did not appear that the testimony had penetrated the distressed old man, and we said no more except, "Just remember." Some days later, I visited the hospital and saw a radiant figure with a healed leg.

"What about the heroin? Did they give you medication?"

"No, I am fine. I did what you said. I called on Jesus and it all went away. I am fine. No pain."

He was off drugs. So then, what to do? He had no family in Hong Kong, as they were in Mainland China. He had no future in the Walled City or South Wall Road. I invited him to live with us. By this time we were all over the place. The former Houses of Stephen had merely rehabilitated the hopeless for a while but gave no permanence for the future. Helpful Hong Kong government individuals had offered a variety of old locations, which were unusable for their purposes at that time but where we could continue to grow up our old men and prepare them to help others or give them time for re-entering society.

Hang Fook Camp was a worn-out tin-hut area meant as temporary lodging for those waiting for government-subsidized accommodation. There were 12 long huts comprising of 10 or so units, each already past their use-by date. We loved them and enthusiastically repaired the multiple rooms. Tiny spaces had formerly contained whole families, but we now housed several men in each. We made a couple of huts into a huge sanctuary by stripping the sides and erecting a plastic roof courtesy of the British Army. It was like a tent with open boundaries, so as many as several thousand would come to worship and gawk, too.

Grandpa Chau Bat became as famous as Hang Fook Camp. He got new teeth and clacked about most possessively. He called me "my daughter," and we adopted each other. Now I had a Chinese mother and father.

"Here is my offering."

He handed me most of his government old-age allowance. Times had changed, and now he had our help as well as local assistance. With the rest of his monthly sum, he bought buns and bananas for me and my secretary. We passed them on secretly to those who liked buns and bananas.

"I need to see my daughter in China."

His leg had been healed in the hospital and his heart's desire for love and acceptance had been met by Jesus and us. He had been healed by Jesus in many ways. We helped him apply for his daughter, who he had not seen in decades, to stay with us for a month in Hang Fook Camp. She came and saw her father—the craggy-faced, occasionally toothless, geriatric patrician—and she also saw his Lord. And then she became our heart responsibility, too. And her family. And her village in China. Equally poor. Hundreds of them. I had dreamed of the hundreds and yet could hardly cope with the few.


This is how it had come about. Back in the last House of Stephen, nearing the 1980s, the Willanses had left Hong Kong and this book's 15 chapters of history in suspense. A plump Hong Kong man had helped for a while. I took him to the Walled City, and he also assisted in the new-boy house stuffed with over 10 new men. I thought I was training him, although that really meant, "Come with me." I sent him to New Zealand to learn more. Sadly for me, he returned with new ideas.

"I feel a burden to work with children," he pronounced sweetly.

I was not impressed. I did not understand his language.

"I need to leave and pursue this," he persisted.

"But there are children affected by everyone we meet. Can you not stay and find a way to reach them? The way is open for you," I almost begged.

However, he had seen a more sophisticated church community where its members were separated into "ministries." And he did have a way with kids. He left. I was devastated.

It happened that at that moment I was sitting in a little room in our last House of Stephen. No Willanses. No foreign helpers. Just 12 men doing so-so and Jesus doing good. I began to weep. I could only think that it had taken so long to train one man to help and now I would have to start again. Alone. Again. I cried and cried.

Through the door came plates (barbecued pork on toothpicks). Then flowers. Then tissues as I went on grieving.

"We are praying for you," came the messages from those I lived with, "that you will get better enough to care for all the people in Hong Kong who still need you."

That was not comforting, and it made me howl even harder.

"You do not understand," I tried to say.

"We pray Jesus gives you comfort," they continued.

"I do not *need* comfort," I retorted in frustration. "You do not understand. I do not need you to pray that I get better to go on. I want you to do what I have been doing. I am only one person."

The trouble was that it looked so easy. Already I had seen Jesus reach men, touch men, heal and change them; the drawback was that as one person, I could only physically do so much, even if that were mightily empowered. Even Jesus handed

over the world to 12 problem-ridden men. Where were mine?
Twelve problem-ridden men I had without a doubt, but they
expected me to do it all. And so much of the rest of the Church
was engaged in discovering their giftings rather than giving. I
went on crying and saw, over a period of three days and three
nights, many faces. I knew them all. They slept under flyovers
and lived in cages. The old women gathered in parks and all
were easy to reach. They just needed someone with time to
touch them.

In Hang Fook Camp, we began to see the outworking of my
frustration, which some angelic soul described later as interces-
sion. Teams were formed from the broken to reach the broken.
The limping helped the limping. Perhaps we should have
renamed ourselves Jacob instead of Stephen, although we
retained that name.[5] And so hundreds more were touched not
by me but by those, like me, who were hardly healed themselves.
Again I was part of an unfair multiplication. Hundreds
thanked God or me, although by now I was but remotely associated with their lives. I still connected with the streets and the
addicts seeking help. I still visited the prisons, although most
of the walking was done by those who had been touched themselves and served in gratitude. I watched them make the same
mistakes that I had done and deal with them rather better.

Elfrida joined a team, too. Her life had been a catalogue of
horror. Born to a father with two wives and a mother who was
probably his mistress, she was brought up by an aunt after her
mother committed suicide. This woman was a lesbian, and
Elfrida was exposed to all the permutations of her affairs,
which included one with Elfrida's father's wife. At 17, she had
a boyfriend and was going to marry him, but she was thrown
out of the house when it was discovered that she had been
seduced by him. Sexually confused, not knowing whether she
loved or hated men, Elfrida became a prostitute and dulled her
senses with heroin.

For years we had been renting apartments in which men could withdraw from drugs. They were always full, and there was no room for women. I had avoided the old woman's street. The dark, weeping ghost was persistent in her cries, however, and so came the day when I could resist her no longer and took her in.

In a small room six foot by four, Elfrida prepared to come off drugs. Her back was covered with old black bruises, and she was so weak and frail that my friend took her in her arms and carried her to the bath. She soaked a while and was carried back. We laid her down on her mattress and spoke peace to her. She was healed from that moment. When Hang Fook Camp became available, she moved in and it became home. She worshiped Jesus, washed and ironed and slept a lot. She also cried a lot.

I watched with many questions in my heart and mind. We had learned something of praying for those with past hurts, and I had observed both the courage of those who opened up old wounds still infected with fear and violence and the eventual resolution as the cross of Jesus cancelled the pain and offered forgiveness to the perpetrators. But in her case, how long would it take?

I wondered whether we would have to take her through each nightmare separately. That would take as many years as the afflictions themselves. The cross ought to be quicker. There had to be a solution.

Elfrida went with a team from Hang Fook Camp who visited the poor, wretched and unwanted. She saw sadness and lack of love in the lives of others and realized how much she had been given. One day, she came back from an old people's home obviously incensed.

"They give them beds and vegetables, but that is all. They do not pray for them like we do," she proudly opined, as if the omission was obvious.

So she went back, and as she visited came the desire to share what she had received herself. As she bathed the elderly, she prayed for them, too. Elfrida went to see street sleepers with her team and also found some of the old prostitutes whom she had known before in the Walled City. One was lying incontinent in her urine, having lost the need for a protector. Elfrida washed her body, washed her nit-ridden hair, and spoke of her new life and her Christ.

She loved much, for she had been forgiven much.

This new woman shed pain, bitterness and, as long as she served others, self pity. She seemed to shed years, too, and became so attractive that she found a suitor. Their wedding preparations were hilarious as she planned for the day she had been dreaming of most of her life. Bridesmaids. Flowers. Vows. Rings.

So, in her 70s, she married in virginal white and gracefully walked down the aisle to her future husband. It was a glorious day—a picture of how all things can become new.[6]

They had a few problems, however. She had not actually thought, in the euphoria of the wedding, about living out a married life. They behaved just like a young couple and had to grow into their new life. One day, she came to my hut. Another elderly lady—Hing Jeh, a widow—was also preparing to get married.

"She asked me if she could borrow my wedding dress, and I said she could," Elfrida told me, "but she can't. She cannot wear white—she has been married before!"

Ah, well.

# YOUNG MEN'S VISIONS[1]

The young man walked down a rural path before climbing the mountain leading to the next village. He had no spare clothes, although the journey had started with him carrying a bundle of old ones, and he had also worn several sets himself. He had left them all in previous country settlements as he traveled from day to day. He had no bicycle, either. He had given that away, too. In his pocket was a sweet potato donated by the grateful villagers who subsisted on them and had nothing else to give except a blessing.

He had walked into the countryside and told those he met about his Lord. They welcomed him and his Jesus too. He prayed for them, and many were miraculously healed of diseases. Then he took his Bible and tore a few pages out, for they had none. He laid his hands on them that they could receive the power of the Holy Spirit and pray for the sick. Then he left a changed people and walked on, promising to return when he could.

Another young man lived in an urban block 30-odd stories high, with multitudes on every floor. He had no contact with other believers, for it was an era when this was forbidden. But he had been curiously transformed in his own life when some time before his heroin habit had overwhelmed his veins. How strange that a dead Jesus, apparently alive again, could physically quiet a body and urge a heart into leaping joy.

With the track marks yet on his arms but a deeper impression on his heart, this youth had found hope and a reason to live. After he had come off drugs when someone prayed for him in this living Lord's name, he was transformed body and soul.

He sang in his one-room apartment. He shared what had happened with his elderly neighbor who lived alone and had an aching pain in her wrist. She was healed, too, and then they sometimes sang together. Then they found a homeless tramp who camped on the landing, and they touched him too . . .

These were my dreams. Knowing not what the future might bring in a political sense or what would be permitted in terms of formal structure, I had always wished for such simplicity, no need for organization. One poor man reaching one poor man. "Love your neighbor as yourself" seemed to sum it up.[2]

Our young people are unlikely dragon slayers. Most have failed society, school and parents. But they have an unearthly courage. A group of them used to visit a certain city in Asia and found, over time, a gang of flower-sellers. They were children. They were slaves. These were children who, along with others, had left home, which was often several days away by train. Some of them had been unwanted. One of them had been sold several times as he was an orphan and some families wanted a son or a worker. He was beaten and ill-treated and ran away, only to be sold again. Another was already bent like an old person for, as a young child, he had to carry boulders strung to his back like the adults did.

They came to the city hoping for money. They slept by the railway station and found a way to make some money. Some sold their bodies, and many contracted diseases of a deadly nature. The very young ones sold flowers to tourists. But they never kept their money. The boss who gave them flowers took their earnings and their precarious freedom. He controlled them.

Ah Chi, with her team of lame young people, met them and slowly made friends. They loved them and took them to eat noodles or hamburgers. One famous franchise holder noticed this and allowed them to meet in his outlet. He had seen the plight of the kids and the persistence of the Hong Kong teenagers.

One young girl waited in wonder for the group who loved her, touched her, washed her and prayed for her. Her situation was not good. Although she had found Jesus, she still lived on the streets under the imprisonment of her controller. She had no money and nowhere to go.

Ah Chi found the flower-seller boss and pleaded for the little girl's freedom. In one short explosion, the exploiter apparently was bombed. What had hit him, he knew not, but suddenly the man cried and cried. He did not understand why he was so moved but, as Ah Chi talked, the boss was unbelievably awash with contrition. She told him of the God who sent His Son to die for the child and for him, too, that both could be truly free. He gladly accepted such a Savior and released the girl as well.

One of the team bought train tickets, although he himself had little money. We could not finance him, so he had to pray, like us, for rice and travel money. Having spent all, he took the child with him back to her original family. They rode the train for days and nights to reach their destination. This story has been repeated numerous times except that, in each instance, it is a different boy or girl. Often the families receive them back gladly and are, themselves, greatly affected by a love that they had never heard or guessed of.[3]


Ah Leung was taken home in this fashion. On arriving at his house, his mother rushed out in tears. She had remarried when he was young and the second husband had rejected her son, so he ran away and was lost for years.

"Let me tell you what happened to me," she blubbered and heaved. "Let me tell you." It turned out that six months before she had somehow heard of Jesus and had become a believer. Since then she had prayed non-stop.

"I did not know where Ah Leung was. I did not know which city he was in. I did not know how to find him, so I prayed, 'Please

God, wherever my son is, please send some Christians to him.'"
    Her prayer was answered.
    My dreams came true.[4]


Ka Ming and Esther were the ones who reached out to a new
generation in Hong Kong with the same problems as the previous ones but set in quite different living conditions. A new middle class had emerged and a wider form of social security. The
new youth were able to enjoy compulsory secondary education
and a higher standard of living than their parents had. Many
were given watches, credit cards, roller blades and material
possessions. A great number, though, still missed out on being
listened to or cared for. They were pressed into performance-
oriented schooling and fell out of the system.
    If you have fallen out, it is hard to get back. Ka Ming tried to
give them some hope through meeting them in playgrounds and
befriending them. Many, however, had already joined another
system and followed the hordes that seldom went home, slept
outside and experimented with drugs and sex.
    "I do not see them as problems, though," Ka Ming told me
with stars in his eyes. "If God could change me, then he can help
them, too."
    He saw them as possible dragon slayers: a band of young
men with new hearts and godly values willing to use their vigor
and lives to serve the unlovely and unfound. He saw the cities
of Asia touched in practical and miraculous ways by a youth
who would choose different values than those that their parents had been trapped into serving for survival or promotion.
He saw teens and young people in their 20s not trying to go up
in the world but willing to reach down.[5]


Chi Ho, who had tattoos up and down both legs, found himself
in someone else's city. He still had gelled hair nicely done in
spikes and that year wore trousers that looked as if they would

fall off any moment. Certainly chains had fallen off his own life, although part of the current gear necessitated them trailing from his low-slung belt. He came across an old lady who was blind in two eyes and pained in one leg.

"Please pray for her sight," he was invited by the team leader who lived in that city. Chi Ho did not feel quite up to praying for her blindness but thought he could manage the leg. He laid his hands on it and, as had been done for himself just one year previously, he said, "In Jesus' name, be healed."

The woman squawked in her language and thrashed around in huge emotion.

"What happened?" he asked of the interpreter. "How is the leg?"

"She says, she says," stuttered the interpreter, "she can see clearly through both eyes."

# BIBLICAL REFERENCES

**Chapter 1**
1. John 15:13.
2. Luke 10:31.
3. Romans 5:6-10.

**Chapter 2**
1. Isaiah 43:25.
2. John 14:6.
3. John 3:36; 6:40.
4. Proverbs 3:5-6.
5. Psalm 32:8.
6. Hebrews 11:8-9.

**Chapter 3**
1. Hebrews 11:10.

**Chapter 4**
1. Matthew 5:41.

**Chapter 5**
1. Romans 8:9-16; Galatians 4:6; 1 John 3:24; 4:13; 5:6.
2. 1 Corinthians 14:2,14.
3. 1 Corinthians 12:8-11.
4. 1 Corinthians 12-14.
5. 2 Timothy 1:7.
6. 1 Corinthians 14:4.
7. Acts 1:8.
8. 1 Corinthians 14:23.
9. 1 Corinthians 14:32.
10. 1 Corinthians 4:10.
11. Romans 8:26-27.

**Chapter 6**
1. Luke 5:32; 1 Timothy 1:15.
2. 2 Kings 5:1-19.
3. 1 Corinthians 14:27.
4. Luke 23:34; Romans 5:8; 1 Thessalonians 5:10; 1 John 4:10.
5. Luke 7:22-23.
6. Isaiah 53:6,12.
7. 2 Corinthians 5:21.
8. Matthew 5:9.
9. Matthew 6:31-33.

**Chapter 7**
1. Matthew 5:39,44.
2. Romans 5:3.
3. Matthew 6:24.
4. 1 Corinthians 15:58.
5. Matthew 10:19-20.

**Chapter 8**
1. Matthew 27:38.
2. Luke 23:39-43.
3. 1 Peter 2:24.

**Chapter 9**
1. James 2:14-17.
2. John 3:16.
3. John 6:35.
4. Mark 10:29-30.
5. 2 Corinthians 5:17.
6. Matthew 9:37-38.

7. Psalms 126:5-6; 127:1-2
8. 1 Corinthians 14:12,26.
9. Philippians 4:19
10. 1 Peter 1:18-19; Titus 2:14.
11. John 16:21.

## Chapter 10
1. Luke 7–8.
2. Luke 7:47-48;
   Romans 5:20-21.
3. Philippians 1:6.
4. 1 Corinthians 14:27.

## Chapter 11
1. John 3:3.
2. Matthew 10:39.
3. Ezekiel 36:26.

## Chapter 12
1. 1 Corinthians 12:8.
2. Matthew 6:19-21.
3. Judges 7–8;
   2 Chronicles 20.
4. Luke 7:36-50.

## Chapter 13
1. Isaiah 40:12-17,26-31;
   Psalm 8.
2. 1 Corinthians 3:16.
3. Matthew 5:17-18.
4. Matthew 5:37.

## Chapter 14
1. Matthew 6:15.
2. John 6:68.
3. 1 Timothy 1:15-16.

## Chapter 15
1. Galatians 5:16,25.
2. 2 Corinthians 6:2.

## Chapter 16
1. Acts 2:17; Joel 2:28.
2. 1 Chronicles 16:24-25;
   Galatians 5:6
3. Romans 2:2-5.
4. John 2:10-11.
5. Genesis 32:28-32.
6. 1 Corinthians 1:20-31.

## Chapter 17
1  Acts 2:17; Joel 2:28.
2. Luke 10:27.
3. 1 Corinthians 2:9-10.
4. Psalm 126:1-3.
5. Hebrews 11:14-16.

# ALSO AVAILABLE

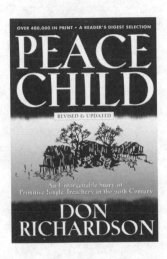

## PEACE CHILD
An Unforgettable Story of Primitive Jungle
Treachery in the Twentieth Century

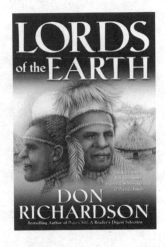

## LORDS OF THE EARTH
An Incredible but True Story from the Stone-
Age Hell of Papua's Jungle

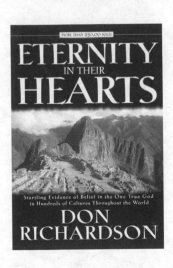

## ETERNITY IN THEIR HEARTS
Startling Evidence of Belief in the One True God
in Hundreds of Cultures Throughout the World

Available at
Bookstores
Everywhere!